BABY NAMES
WHY THEY COUNT

For A Lifetime !!!

More Than 18,000 Names

Including the Meaning

Of Every Name

by

Lance Shaler

Published by:

Sci-Com Data Services Ltd.
402 – 1488 Hornby Street
Vancouver, B.C. V6Z 1X3
www.numbers-count.com

Logo Trademark TMA369,120 by Lance Shaler

ISBN 978-0-9866217-1-0

1. Family   2. Relationships   3. Self Help   4. Spirituality
5. Psychology

Cover Art & Illustrations by Eve Lees
evelees@telus.net
www.artnews-healthnews.com

Book Design by Lance Shaler
lance@numbers-count.com
www.numbers-count.com

Printed in USA
2010 1st Printing

BOOK COVER

The book cover depicts numbers as a common thread weaving themselves throughout the universe. The background stars are the Pleiades, also known as the Seven Sisters.

DEDICATED TO:

The Children of the World

& Their Happiness

ACKNOWLEDGEMENTS

Numerology appears to be as old as time itself. Pythagoras of Samos, known as the Father Of Numerology, acquired his initial insights from the Egyptians about 600 B.C. The symbology of numbers is common to most mythologies, religions, and oracles such as the tarot, astrology, and the I Ching.

For example, in Christianity, the days of creation reflect the qualities of numbers, the Old Testament contains a Book Of Numbers, the Baptism asks, "*Who gave this child this name, and what will this name do for this child?*" In Revelations, "*One is given a white stone. Within the white stone is inscribed a new name only to be known unto oneself.*" In Christianity, there are many name changes such as "*Saul changed his name to Paul and he became ... Sarai to Sarah and she became*". The Jewish Kabbalah is infused with numerological references as is the Order of Rosicrucians and Freemasonry.

To specifically acknowledge each person and event which has contributed to this book would be quite impossible. However, it is important for me to acknowledge the ancients for their wisdom and all those who build on their foundation through to this present era of insight and radical change.

Within our changing world, this book speaks of my conviction that life has purpose, meaning, and an inherent design — that life is not a random happenstance of unrelated events. I believe that the people of this planet will become increasingly willing to embrace reasonable solutions as the conscious awareness of hope, purpose, and the inherent design of life become more apparent. As we become progressively more responsible for our environment, both personally and globally, we will establish a sustainable future.

Although the ideas of this book are only one piece of the huge

---

puzzle of life, for the picture to be complete, all pieces of the puzzle must be included in appropriate perspective.

Specifically, I want to acknowledge all those who for years pestered me to write this book and encouraged me to pursue what I love to do. For their loving support, I acknowledge Desiree Panico, Dawn Macaskill, Paulette Tomasson, Donalei Tabak, Lesley Tomlin, Joan Sutton-Brown, Carol Johnson, Les Atchison, Chuck Spezzano, Nancy Shipley Rubin, Cynthia deHay, Terry & Athena Ferguson, Glenn Urquhart, Steffany Caldwell, Andy Bryce, Andy Mar, Teya Danel, Robert-Michael Kaplan, and Donna Johnson. Plus a special thank you to my Mother for her words of encouragement.

For her impeccable editing and enduring support, a special thank you to Karmel Shaler. For their editorial comments and honesty, I acknowledge Kelly Henderson, Debrah Rafel, Rae Armour, Sabrina Braham, and John Clancy.

I thank everyone who has made use of this book and is searching to understand life's purpose.

TABLE OF CONTENTS

WHAT IS NUMEROLOGY?

Cymatics – Frequency and Form

Cymatics, commonly called "visible sound", is a study that demonstrates how frequency affects matter and creates form. Although names generate a sound when spoken and hence have a relationship to form, I suggest the relationship of a name's frequency affects form at levels deeper than the spoken word.

The relationship of frequency to form is all encompassing and can be found throughout life from the patterns on butterfly wings, bird feather designs, tortoise shells and to the basic structure and design of all life forms.

To view the relationship of frequency and form, Google "Cymatics" and watch some of the videos noted below or peruse some of the books on the topic.

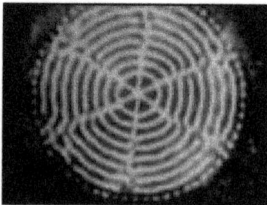

http://www.youtube.com/watch?v=oCmGjD9j9bU&feature=related

http://www.youtube.com/watch?v=bxV0FrFMxUY&feature=related

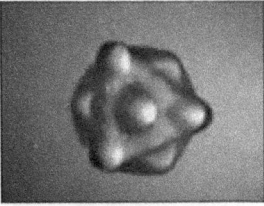

http://www.youtube.com/watch?v=fCXZF3NiPIk&feature=related

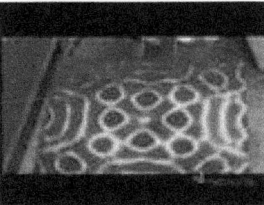

http://www.youtube.com/watch?v=EQPMhwuYMy4&NR=1

Forms become more explicit as frequency increases.

For example, the following snapshots are very reflective of a *dragon fly* and *brain coral*:

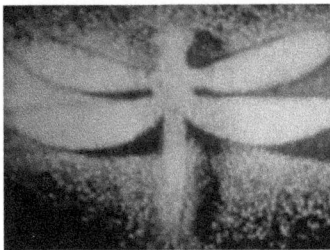

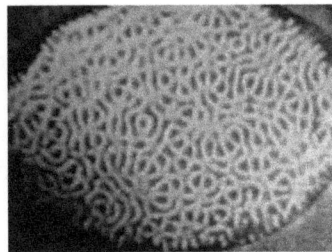

http://www.youtube.com/watch?v=05lo6lop3mk&feature=related

The following images, © Dan Blore, can be found at www.cymatics.org,

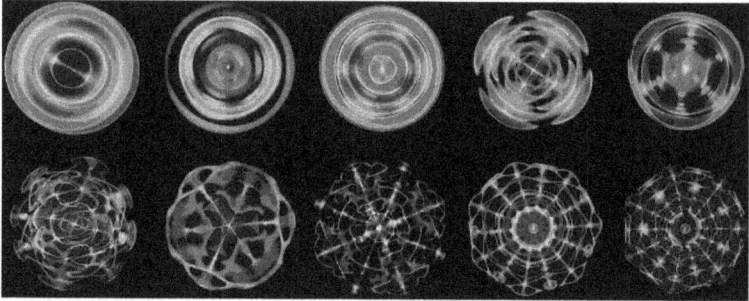

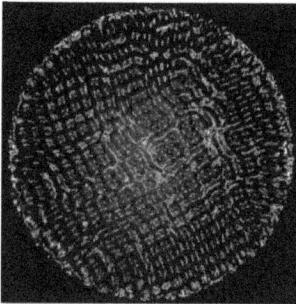

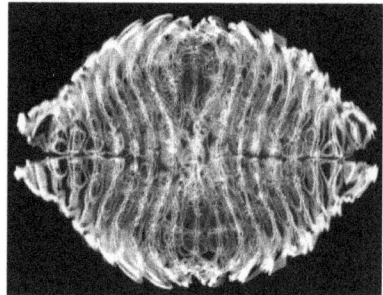

You may also wish to explore: http://cymaticsource.com/ and http://cymatica.net/

An interesting book to consider is:

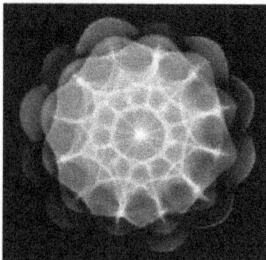

Cymatics: A Study of Wave Phenomena by Hans Jenny

Symbology and Names

Written language is a very recent development in the evolution of human consciousness. The earliest forms of written language were pictures directly representing things and events — known as pictographs. In some ways, pictographs are similar to the oriental form of logograms. The distinct disadvantage of these systems is the huge number of symbols which must be memorized in order to become literate. For example, one must master a minimum of 3,000 logograms to be minimally literate, and over 50,000 to be fully literate.

The Sumerians' addition of phonetic elements around 3800 B.C. was a vital and progressive step towards simplifying the complexity of written language. Three thousand years later, the Greeks added vowels to the Sumerians' symbols which gave birth to the alphabet proper. While it was considered to take 20 years to fully master the system of logograms, the addition of the vowels by the Greeks reduced the learning period to 3 years. This remarkable contribution occurred about 800 B.C.

In our familiarity with written language, we forget that each letter of an alphabet was chosen to **symbolically** represent and communicate a specific conscious intention. We overlook that words are a precise combination of letters each designed to symbolically communicate their own unique meaning, flavour, tone and quality of intelligence.

The fundamental point is that all words, in every language, are symbolic representations of emotions and concepts. **Unfortunately, we cease to apply the same recognition to people's names.**

Why Numbers?

Numbers do <u>not</u> have intrinsic powers that dictate specific consequences any more than the words written on this page do. They are convenient, *symbolic* representations of parts of the whole cosmology of life. Although other symbols have a broader universal import than numbers, the numbers 1 to 9 form a primary logic set that are common to most languages of our world.

Imagine a triangular prism that separates white light into the colors of the rainbow. Similarly, imagine the numbers from 1 to 9 within the prism and diffusing the full spectrum of the qualities of life into 9 separate categories. In this sense, numbers are referred to as the grandparent of all the various oracles such as astrology, the tarot, the I-Ching, etc. As such, they are more generalized in their definition, whereas the details of astrology are extensive, indeed.

As the grandparent of all the oracles, the qualities of the numbers are common to most of the world's mythologies, religions and philosophies which affords another good reason to become familiar with the symbology of numbers.

Identity and Names

Your name is like a mantra, a rhythmic chant that you use in your mind, possibly, hundreds of times every day. It is like a tuning fork that each of us takes note of and responds to in accordance with the intensity and degree of chord or 'dischord' that the set of symbols invoke.

Consider a set of piano keys — would you choose a harmonious chord, a semitone or a complete discord of sound to reverberate throughout your entire being dozens of times per day? Or, imagine that every time someone says your name or you think of yourself consciously or unconsciously, your name resonates like squeaky chalk on a blackboard. How long would it take before you would become irritable? After several years, what would be the cumulative effect of hearing such an irritable sound hundreds of times a day? Just because you get used to the road noise, doesn't mean that the constant drone is not wearing on the emotions and the body.

Your name is possibly the most important source of your identity. Most people, when asked "*Who are you?*" respond by giving their name. If you think you are not attached to your name, take a moment and consider changing your name to something completely different. Seemingly from out of nowhere, the "*hums and haws*" begin and it becomes apparent that people are very attached to their names, identifying strongly with what they are called.

In short, your names are very important to you and you consciously and unconsciously identify strongly with them. In addition, their symbolic resonance has outstanding impact on your character and your life's experience. This book can help you understand that impact and substantiate many of your own personal insights and awareness of yourself.

ABOUT THE AUTHOR

I spent the last 40 years of my career as the CEO and/or President of a number of companies determining what was real and what was not. Time and again, scepticism proved to be a valuable ally although I found it needs to be partnered with an open mind and a willingness to embrace new ideas.

Turning the clock back, I was introduced to numerology in 1969 by a friend who had a reputation for going from one strange encounter to the next. He was passionately enthralled with his latest discovery, and I decided to acquire some background information to effectively counter his arguments. At the time, I was teaching computer technology, having come from an educational background in electronics, industrial process controls and the advanced technological measurement of physical phenomena. At the time, I believed the universe ran strictly on known scientific law.

When I signed up for an introductory course, my intention was to acquire sufficient knowledge to invalidate numerology and therefore rescue my friend from another of his hair-brained ideas.

I studied with vigour and each time I believed I had found a loophole, I challenged my instructor who patiently pointed out the fallacies of my logic. After six months of concerted effort to invalidate numerology, I reluctantly decided to change my attitude and adopt a more positive approach.

It's now more than 40 years since I was introduced to numerology and it has been the core measuring stick of my life and an exceptionally helpful tool for investigating other belief systems. Seldom is there a day when I don't counsel at least one person on their life's experience based on the tools of numerology. Each day offers me deeper insights into the process of life through the metaphor of numbers.

Even so, sometimes I get obstinate and decide that I am allowing numbers and the natural cycles articulated by numerology to dictate my life. At such times, I say *"To heck with numerology, I'm going to do it anyway"*. Those times have fostered the major losses of my life. Slowly I'm becoming more accepting of life and allowing it to be the way it is rather than the way I think it's supposed to be.

During my early studies of numerology, I was plagued with the desire to make the process of learning it more inviting and credible. I'm grateful for the opportunity to share my insights with you.

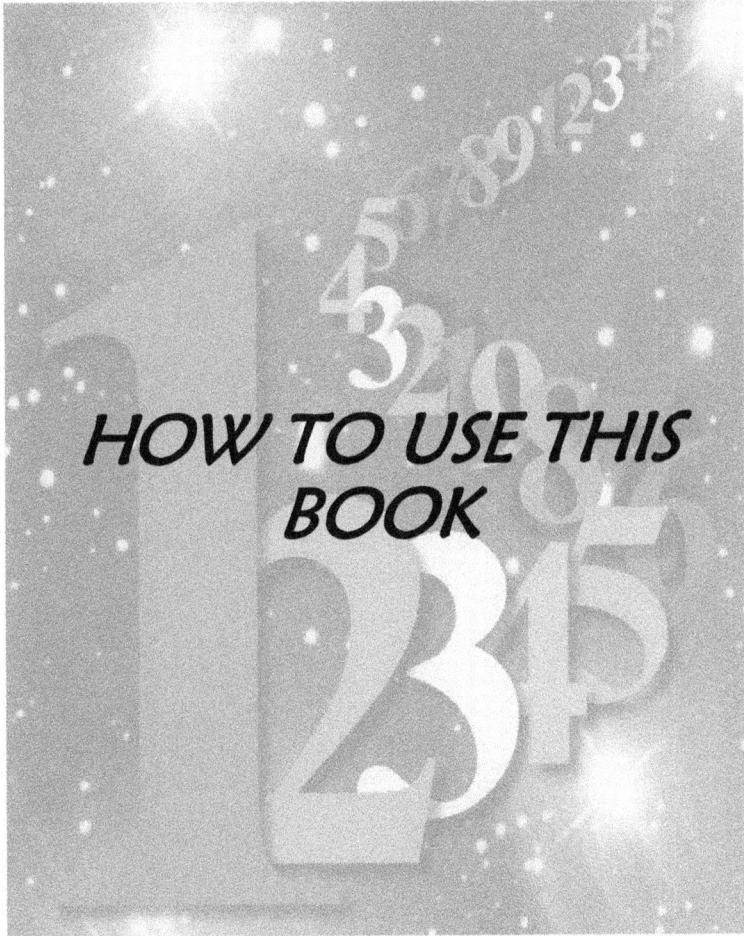

HOW TO USE THIS
BOOK

HOW TO USE THIS BOOK.

This book offers 3 sets of best possible names for your child. If you have a name or names in mind, hopefully they will be in one of the 3 sets.

If not, look up your name choices in the *Alphabetic Index of All Names* (page 121). There you will find a 3 digit reference code to the right of the name. Next look up the reference code in *What Each Name Means* (page 65) and read about the qualities of the name.

Once you have a name that has qualities you like, you need to determine how the name fits with your surname. To do this, you may want to go to www.numbers-count.com and download my name calculator from the section Free Downloads. Type in the name being considered along with your surname. A numeric combination will be generated which is the Destiny Combination of the first and surname. Return to *What Each Name Means* (page 65) and read about the qualities of the destiny combination. If the qualities are to your liking, shout "eureka". If not, follow the above process with your next choice of name. The right name may show itself quickly or it may take some time. But remember, whatever you chose will be with your child for a lifetime.

WHICH NAME IS BEST FOR MY CHILD?

Without question, the very best name combination for your child is one that balances with your family name and is related to the innate potential of your child as determined from his/her birthdate. Consider reading *Why Do Numbers Count* for a full understanding.

In the final analysis, either there is something in a name or there is nothing. If there is nothing in a name, you have nothing to lose by choosing a name from this book. On the other hand, if there is something in a name, you have everything to gain by giving this book every consideration.

BEST POSSIBLE NAMES

MAYBE......

The big question is this:

Do the following "best possible names"

work with <u>YOUR surname</u>?

Please use my Name Calculator to confirm your choice. My
Name Calculator can be found in the download section at
<u>www.numbers-count.com</u>

BEST FEMALE NAMES

Female 3-3-6

The accountable and responsible instincts of the 6 draw out the positive aspects of the 3 and create a particularly congenial and wholesome personality. People with this combination have a superb sense of humour and, at the same time, they are very clear on their direction in life and on their goals. They prefer to do business in an easygoing manner but do not hesitate to back up their smile with conviction and strength. This is a completely balanced combination that offers the best of all possible worlds. They are artistic, creative, practical, and systematic. There is little they cannot do if they set their mind to it. They have a mature, robust, and well balanced physical appearance.

Abagail	Adabelle	Adamma	Aeriela	Alannah
Amarrah	Ambrosine	Antonie	Aphrodite	Arnalda
Atalya	Atlanta	Barbarah	Belloma	Bharbara
Buffy	Bunni	Calantha	Carmacita	Cathlaina
Corenda	Coro	Dammara	Danielea	Derorah
Dhorea	Doneal	Dorothy	Drusy	Eliora
Elora	Eroca	Esmeralda	Guin	Harriotte
Ilu	Iolande	Jaromey	Jenafor	Jeysoca
Jocelan	Jollean	Jollena	Josanne	Judy
Juhli	Kakalina	Kasandra	Katannya	Koraley
Koresa	Kori Anne	Kori-Anne	Korianne	Laara
Lavana	Lavone	Leonda	Leondra	Leora
Levona	Lindoro	Loraleigh	Lorea	Lorenda
Loriennah	Lorihanne	Lu	Lucill	Mahara
Malonie	Mararah	Marceane	Marelena	Margarethe
Margharita	Marihannah	Marjorye	Marlowe	Mary Anna
Maryanna	Meralon	Moneca	Monela	Moreah
Morganne	Morgenna	Morlaine	Nathollie	Nattanya
Nokomis	Novelia	Nunki	Oralie	Orela
Orelee	Orelia	Orlande	Orlea	Orlenda
Polly Anne	Ranalda	Raphaelle	Rayana	Robertha

Rolande	Ronalde	Ronaye	Ronelda	Rosalynne
Rose-Mary	Rosemary	Roseta	Rossanne	Royane
Rusti	Safarina	Samaya	Sharie Lea	Sharlannah
Sharole	Sharra-Lee	Shera-Lea	Sheralea	Sheyona
Sigrud	Sigurd	Soledad	Stevona	Suki
Suti	Taronne	Taylore	Tennora	Toinon
Tomasine	Tonnae	Toranne	Toresa	Torranne
Tosea	Toseia	Toyace	Valana	Varaza
Veronica	Violaine	Wakana		

Female 6-9-6

This combination is responsible, accountable, sensible, paternal, maternal, affectionate, artistic, stable, wise, congenial, and wholesome of character. They are most capable of doing anything they choose to do, both artistic or practical. They create a wonderful home atmosphere and participate fully in community activities, offering their wisdom and support wherever they go. Sometimes they can be a bit on the bossy side and assume that they have all of the answers which is reflected in their favourite expression of "I know". They are so used to being tuned into a global knowingness, that even when they have no idea of what they are being told, they habitually interject "I know. Yes, I know." This habit is exasperating to those close to them.

All-in-all, this is a superb combination. They certainly make excellent counsellors and educators. Their only weakness stems from assuming too much responsibility for themselves and others. As a result, they can suffer from mental stress in the form of migraine headaches.

Abdel	Adine	Adrien	Aiden	Ainslie
Alex	Alexi	Alfie	Alisen	Amine
Andie	Andre	Anett	Anikke	Annze
Arden	Ardine	Arleigh	Armine	Ashe
Ashleigh	Aurore	Belva	Belvia	Benigma
Benita	Bernita	Bertina	Betina	Beverle
Beverlie	Bianche	Bibiane	Bonnilyn	Brittaney
Cacilie	Calle	Callie	Catherin	Cathrine
Cecilia	Celeste	Cella	Clarice	Clemence
Cressida	Cybella	Dabney	Daren	Delilah
Delphina	Delphinia	Delta	Dena	Desma
Diane	Dion	Edina	Edna	Emina
Ermina	Erminia	Ervina	Ervinia	Estelle
Etheline	Fairlie	Fealty	Fela	Felisha
Flo	Flor	Flori	Florri	Flossy

Gabbey	Gabie	Gerta	Gillane	Gillean
Gizale	Gizela	Gladdie	Gratie	Gressa
Greta	Grizela	Hailey	Haley	Hanne
Hannie	Harley	Heath	Hedvika	Helga
Hertha	Imena	Jammie	Janel	Janice
Jaquenetta	Jelene	Jemima	Jeminah	Jemma
Jenica	Jenilee	Jessalyn	Jhande	Jhandie
Jhanett	Jhenda	Jonny	Josy	Joyous
Joys	Kachine	Kamile	Karey	Karmel
Katine	Katrine	Kaye	Kelda	Keziah
Kineta	Korry	Kory	Krystalle	Kymberlee
Lallie	Lancey	Larell	Leagh	Leigha
Lella	Lencay	Levka	Lexa	Lilyane
Lorill	Lorilyn	Louella	Mabel	Mable
Maggie	Maible	Mairen	Manie	Maren
Margery	Maribel	Marien	Marine	Marinie
Marne	Marnie	Marren	Martel	Martyne
Mazell	Melady	Melba	Melissa	Melita
Melka	Melta	Mena	Meredeth	Meredithe
Meriwa	Merna	Michael	Micheal	Mirabel
Mirable	Mirean	Mizella	Namie	Natike
Nattie	Neda	Nedia	Neida	Neinah
Nemia	Nenah	Nerima	Netika	Netka
Netta	Neva	Nidea	Nieda	Nienah
Nolly	Nomi	Normi	Ori	Parke
Pazice	Pernelle	Peta	Petra	Phelia
Pietra	Rachilde	Rae	Rande	Randie
Ranitte	Raven	Raylynne	Raynell	Rea
Remina	Ro	Robbin	Rori	Roslin
Sammie	Scarlet	Seleen	Selene	Selina
Shae	Shandie	Shanneh	Sharie	Sharllyne
Shaylynne	Shea	Shelagh	Shera	Sheree
Sheylah	Sibella	Sigfreda	Sigfrieda	Slena
Slenia	Sonny	Stefa	Steffany	Stella
Stepha	Strella	Suzu	Svetta	Tansley
Terzah	Teya	Theckla	Tory	Velika
Veradis	Verene	Verina	Verna	Victori
Vilhelmina	Vivianne	Vivienna	Von	Voni
Wilfreda	Wilfreida	Wilfrieda	York	Zanne
Zenina	Zenna	Zjandre	Zjeria	

Female 9-6-6

This is one of the more delightful and wholesome combinations available. It is referred to in Chapter 23 in the discussion of destiny combinations. This combination offers the best of many worlds because the accountable, responsible, and sensible 6 draws out all of the positive qualities of the 9. In this case, the humanitarian and altruistic nature of the 9 finds expression in unconditional love, forgiveness, compassion, empathy, and tolerance. Plus all the intuitive, musical, artistic, and visionary qualities of the 9 are enhanced by the 6 expression. The result is a well balanced, affectionate, artistic, stable, wise and congenial nature that embraces life and achieves their goals.

Billy	Bird	Bitki	Blinni	Britt
Claudine	Cristi	Cybil	Dilys	Dorotea
Dulcinea	Dupetta	Georgeanna	Ginny	Gizi
Godgifu	Heniuta	Hild	Jaquelyn	Julieta
Juno	Kim	Kimi	Kitti	Kivi
Laurel	Laurice	Lauryne	Lici	Lil
Lili	Lotus	Loulou	Luela	Lunneta
Michi	Miki	Mildrid	Miquela	Nurianne
Pauline	Roux	Rubetta	Ruella	Suelita
Teodora	Theodosia	Tilly	Tim	Timi
Trixy	Tulanne	Viki	Vikky	Winn
Winni				

BEST MALE NAMES

Male 3-5-8

In this case, the magnetic, optimistic, gregarious, cosmopolitan, articulate, and imaginative 3 source finds expression through the 8 which is the number of material fruition. The 8 expression adds discrimination, balance, leadership, and efficiency to the 3 source. In other words, the 8 draws the 3 to completion and capitalizes on its imaginative, artistic, and entertaining qualities. The 8 insists on results and doesn't allow the 3 to become scattered, unfocused, or superficial.

Abraham	Aeron	Alessio	Amasa	Balthazar
Boony	Brooks	Bucky	Burc	Burl
Burny	Clodomir	Constantine	Cornalle	Cullin
Curt	Cut	Cutty	Daelton	Daganya
Duffy	Dunn	Durwin	Dusty	Eamonn
Erasmo	Ermanno	Eustasius	Geraldo	Gilburt
Giorgio	Greagoir	Greiogair	Guy	Hoibeard
Hugh	Hull	Hux	Isadore	Isidoro
Jaysone	Jud	Justis	Kaseko	Kistur
Knoton	Kurtis	Langstone	Milburn	Montagne
Nathanial	Nealson	Niccolo	Normane	Nortrop
Nur	Nuri	Obediah	Octavien	Onslow
Orino	Orion	Osmond	Pacome	Quill
Quincy	Reamonn	Rickwood	Rogatien	Romford
Ruck	Rurick	Seosaidh	Sholto	Stanhope
Sully	Teagon	Thomae	Thormond	Titus
Tucky	Turpin	Ulrich	Zaccaria	Zahaval

Male 6-2-8

This is a balanced combination in the sense that the 8 expression draws the energy of the 6 to a point of completion and fruition. Material success is typically substantial given that this combination begins with the capable, intelligent, responsible qualities of the 6 and completes with the discriminating and results oriented nature of the 8. These people have a very strong sense of commitment to home, family, business, and community. They stay clear, focused, and self-contained in times of conflict. This combination fosters an exceptionally capable administrator who embraces a deep sense of concern and respect for those who he manages. On a less positive note, the 8 doesn't add much humour or relaxation to the rather serious 6.

Although this is a balanced combination, it is very results oriented and is not suitable for everyone. This is especially true for women because the external material focus of the 8 is at odds with the energy of the internal female genitals. The administrative and material gains that this combination offers are typically offset by reproductive disorders for women using these numbers.

Abbey	Abe	Abie	Aldred	Allen
Alsten	Amery	Anastatius	Anstice	Archer
Archie	Arte	Artie	Arvey	Aswine
Avery	Aymer	Azriel	Baden	Baghel
Bainbridge	Barnett	Barrie	Bartlett	Bartolomeo
Bear	Beaty	Bernard	Bevan	Blasien
Blayze	Bo	Bond	Bor	Bozsi
Braden	Brainerd	Brande	Brander	Brandie
Brodrick	Caisey	Calen	Casey	Casper
Cho	Christoph	Claine	Clane	Claybirne
Claybourne	Clayten	Clovis	Colin	Conny
Costin	Dalbert	Dannisen	Dante	Dareld
Darmel	Daye	Delmar	Dennisan	Derald

Devland	Dominy	Dory	Doy	Driscol
Drydane	Edgar	Eliezer	Elstan	Eustazio
Ezzard	Fabrice	Fane	Farren	Fernand
Ferran	Floyd	Fraine	Frankye	Frean
Gabbie	Garde	Gardie	Garett	Garfield
Garrett	Garvie	Gerard	Gerrard	Gersham
Glenndan	Gord	Graem	Graysen	Gresham
Greysan	Griswold	Hagen	Haile	Halden
Hale	Hamdrem	Hamelin	Hamlen	Hanssen
Harel	Hartley	Hearst	Helvan	Hilaire
Hildon	Horst	Ingelran	Jabez	Jase
Jefferey	Jonn	Joris	Jyotis	Karlens
Karre	Kelsan	Kerbay	Kevan	Koby
Laddie	Lambert	Lance	Lawler	Lawney
Leah	Lenaic	Leverett	Lonny	Lorinc
Lysander	Magre	Marten	Mayer	Medlar
Meynard	Millford	Millos	Monti	Morry
Mortin	Mory	Nathen	Neall	Nichols
Nicol	Nicoli	Niklos	Noll	Obour
Ody	Oki	Olwyn	Othis	Padget
Patrek	Pattie	Paxten	Pov	Primo
Radbourne	Raymie	Razel	Reyhan	Rob
Robby	Roch	Rollin	Ross	Royd
Sanders	Saville	Seabright	Seann	Seeley
Shepard	Simson	Slawek	Steffan	Tadewi
Tebald	Teman	Tibold	Tierman	Timon
Tivon	Toby	Tor	Torr	Torri
Tremain	Tycho	Valentijn	Waller	Wallie
Walters	Waylen	Welland	Wendall	Willdon
Worrill	Yarde	Yvor	Zackery	

Male 6-9-6

This combination is responsible, accountable, sensible, paternal, maternal, affectionate, artistic, stable, wise, congenial, and wholesome of character. They are most capable of doing anything they choose to do both artistic or practical. They create a wonderful home atmosphere and participate fully in community activities, offering their wisdom and support wherever they go. Sometimes they can be a bit on the bossy side and assume that they have all of the answers which is reflected in their favourite expression of "I know". They are so used to being tuned into a global knowingness, that even when they have no idea of what they are being told, they habitually interject "I know. Yes, I know." This habit is exasperating to those close to them.

All-in-all, this is a superb combination. They certainly make excellent counsellors and educators. Their only weakness stems from assuming too much responsibility for themselves and others. As a result, they can suffer from mental stress in the form of migraine headaches.

Abdel	Abey	Aden	Adrien	Aiden
Aimen	Albrecht	Aldridge	Alex	Alexi
Alfie	Alleyn	Allister	Allyne	Alphie
Ander	Andie	Andre	Andrei	Angell
Ansel	Arden	Arend	Arie	Armen
Arnett	Ashbey	Asher	Avner	Axel
Balder	Baltek	Barnet	Barten	Bartlet
Baye	Bertan	Beval	Bishop	Blade
Blom	Bodil	Bondy	Borg	Boy
Bradlie	Bradney	Briante	Brodny	Carlile
Carsen	Castel	Cawley	Chalmer	Chapmen
Cirillo	Clayne	Clemence	Clinton	Crandell
Cranley	Dabney	Dalziel	Dane	Danie
Daren	Darren	Davidsen	Dean	Demas
Denbay	Denman	Derrack	Desmand	Dino

	Dominick	Domnin	Don	Doni
D...	Dorn	Dow	Earvin	Edan
Eldredge	Elsan	Eman	Erai	Evan
Eward	Ezkah	Fairlie	Farlie	Farrel
Fentan	Fernald	Flavien	Frayne	Gabe
Gabie	Garek	Garrek	Garret	Garvey
Gibor	Ginson	Gladdie	Godfrith	Gordy
Gradey	Haggen	Hailey	Haley	Halsted
Hamelyn	Handley	Hareth	Harley	Hazzel
Heath	Heathcliff	Hilton	Howin	Ivon
Jarlen	Jasper	Jhae	Jodocus	Joh
Jonny	Kamel	Karey	Keary	Kemal
Kiyoshi	Kory	Lafe	Lancey	Latimer
Lawley	Leicester	Lensar	Lewas	Linford
Livingston	Louison	Lowis	Maddisen	Marcellin
Marien	Marreck	Marren	Martel	Maxwel
Medwan	Mehemet	Mensah	Merrack	Michael
Michale	Micheal	Mikael	Mikol	Minor
Montague	Monty	Morin	Nattie	Nolly
Norm	Normi	Oby	Odin	Ormin
Orvin	Ossy	Parke	Parker	Parnell
Parrnell	Pate	Peeter	Petar	Petria
Philo	Philpot	Pickworth	Piotr	Port
Radvers	Rae	Raiden	Ralegh	Raleigh
Ralphie	Rande	Randie	Renard	Rimon
Robbin	Rodrick	Roi	Rolf	Rolph
Roslin	Rossy	Rycroft	Sammie	Sayers
Sayres	Shae	Shea	Sheppard	Sheremen
Sheridan	Sherman	Shiro	Shurwood	Simpson
Slane	Sonny	Stanley	Swayne	Sweeney
Swinton	Talbert	Tanek	Thaxter	Therstan
Tobin	Tonik	Torry	Traye	Tredway
Troy	Tullius	Tymon	Vachel	Vareck
Varne	Varner	Victoir	Victor	Von
Wade	Walfred	Walther	Warde	Warfield
Wattie	Westlay	Whane	Wido	Wilford
Winston	Winthrop	York	Yutu	

Male 9-6-6

This is one of the more delightful and wholesome combinations available. This combination offers the best of many worlds because the accountable, responsible, and sensible 6 draws out all of the positive qualities of the 9. In this case, the humanitarian and altruistic nature of the 9 finds expression in unconditional love, forgiveness, compassion, empathy, and tolerance. Plus all the intuitive, musical, artistic, and visionary qualities of the 9 are enhanced by the 6 expression. The result is a well balanced, affectionate, artistic, stable, wise and congenial nature that embraces life and achieves their goals.

Bartholomew	Billy	Britt	Chim	Curcio
Dik	Dirk	Duarte	Erasmus	Firmin
Gilchrist	Giustino	Griffin	Griz	Holbrook
Hugo	Huxford	Irwinn	Jin	Kasoleo
Killy	Kim	Knight	Krispin	Loulou
Lucio	Ludlow	Luigino	Mich	Michi
Miki	Mirit	Myrddin	Roxbury	Rufo
Seamus	Seumas	Sissil	Skippy	Smith
Sprague	Stephanus	Tim	Tormund	Tudor
Urson	Vandute	Vik	Whit	Whitby
Winn	Wirth	Wulcott		

SECOND BEST NAMES

MAYBE.....

The big question is this:

Do the following "second best possible names"

work with <u>YOUR surname</u>?

Please use my Name Calculator to confirm your choice. My
Name Calculator can be found in the download section at
www.numbers-count.com

SECOND BEST FEMALE NAMES

Female 6-5-2

These are very intelligent, capable, responsible people who are gracious and easygoing. They always have something pleasant to say about everybody and are a perfect choice for giving a toast to the bride or grace at the supper table. Their intelligence comes across in a smooth and friendly manner. They are excellent diplomats, combining a superb depth of mind with diplomacy and tact. As delightful as they are to be with from a social standpoint, living or working with them can be another matter because, in the end, they have a very definite tendency to procrastinate. Apart from their procrastinating ways, these people enjoy a wholesome, well-balanced personality.

Aggie	Aine	Alike	Ane	Ann Louise
Arbel	Ardyce	Aren	Averyl	Baptiste
Bela	Belia	Belinda	Blaire	Brandice
Carisse	Carlynne	Cassaundra	Cassie	Cate
Catie	Celah	Celestine	Charlie	Chartsie
Chela	Chryseida	Cody	Cordy	Coriss
Crescente	Dacey	Dagney	Daisie	Dannie
Darcey	Darilye	Dasie	Dayle	Denna
Desa	Desiree	Dezba	Dianne	Donni
Doris	Dorris	Dorthi	Dosi	Eadith
Editha	Edwina	Eidann	Eireen	Eirene
Elissa	Elita	Elka	Elyette	Emelye
Emmalyn	Emylee	Ena	Eran	Ericka
Erina	Erna	Esma	Ethered	Eudosia
Ewa	Faline	Fancie	Faythe	France
Francie	Freyja	Garnet	Gaye	Gilberta
Gisella	Gleda	Goldi	Grenta	Gretna
Grishelda	Gwenhwyvar	Hallie	Holli	Imperial
Ireene	Irena	Irenee	Ivanne	Jade
Jaemi	Jaime	Jaimie	Jamie	Jannel
Jelenne	Jennica	Jennilee	Jessalynn	Jessamy

Jesselynne	Jessika	Jetta	Jezebel	Jodi
Jomi	Jonsy	Joylyn	Kacie	Kaile
Kailie	Kandice	Karel	Karlie	Karstie
Karyne	Kelee	Kelia	Kelvina	Kerral
Klare	Kristae	Kristea	Kyrena	Kyrenia
Larke	Larousse	Lassie	Leilah	Lelah
Leta	Letisha	Liko	Lilliane	Lilyanne
Lizabeth	Lorilynn	Lotty	Madelyn	Maecy
Magnilde	Maisie	Mannie	Marje	Marjie
Marley	Marsie	Marthe	Martynne	Mary Beth
Marybeth	Maxime	Mendeley	Merja	Mertah
Michelina	Myrale	Nadine	Nandie	Narie
Nashie	Neisha	Nera	Nevan	Ninetta
Nishera	Nori	Norri	Oni	Page
Paige	Palmer	Pauletto	Penta	Perlette
Petrina	Pryor	Rachel	Raine	Rakel
Razell	Reina	Relba	Remja	Rena
Renee	Resida	Riane	Richela	Riena
Robyn	Roni	Roslindis	Row	Sadie
Sapphire	Seda	Sedee	Selewine	Semira
Septima	Shaine	Shane	Shanie	Shanleigh
Sharen	Shena	Sheran	Sibeta	Sileas
Solly	Sophy	Stefani	Stephani	Stephenie
Stormy	Tabithe	Tace	Tacie	Tareyn
Taryne	Teca	Theda	Thema	Tony
Totsi	Tourmaline	Tracie	Trescha	Valery
Vannie	Vicenta	Vonni	Wandie	Wenda
Winema	Yonit	Zella	Zhorzh	→

Female 6-3-9

The 9 draws out the artistic, musical, and community-minded qualities of the 6 and adds a flair of inspiration to an already wholesome and congenial nature. This combination has a strong humanitarian side that is generous, compassionate, and empathic. They have a good sense of rhythm and appreciate music. These people can have intense moments of jealousy, temper, and possessiveness which pass rather quickly. Although they can worry extensively about the welfare of family, friends, and community, they always maintain an atmosphere of responsibility. This is one of the better first name combinations.

Adlen	Ailie	Alie	Alvine	Amsey
Andrel	Ange	Angie	Areli	Ariel
Arlie	Asber	Aurelea	Balbine	Beatriz
Bertha	Bethia	Birdella	Blanche	Blondy
Bonni	Brandeis	Brenna	Brianne	Caire
Caldwell	Candie	Candre	Carie	Carmen
Carmine	Carrie	Cassey	Cecilla	Charmell
Cipressa	Clianthe	Consuela	Cori	Corri
Daisey	Dalien	Danice	Danlei	Dannye
Darline	Darsey	Delina	Dextra	Donny
Dorthy	Dyanne	Edeline	Edwyna	Effia
Effra	Ela	Elbertine	Elisha	Elizsa
Elmina	Elvina	Elyssa	Emeline	Erica
Esta	Estee	Etheldred	Eveline	Felcia
Felicia	Filbertha	Fredrika	Friederike	Gabriel
Gena	Genia	Goldy	Gretal	Grizella
Gwenda	Gwenette	Haidie	Halley	Hattie
Heda	Hedia	Heida	Helsa	Herma
Hermia	Holly	Idaline	Ingaberg	Ingibiorg
Jackelyn	Jacquenetta	Jakie	Jamey	Janifer
Janthine	Jayme	Jaymie	Jessa	Jewelle
Jillane	Jobi	Jody	Kacey	Kailey
Kamille	Karesi	Kathe	Kathie	Katline
Kayle	Keeley	Keitha	Kenna	Keriann
Kerri-Ann	Kerwina	Kesia	Kessiah	Ketzia
Konni	Lavinie	Lea	Leia	Leisha
Lenette	Lerinda	Leshia	Levina	Linetta
Lori	Lorri	Maddie	Maisey	Marcine
Marilen	Marjery	Marline	Maryse	Mathilde
Mechelle	Mehira	Melan	Melenie	Melina
Memtba	Mercedes	Merleen	Merlene	Merlina
Michella	Mignon	Milena	Monic	Nelda
Nepa	Neya	Nezza	Nineta	Norry
Patrice	Philbertha	Poni	Rainey	Raychel
Regan	Regina	Reyna	Rhetta	Rheva
Rhodi	Roslynn	Sadey	Sadye	Sayde

Shayne	Sheila	Shela	Shelia	Sherlee
Siko	Stepka	Stesha	Tacye	Tannie
Tarres	Tawnie	Tawrine	Tayler	Terese
Terisa	Tesia	Tracey	Treacy	Trenna
Tresa	Triso	Vedette	Vonny	Welda
Welma	Xanthe	Zetta	Zeva	

Female 2-4-6

This is a delightful, gracious, warm, loving combination that will always go the extra mile to seek understanding. At the same time, they will not give themselves away with excessive procrastination or an inability to say no. They are a delight to be with and always find something loving and supportive to say about everyone. Their compassionate and tactful nature embraces both practical and artistic skills. They have a strong love for home and family and can also do well in the business world.

This is a desirable combination for a woman because the 2 source number is in tune with her instinctual nature. On the other hand, males using this combination can be very gentle, if not passive. Robert is often called Bob which is a 6-4-1 and affords Robert a strong measure of male energy.

Ada	Adar	Adelphe	Adira	Adria
Agnese	Ahimsa	Aida	Aimee	Aleksey
Alethe	Alisa	Alithia	Alitza	Alizka
Althee	Ama	Amandi	Amira	Anselme
Arda	Ardere	Ardia	Ardra	Arette
Arva	Ava	Avira	Barbee	Barbra
Bergetta	Bertrande	Blanca	Bobbye	Callida
Camilla	Carmilla	Carneen	Carnene	Casia
Catalin	Catha	Cathee	Cayla	Chaitra
Charissa	Charita	Cherolynn	Chistabelle	Christabelle
Clementina	Collett	Connie	Corinne	Corrinne
Danette	Danyelle	Dara	Daria	Darree

Dasha	Daveen	Davina	Derori	Devon
Diahann	Diandra	Doe	Dore	Dorie
Dorrie	Eadie	Edouardine	Edrea	Eglantine
Elaise	Elfreda	Elfreida	Elfrieda	Ellenita
Emera	Ernaline	Ethelinda	Evadne	Falda
Falma	Fatina	Federica	Flavia	Franceline
Fraya	Frederica	Gayleen	Gaylene	Grizemalie
Hana	Ignatzia	Ilanna	Inalani	Innogen
Iodie	Jacinda	Jaryeen	Jaryene	Jascha
Jeraldine	Jeremiah	Joaquima	Joice	Jolie
Joscelin	Kagami	Kajsa	Kalah	Karissa
Karita	Kassia	Kata	Katee	Kathy Lee
Katia	Keiko	Kristabelle	Lanna	Larisa
Lavelle	Layla	Leanne	Lee Ann	LeeAnn
Leesa	Leianne	Leonn	Lianna	Liranna
Lisandra	Loise	Lonnie	Louanna	Loyce
Lyaksandr	Mackenzie	Magnhilda	Maia	Mairee
Manda	Manette	Mara	Marcelle	Maria
Mariee	Marinda	Marinette	Marisha	Marnette
Marsha	Martinka	Mary Ellen	Maryellen	Masha
Matilda	Matyash	Melanthe	Mellony	Miranda
Moe	Moire	Morie	Morrie	Nadette
Nalani	Nancee	Nasya	Nicholle	Niyanna
Palila	Panthia	Penthea	Pollie	Rama
Rashida	Rayelle	Rebeka	Reeva	Rhiana
Rhodes	Rihana	Robbie	Rodie	Rosel
Roxey	Rozine	Sabinna	Sabrinna	Sala
Salvina	Santina	Sanya	Sascha	Shada
Sharette	Sharma	Sheehan	Silvana	Stasa
Tabia	Taka	Tammany	Tanhya	Tara Lynn
Teressa	Thalia	Tobe	Tobie	Ursule
Vanda	Viridiana	Viviana	Wilone	Wynone
Zarina	Zarrna	Zeena	Ziyanta	Zorine

Female 2-6-8

The 2-4-6 and the 2-6-8 are similar in many ways. Both are very considerate, loving, and affectionate, yet they know how to stand their ground and not give themselves away. This is a very charming personality that can do exceptionally well as a mediator or a diplomat. The 2-6-8 is much more materially oriented than is the 2-4-6 and favours business over home and family life. Like the 2-4-6, the 2-6-8 combination is very gentle for a male. These people desire quality and quantity but are short on the ambition required for the fulfilment of their dreams. They frequently fantasize about winning the lottery or inheriting money.

Although this combination creates a very pleasant ambience for a female, it is not a good combination for a woman from a health standpoint. The source number of 2 which is directly related to feminine energy is in contradiction to the 8 which is externally oriented. The contrast can manifest in reproductive system disorders.

Aeriell	Affrica	Afra	Agathy	Ajani
Alica	Alicia	Alla	Aloula	Althita
Alyeen	Alyene	Amissa	Anais	Angele
Annan	Anthia	Aphra	Arielle	Arleyne
Atheen	Athene	Atida	Ayaz	Babita
Basilia	Bastienne	Beattie	Benedette	Benedikta
Blasia	Bobbe	Bobbie	Cacia	Cadence
Calinda	Calvina	Carla	Carlee	Carmeline
Casta	Cerelia	Chelsae	Chelsea	Cipriana
Clara	Clarinda	Cleo	Cloe	Clorinde
Clotilde	Cynara	Dagmar	Dahlia	Danelle
Danielle	Daphna	Darlleen	Debor	Derorit
Dorek	Elayne	Elizabet	Elladine	Emillion
Eranthe	Evalynne	Fara	Farand	Faria
Farra	Farrand	Farrar	Ferdinande	Filantha
Fiore	Fredericka	Fronde	Gabrielle	Galina

Galna	Gerhardine	Gilana	Grazia	Gretalle
Grisolde	Hagar	Hagia	Halette	Hebernia
Henrieta	Henryetta	Herleva	Holde	Hope
Hyacintha	Hyacinthia	Hypatia	Iantha	Ignacia
Isobel	Jana	Jania	Jeane	Jeanie
Joliet	Jolisse	Jonie	Jonnett	Kalyca
Kama	Karida	Karitta	Karma	Katharyn
Kathi Lee	Katta	Kavindra	Klarrisa	Lacee
Laila	Lala	Laynee	Leela	Liadah
Macha	Magda	Maralynn	Marceline	Margalis
Margalith	Margarid	Margette	Mariellen	Marika
Marishka	Marissa	Marita	Marka	Marrissa
Marta	Maryam	Maxene	Mayda	Milleena
Moswen	Mozel	Myrlanna	Nanna	Nasia
Natha	Nealey	Neathe	Nonnie	Ollie
Paza	Pazia	Pearline	Philantha	Prosper
Rafa	Rayleen	Raylene	Rebekka	Rejane
Rejean	Richarda	Rikarda	Rosine	Rothnie
Roxie	Sarene	Sarina	Sawa	Seena
Seon	Serena	Sharra-Lyn	Shondell	Siana
Sidonne	Simonne	Sitala	Stacee	Stacia
Starla	Suletu	Tacitah	Taima	Talasi
Talitha	Tama	Tamar	Tamee	Tamra
Tavia	Tottie	Tove	Trava	Wakiza
Yelena	Yevetta	Ysolde	Zabina	Zabrina
Zanete				

Female 3-5-8

In this case, the magnetic, optimistic, gregarious, cosmopolitan, articulate, and imaginative 3 source finds expression through the 8 which is the number of material fruition. The 8 expression adds discrimination, balance, leadership, and efficiency to the 3 source. In other words, the 8 draws the 3 to completion and capitalizes on its imaginative, artistic, and entertaining qualities. The 8 insists on results and doesn't allow the 3 to become scattered, unfocused, or superficial.

Adrianna	Aletea	Alexandrine	Alexena	Amaliya
Ananda	Andriana	Annaliese	Annemarie	Annmaria
Arabele	Ardatha	Ariana	Aridatha	Atalia
Avasa	Berengaria	Brooks	Carolynne	Cassandra
Clarabelle	Conchetta	Constantine	Deborah	Desmona
Dorothi	Dorthea	Drucy	Drus	Drusi
Dusty	Elizabetha	Ezraella	Gaetane	Georgee
Georgia	Gratiana	Gregoria	Hasana	Hollea
Isadore	Johane	Jonalen	Judi	Justinn
Kamarah	Karalai	Karalee	Karayan	Karole
Katannia	Konstanze	Koralie	Latashia	Leonelle
Leota	Loralynne	Madalyna	Magdaleen	Magdalene
Mahalah	Marianna	Marjorie	Misu	Moranne
Nikoletta	Noor	Norea	Novena	Obelia
Oleta	Orabel	Oriane	Petronia	Ronae
Rosetta	Rozalle	Rozella	Samara	Samaria
Savannah	Shenoa	Sheona	Sherona	Simonetta
Sudi	Sumi	Sutki	Suzin	Tabatha
Tamarah	Tara Lee	Taralee	Tatianna	Thorberta
Unity	Valorey	Vernona	Violante	Volante
Wenonah	Yosepha	Yovela		

SECOND BEST MALE NAMES

Male 6-5-2

These are very intelligent, capable, responsible people who are gracious and easygoing.   They always have something pleasant to say about everybody and are a perfect choice for giving a toast to the bride or grace at the supper table. Their intelligence comes across in a smooth and friendly manner. They are excellent diplomats, combining a superb depth of mind with diplomacy and tact. As delightful as they are to be with from a social standpoint, living or working with them can be another matter because, in the end, they have a very definite tendency to procrastinate.   Apart from their procrastinating ways, these people enjoy a wholesome, well-balanced personality.

Abel	Acker	Albie	Alek	Alter
Ancell	Andrew	Andrien	Arciet	Arcite
Ardley	Aren	Arlet	Arne	Arnie
Atuanya	Averyl	Aylmer	Aymeric	Bailie
Bale	Baptiste	Barney	Bartley	Beal
Bela	Benyamin	Berenger	Berkeley	Berklay
Blaire	Blakey	Boski	Broc	Brocky
Brutus	Bryane	Bryon	Byron	Camey
Carter	Carvey	Cassie	Chale	Chandler
Chaney	Charlie	Chico	Chilo	Cob
Cobby	Cody	Collin	Cordy	Cort
Cross	Cvetan	Dacey	Dagney	Dannie
Darcey	Darwen	Daryle	Deverell	Dewain
Dickon	Dinsmor	Donn	Donni	Driscoll
Dwaen	Dwaine	Dwane	Eadwin	Ealdfrith
Ean	Einar	Everley	Farlen	Farnel
Filippo	Fraze	Frazer	Frazier	Gadiel
Gage	Galmier	Gamiel	Garey	Garnet
Gatien	Geary	Geraint	Gerald	Gerrald
Gifford	Gilead	Graige	Grayden	Graye
Grigori	Hakem	Hanley	Hasen	Haskel

Hawley	Hazlett	Heall	Hephzibah	Ignate
Isidor	Isidro	Jaem	Jaime	Jaimie
Jamie	Jared	Jarett	Jarred	Jarrett
Javier	Jehan	Jerad	Jereme	Jeremie
Jhon	Jodi	John	Julius	Justus
Kale	Kalven	Karel	Karle	Karney
Kayne	Keegen	Keeler	Kelemen	Kelman
Kelvan	Kendal	Klare	Knolls	Kolmin
Kosti	Kristo	Lache	Loyd	Macey
Madisen	Maecy	Maje	Manleich	Mannie
Mansfield	Marcinek	Marley	Marsden	Mathe
Mather	Maxime	Mehtar	Milton	Moris
Moritz	Morly	Morris	Mos	Mosi
Mylo	Neree	Newlands	Nilson	Noby
Nodin	Norby	Norvin	Nuru	Orin
Orrick	Orrin	Ozzy	Page	Paige
Palmer	Parge	Paten	Pavel	Peverel
Phelan	Primael	Pryor	Radley	Rahmet
Rainer	Rainier	Ramsden	Rancell	Rane
Rawleigh	Rennard	Ridgeway	Rock	Rolt
Ron	Ryton	Sahen	Shaine	Shane
Shino	Shipton	Shon	Skeat	Skeeter
Solly	Spangler	Stefan	Stephan	Stinson
Tancred	Thatcher	Theudobald	Thom	Tidzio
Timothy	Titos	Toli	Tomlin	Tony
Toski	Trace	Tracie	Valient	Vernan
Victorin	Virgilio	Warden	Ware	Wemilat
Whitelaw	Whitlock	Wilmot	Wilson	Winstonn
Witton	Wolf	Wyot	Yogi	Yonit
Zenas				

Male 6-3-9

The 9 draws out the artistic, musical, and community-minded qualities of the 6 and adds a flair of inspiration to an already wholesome and congenial nature. This combination has a strong humanitarian side that is generous, compassionate, and empathic. They have a good sense of rhythm and appreciate music. These people can have intense moments of jealousy, temper, and possessiveness which pass rather quickly. Although they can worry extensively about the welfare of family, friends, and community, they always maintain an atmosphere of responsibility. This is one of the better first name combinations.

Ace	Acie	Adelin	Airel	Alden
Ange	Angie	Ansell	Anshelm	Archaimbaud
Archambaud	Ardlen	Arel	Ariel	Arlie
Arminel	Arney	Arshile	Asker	Atley
Aurelio	Avniel	Axell	Bailey	Barse
Base	Basie	Beltran	Bentlee	Bertramd
Blagden	Bonds	Boris	Both	Bryony
Caldwell	Calliste	Calvert	Care	Carmen
Carmine	Castell	Charley	Chase	Chilton
Christophorus	Cirio	Ciro	Columbo	Corby
Cori	Cormick	Corty	Crichton	Dalziell
Daniel	Darsey	Davide	Delain	Donny
Dwayne	Earl	Edvard	Egan	Elia
Elijah	Elisha	Emelen	Erhard	Erland
Ernald	Etienne	Ewald	Ezard	Farnley
Farrell	Fineas	Fitzgerald	Fons	Friederike
Fritzino	Gable	Gabriel	Gainer	Garner
Garnier	Geralt	Gerhardt	Gervais	Gilot
Gino	Godwin	Gregary	Gualterio	Gualtiero
Hadden	Hadleigh	Halley	Harbert	Hardie
Hartwell	Harve	Harvie	Hazen	Hod
Houghton	Inigo	Jabe	Jake	Jakie
Jamey	Jareb	Jarek	Jaret	Jarret
Jarvey	Jayme	Jaymie	Jessee	Job

Jody	Johny	Kaiser	Kase	Keath
Keeley	Kenan	Kesar	Kienan	Kiernan
Lander	Lavern	Lenard	Lio	Litton
Lori	Loudon	Maddie	Marlen	Matthew
Matthiew	Maxwell	Medard	Melan	Napier
Nicolis	Norry	Norvil	Norvyn	Noy
Ogin	Otis	Paine	Patrice	Phineas
Pippo	Prane	Race	Rafferty	Rainger
Ramsey	Randle	Range	Ranger	Ransell
Rayner	Redpath	Reece	Regan	Rehard
Reinald	Renald	Rico	Ringo	Risto
Roc	Rocky	Rollins	Ryane	Ryon
Saber	Sacher	Sahile	Seba	Seraphin
Sewall	Shayne	Sheldan	Sigmond	Sinclaire
Sinclare	Standcliffe	Stanfield	Steward	Storr
Tanner	Tannie	Tayler	Thacher	Tiernan
Tilton	Town	Tracey	Trentham	Tymothy
Vance	Vianney	Wetherell	Wolfy	Woodruff
Xylon	Yardley	Yogy	Yorick	Yoshin
Zared	Zolly			

Male 5-1-6

This is a vibrant, alive and dynamic combination. No moss grows under the feet of the 5 who has outstanding analytical skills and a determination to move forward at every opportunity. The 6 expression offers a clear channel for the aliveness of the 5. The 6 also helps to stabilize the 5 by adding an air of caution, responsibility, and accountability. Internally, these people are intense. Externally, they are congenial and progressive. They exude a great deal of confidence and trust in their lightning fast mental abilities. They have no fear of getting backed into a corner or of being taken advantage of in any way at any time. This combination is in the top 20% of all possible combinations.

Adalfuns	Anatolio	Barnabus	Benci	Benny
Bently	Bryse	Cedric	Cerdic	Clem
Clive	Dell	Demmy	Denis	Dex
Diderik	Dillie	Dinse	Dumaka	Edlyn
Eldric	Elvyn	Ely	Emlyn	Emmit
Erwin	Eskild	Fedir	Ferd	Ferguson
Filley	Fred	Fredi	Fyfe	Giffie
Gilbey	Gile	Griffie	Hendrik	Herb
Hermy	Huata	Hyde	Hymie	Jer
Jerri	Jessy	Kaluwa	Kenny	Kenric
Kevitt	Kimmie	Kineks	Kjeld	Mell
Merill	Merrill	Mikelis	Miller	Nickie
Pepin	Peppy	Perc	Phillipe	Price
Riley	Ryle	Rylie	Sheffy	Sherwin
Simen	Skerry	Skye	Smedly	Sven
Tedd	Thaddaus	Thedrick	Tibbles	Timmie
Tristen	Truesdale	Verill	Verrill	Vincent
Welch	Wen	Whistler	Whitfield	Wicek
Wilek	Wilkie	Witney	Wren	Zeb
Zeki	Zerk			

Male 9-8-8

The universal ideals of the 9 strive to find expression through the 8 in the material world. Ask these people how they are doing and they will tell you about the big business deal that didn't quite make it. But there is one cooking now that will be "the big one", putting them on easy street for the rest of their lives. The 9 quality is inspired and visionary but lacks the practicality to put their ideals into action. The 8 expression helps this process considerably. Unfortunately, the 8 also has huge plans for material success and between the two of them, they get carried away with schemes to become billionaires. They want immediate results and lack the patience and willingness to make the effort required to achieve their goals. Remember, the 8 is an administrator and not the worker. These people can have an air of being pompous and good-natured at the same time.

Athanasios	Austen	Bill	Bix	Bixby
Bohumil	Briggs	Brough	Chauncey	Chill
Dilly	Dimitry	Dixy	Donatello	Dwight
Eadmund	Eduard	Gauthier	Giffy	Griffy
Gris	Hi	Hutton	Iz	Khoury
Kimmy	Kylin	Lauren	Lin	Lockwood
Mattheus	Mikk	Mitch	Nic	Nicky
Nil	Osburn	Pauley	Philips	Phillipp
Rodmund	Samuel	Shurlock	Sig	Skipp
Slim	Thebault	Thorburn	Timmy	Todorko
Valerius	Vilis	Willoughby	Zupeika	

THIRD BEST NAMES

MAYBE.....

The big question is this:

Do the following "third best possible names"

work with <u>YOUR surname</u>?

Please use my Name Calculator to confirm your choice. My
Name Calculator can be found in the download section at
<u>www.numbers-count.com</u>

THIRD BEST FEMALE NAMES

Female 1-5-6

Although this combination can be very self-centered, headstrong, and independent, they always return to an atmosphere of sensibility and congeniality. Primarily, they look out first for themselves and second they keep an eye on the needs of their family. This combination creates a strong willed individual who knows what they want and goes straight after their desires. Their nature lends itself to being good bosses in the sense that they uphold firm convictions and are not upset by the emotional needs of others. Yet, they are sufficiently receptive to new ideas that others see them as being reasonable. These people can be very creative in a practical sense. Women with this combination are competitive and do not take a back seat to their mates at any time. These numbers are in the top 20% of all the possible combinations.

Aggi	Aislinn	Akili	Aliss	Allys
An	Ani	Ardis	Ardith	Avis
Avyril	Babs	Berney	Binga	Blair
Bryna	Cabby	Carlynn	Cass	Cassi
Cati	Celestin	Charil	Chastity	Cherice
Chitsa	Christa	Christia	Chyna	Cilehe
Claudetta	Clemmie	Crescent	Cyma	Dacy
Daffy	Dagny	Daisi	Danni	Darcy
Darryl	Daryl	Dasi	Dathi	Dawn
Dennie	Desire	Diann	Disa	Drisa
Edithe	Edwine	Elke	Emyle	Eppie
Erine	Esme	Fanny	Fayth	Felicite
Filippa	Flan	Franci	Franny	Freddie
Fynnia	Gay	Gennifer	Gilberte	Gilda
Giselle	Glad	Gladi	Gray	Grishelde
Grishilda	Halli	Hedvige	Helice	Ian
Ierne	Ilka	Ina	Inia	Ireen
Irene	Irina	Jacklin	Jami	Jemie

Jesselynn	Kaili	Kairl	Kali	Kalindi
Karli	Karsti	Karyn	Kele	Kerel
Kerstie	Kester	Kial	Kiele	Kimball
Kiral	Kirila	Kirstee	Kiska	Klair
Krista	Kristee	Kyna	Kyrene	Lark
Lesley	Levey	Lexine	Lezlie	Licha
Lidiya	Liesse	Lilah	Lillani	Lillian
Lirissa	Lissa	Lita	Liviya	Lyda
Lydia	Lykka	Marcy	Maris	Marji
Marris	Marsi	Mary Lou	Maryl	Marylou
Meryle	Micheline	Mijra	Minna	Mirja
na	Nandi	Nari	Neety	Ninette
Noura	Nyssa	Omusa	Pauletta	Petrine
Philina	Philippa	Phyllida	Prisilla	Rain
Raini	Rani	Reggie	Reine	Rene
Renie	Rickee	Rina	Rivkah	Rosamund
Rosmunda	Sadi	Sakti	Sally	Sam
Sebbie	Shani	Sharin	Sheren	Shifrah
Shina	Shiran	Shirina	Sidra	Sidria
Sima	Siva	Stephine	Taci	Tarryn
Taryn	Tierney	Traci	Tricia	Trista
Tyna	Valry	Vanni	Vernine	Vigilia
Villette	Virgilia	Wendie	Winda	Winnah
Zilla	Ziyah			

Female 7-8-6

This is the only combination beginning with a 7 that has a wholesome balance to it. Why? The 7 is a very refined, delicate quality that needs a great deal of consistent support and understanding for it not to retreat inward and disconnect from the outer world. The 6 is the only number that has sufficient balance, stability, and insight to nurture the 7 into participating openly in life. The 6 draws out the philosophic, spiritual, mystical, inquisitive, refined, poised, and dignified qualities of the 7. At the same time, the 6 helps the 7 to remain practical in its inspiration rather than becoming deeply abstract and aloof. Even so, this is not an easy combination to live because the 7 is constantly striving to comprehend those qualities of life which go beyond words. They prefer a private, reserved life style. This combination is particularly astute at poetry, music, writing, and acting.

Abella	Agathe	Alaine	Alane	Alena
Amedee	Anela	Angelika	Angelita	Aniela
Arlena	Arselma	Asadel	Asenka	Avelsa
Batsheva	Bertrada	Bobette	Carena	Carmencita
Caron	Cherolyne	Cinofila	Clareta	Constancy
Coreen	Corene	Corina	Corlissa	Corrina
Cosette	Cosima	Cyn	Dalenna	Delores
Diahane	Doda	Dorcas	Dorette	Dorlisa
Earleen	Earlene	Edmonde	Elaina	Elana
Elenor	Elinore	Elnore	Ethelreda	Fallon
Florence	Gavriella	Gerianna	Gwenore	Gwyn
Halcyon	Hateya	Hermione	Hildagarde	Hildegaard
Hoa	Hondia	Hondra	Ileana	Ilona
Isabelita	Isolda	Janessa	Janot	Jaynetta
Jezabelle	Jezebella	Jobina	Jonati	Jorgee
Joscelie	Joselle	Joselyne	Josephe	Joya
Karolyn	Katharine	Katherina	La Reina	Lanae
Laraine	Larraine	Latreece	Leana	Lenore
Leoine	Leone	Leonie	Lerone	Levanna
Liona	Lionnette	Lisa Marie	Lisabeta	Litonya
Lizaveta	Lolita	Lona	Lonee	Lorain
Loreen	Lorene	Lorna	Lorrain	Lyn
Majesta	Mallory	Maretta	Marietta	Mariom
Marisol	Marketa	Mary Jane	Mary-Jane	Mattea
Melisanda	Melisandra	Monah	Natesa	Neala
Noelie	Nohma	Nola	Norberthe	Odette
Onele	Orah	Orleen	Orlene	Orlina
Palmela	Pamella	Pelagia	Phoebe	Rhodina
Rhonda	Rochelle	Rondalin	Ronica	Roza
Sabena	Salomi	Samale	Sashenka	Tamiko
Tokriva	Topaz	Ursulette	Vittoria	Yonina
Zariea	Zenaida	Zora		

THIRD BEST MALE NAMES

Male 1-5-6

Although this combination can be very self-centered, headstrong, and independent, they always return to an atmosphere of sensibility and congeniality. Primarily, they look out first for themselves and secondly they keep an eye on the needs of their family. This combination creates a strong willed individual who knows what they want and goes straight after their desires. Their nature lends itself to being good bosses in the sense that they uphold firm convictions and are not upset by the emotional needs of others. Yet, they are sufficiently receptive to new ideas that others see them as being reasonable. These people can be very creative in a practical sense. Women with this combination are competitive and do not take a back seat to their mates at any time. These numbers are in the top 20% of all the possible combinations.

Adolfus	Adolphus	Ahdik	Ahmik	Akil
Alik	Alrik	Alvy	Anwyll	Arick
Arin	ARni	Asid	Bail	Bal
Baldrick	Bali	Bandric	Baptist	Barny
Barric	Belden	Benedic	Bennet	Bergen
Bergren	Berkley	Blair	Bland	Brandyn
Briac	Bryan	Byran	Cab	Cahil
Camp	Cart	Carvy	Cass	Celestin
Chal	Chapin	Chappy	Cheney	Chester
Clemmie	Dacy	Dagny	Daly	Darcy
Darryl	Darwin	Daryl	Dempsey	Dennie
Desire	Dougal	Dwain	Elek	Elert
Elridge	Elwell	Erne	Ernie	Errne
Esme	Everly	Fanny	Farlin	Ferenc
Franc	Franny	Frants	Freddie	Gabin
Ganit	Garry	Gary	Gavil	Gay
Gereld	Giffard	Gilad	Glad	Graig
Grant	Gray	Gredel	Gustavo	Hakim

Halil	Hall	Hans	Hasin	Hazlitt
Henley	Herschel	Iain	Ian	Ibrahim
Jankins	Jarid	Jarrid	Jarv	Jeffers
Joaquin	Kal	Kalvin	Karl	Kasch
Kasib	Kazimir	Keelby	Kele	Keler
Kelven	Kenelm	Kennedy	Kennet	Kester
Kijika	Kimball	Kincaid	Klair	Lach
Lat	Latty	Lesley	Levey	Lezlie
Macy	Mappin	Marly	Marmaduke	Marnin
Mars	Marwin	Maxim	Melbourne	Meredydd
Michah	Milap	Millard	Myca	Nee
Nepter	Nickolaus	Palm	Parkin	Parry
Patin	Patrick	Patrin	Pepe	Peveril
Platt	Preben	Prewet	Rani	Rawlins
Redley	Reggie	Rene	Rian	Rickward
Sally	Sam	Sami	Samir	Sebert
Selwen	Shan	Shaw	Shoushan	Silas
Skeet	Spense	Spenser	Stephen	Stillmann
Tadzi	Takis	Tal	Terrel	Thad
Thatch	Tierney	Trask	Vas	Vawn
Veryle	Wainwright	Warburton	Warri	Wash
Ximenez	Xymenes	Yank	Zacchaeus	Zamit

Male 1-7-8

This combination is interested in results — practical, tangible, physical, demonstrable results. They are not interested in stories or excuses. They operate their lives like a steamroller. If it doesn't work, get a bigger hammer. Their predisposition with material success creates an ambience of "I want what I want, and I want it now, thank you very much." Tact and patience are not among their strong points. They are self-starters, well organized, and have leadership skills.

If this combination gets lost in materiality, they can be the most ego-centric, macho combination of all because the negative side of the 8 is power-hungry, unscrupulous, domineering, oppressive, manipulative, and exploitive.

This is a most undesirable combination for a woman. If there are not offsetting qualities in other names, a woman with this combination is well described as a man in a woman's body. Women with these numbers are very prone to all manner of reproductive system disorders. It is not uncommon for them to have hysterectomies before they are 30 years of age. In addition, sexual intimacy can be extraordinary difficult for women with these numbers. Why is this so? The source number is a 1 which is male energy and the 8 is focused on material externals which is in contradiction to the internal nature of female sexuality.

Even though males with this combination have an exceptionally strong sexual focus, they seldom manifest generative disorders. They are completely preoccupied with money, sex, and power and have little or no understanding of personal intimacy.

Adli	Aikin	Akin	Alfy	Alphonsus
Andry	Andy	Arkin	Armyn	Arnit
Asfour	Bain	Balki	Ban	Banky
Barn	Basyll	Bene	Benedick	Benedict
Bennett	Berne	Bernie	Beverly	Bian
Bradly	Bran	Brandin	Brenden	Brewer
Brian	Bryant	Cad	Cadby	Cam
Carolus	Cassidy	Chadwick	Chan	Clemency
Clemens	Dal	Darci	Daulo	Demsey
Dennet	Denten	Derle	Devlen	Dewey
Dougan	Douglass	Eben	Ebner	Edel
Elbert	Elder	Elme	Elmer	Elvire
Emeric	Emile	Essien	Evel	Ewert
Fairly	Farly	Farris	Felipe	Felten
Fennie	Findlay	Franck	Frewen	Gaby
Gar	Gari	Garvin	Gavin	Gerrie

Girvan	Gladdy	Hamid	Harlin	Harwyn
Haslitt	Hastin	Henney	Ingmar	Ingram
Ingvar	Jacobus	Kabil	Kahlil	Kain
Kalb	Karlik	Kasimir	Keen	Kenleigh
Kennett	Keren	Kerne	Khalil	Kharouf
Kieren	Kinnaird	Kinnard	Kippar	Kleber
Klement	Krishan	Krishna	Kwamin	Lad
Laird	Laughton	Leslie	Liam	Linsay
Lyall	Mac	Mahoud	Makis	Maks
Mal	Malvin	Manvil	Marc	Marceau
Marl	Marts	Mattys	Mauricio	Mendel
Mercer	Meredyth	Merle	Merrel	Merripen
Milward	Mischa	Mychal	Nagid	Nat
Natty	Nefen	Newell	Nihal	Ouray
Parish	Parr	Parrish	Pattin	Peer
Peterkin	Petey	Piere	Pierie	Pierre
Pincas	Prewett	Randy	Ranit	Ray
Renfrew	Ricard	Routledge	Ryman	Sammy
Sax	Shandy	Shay	Sherbourne	Sigvard
Simba	Spence	Spencer	Steve	Stevie
Tan	Tarn	Tauno	Tavis	Telek
Temple	Tibal	Travis	Tybalt	Urbano
Vail	Val	Vassily	Velden	Vendel
Verney	Walwyn	Wasyl	Wat	Watty
Weber	Wesley	Wetherly	Wladimir	Wyatt
Ximenes	Yadin	Yvain	Yvan	

Male 7-8-6

This is the only combination beginning with a 7 that has a wholesome balance to it. Why? The 7 is a very refined, delicate quality that needs a great deal of consistent support and understanding for it not to retreat inward and disconnect from the outer world. The 6 is the only number that has sufficient balance, stability, and insight to nurture the 7 into participating openly in life. The 6 draws out the philosophic, spiritual, mystical, inquisitive, refined, poised, and dignified qualities of the 7. At the same time, the 6 helps the 7 to remain practical in its inspiration rather than becoming deeply abstract and aloof. Even so, this is not an easy combination to live because the 7 is constantly striving to comprehend those qualities of life which go beyond words. They prefer a private, reserved life style. This combination is particularly astute at poetry, music, writing, and acting.

Abbott	Adalwine	Adamer	Adom	Ailean
Alcot	Aloin	Alon	Anael	Aniol
Anntoin	Antonin	Anyon	Ascott	Atworth
Avidor	Avrom	Beathan	Brannon	Cathmor
Crayton	Diamond	Ernesto	Fabio	Faxon
Frederigo	Galton	Gamaliel	Garnock	Garroth
Gawaine	Gaylor	Geoffrey	Gilleabart	Goddart
Godfree	Gwyn	Harmon	Hedeon	Howard
Hy	Ichabod	Jonati	Josephe	Landon
Layton	Leone	Leoner	Lomasi	Lonnard
Lyn	Maddock	Malcolm	Mallory	Marcos
Mohan	Motka	Nikolay	Noland	Orlan
Parsefal	Patrizio	Platon	Pollard	Quasimodo
Rowland	Safford	Sancho	Santo	Scanlon
Seeton	Sherlocke	Somerset	Stamford	Thorald
Tiobaid	Topaz	Urbanus	Waldon	Waldron
Watford	Yoann			

Male 6-8-5

This is a particularly vibrant and alive combination that thrives on newness, change, and travel. They are exceptionally quick of mind and could never be accused of having any grass grow under their feet. They are versatile, self-reliant, decisive, curious, enthusiastic, enterprising, freedom loving, adventurous, and very insightful. Not too many people are willing or capable of keeping up with this combination. Even so, there is a sense of sensibility infused in their character and a wholesomeness that is easy to admire. Life is not all roses for this combination given the 5 expression number which has intense likes and dislikes resulting in some bitter experiences and personal disappointments.

Achille	Addie	Adem	Alberic	Aleck
Ambert	Argyle	Arlen	Asger	Athanasius
Baillie	Baxie	Beall	Benjamin	Bertram
Bickford	Bjarne	Bjorn	Blayne	Bramwell
Brawley	Brennan	Broddy	Caleb	Carlysle
Casimire	Chancey	Clarke	Clemente	Colt
Con	Courtenay	Craggie	Crane	Crow
Dame	Dannel	Dave	Davie	Dido
Dmytro	Dom	Donahue	Dov	Edouard
Eduardo	Emmerie	Ethelbert	Ethelmer	Ethelred
Evered	Everett	Ezia	Ezra	Fabe
Faber	Fabre	Fadey	Farnell	Fernall
Foss	Gannie	Gareth	Garreth	Gawen
Gayle	Gayler	Gerhart	Gilroy	Golding
Gradeigh	Grandville	Granthem	Greeley	Hackett
Haden	Hadrien	Haiden	Haleigh	Hamlet
Hansel	Harden	Harleigh	Haskell	Haven
Heman	Herman	Hildebrand	Hiroshi	Ho
Hoshi	Hoyt	Hulburd	Ihor	Jacme
Janek	Jaye	Jedidiah	Jerald	Jerrald
Johnny	Jory	Kalle	Keefe	Kendall
Kennan	Kimiko	Laidley	Landen	Lane

Lanie	Lawrie	Lennard	Lindon	Lino
Lion	Liron	Lloyd	Lock	Lon
Lorin	Lorn	Maixent	Marve	Matek
Mattie	Matvey	Maxey	Mead	Milford
Milos	Mitsos	Mord	Neal	Nikos
Offin	Olin	Olorun	Osbourn	Oz
Paley	Percival	Peverell	Pinon	Placide
Radbert	Raddie	Rambert	Rance	Reinhard
Reinwald	Riston	Rodd	Ronny	Rosslyn
Roz	Salem	Sarge	Sargie	Savile
Sayer	Sayre	Scott	Scotti	Segar
Selmar	Silvio	Skipton	Slade	Stanberry
Stancliffe	Stane	Stanleigh	Stearn	Symon
Tadek	Tallie	Thayer	Thorfinn	Thorp
Toddy	Tommy	Vidor	Viktor	Viljo
Wace	Wagner	Wakely	Walden	Wayne
Whitaker	Wildon	Winton	Wykeham	Yakez
Zachery	Zivon			

Male 6-7-4

On one hand, the innate intelligence of the 6 is supported by the intellectual skills of the 4 creating an exceptionally capable analyzer who does not tend to get lost in the detail — an analyzer who actually knows when to quit. On the other hand, the 4 is not expressive or spontaneous. This combination is on the reserved side, not favouring surprises or idle talk. The 4th physical sense is hearing. These people are superb listeners who portray a most sincere desire to understand other people's point of view. They have a non-threatening style of asking questions which combined with their ability to intelligently reflect on what they have heard, offers the other person a deep sense of being understood. They strive to understand and do not confuse their convictions with the opinions of others.

Abner	Adler	Adney	Adriel	Ahmed
Aiken	Ailbert	Ainsley	Alberik	Albert
Alder	Alvie	Amiel	Andrey	Ansley
Anwell	Aristide	Armel	Artemis	Arvel
Auberon	Avel	Averil	Aviel	Bane
Barnie	Bartel	Belamy	Bernardin	Bernarr
Beverley	Biron	Blake	Born	Bow
Bradley	Branden	Brendan	Brion	Brock
Bron	Cade	Camden	Candide	Carlyle
Carver	Chane	Chappie	Chicko	Claes
Cobb	Codi	Colis	Conlin	Cord
Dace	Dael	Dale	Darce	Darcie
Darle	Darrel	Davidde	Diggory	Dominic
Edelie	Edwald	Elrad	Elvira	Emele
Etan	Ewart	Fairdell	Fairley	Falkner
Farley	Flory	Floy	Frannie	Fraser
Frasier	Gabey	Gardiner	Gardner	Gare
Garnett	Garrie	Gaven	Gerardin	Germain
Givon	Glanville	Hagley	Halliwell	Harlen
Haslett	Hayes	Haze	Houston	Hylton
Igor	Ingemar	Ingeram	Ishmael	Jasen
Junius	Kaine	Kaleb	Kane	Kasimer
Kean	Kearn	Keene	Kelbee	Kennard
Kenward	Kieran	Landbert	Langley	Lattie
Launcelot	Lemar	Livo	Lucius	Mace
Mael	Malvern	Mandel	Marice	Mariel
Mayne	Milo	Mitros	Myron	Nasser
Nate	Newall	Nickson	Niko	Nixon
Normy	Ornit	Orvil	Paget	Parrie
Patten	Pirro	Porty	Prior	Quintus
Ransley	Rapier	Reading	Redwald	Reynard
Robin	Rodric	Rog	Ronit	Rorry
Rory	Roslyn	Roy	Rufus	Sallie
Saunderson	Saxe	Stedman	Storm	Tades
Thornly	Tino	Toms	Toni	Torin
Torrin	Travers	Tukuli	Tunu	Upwood
Vale	Waite	Wake	Wheeler	Whitford
Yori	Yvon			

Male 4-2-6

The 4-2-6 and the 6-7-4 are amongst the better combinations, given the wholesome, congenial, and responsible influence of the 6. Wherever the 6 is found, there is a strong tendency to bring out the positive qualities of the associated number.

This combination is intellectual, honest, trustworthy, loyal, organized, and persevering. They are excellent listeners and have outstanding analytical skills. Although they are a bit on the reserved side and don't like surprises or being spontaneous, they have a maturity that is inviting. They have a very strong love for home, family, and take an interest in community affairs. They can be on the fussy side and worry a bit too much, but, all-in-all, this combination facilitates an attractive list of positives.

Agdu	Artur	Atwood	Aubi	Audy
Barnum	Baudouin	Bua	Burbank	Burnard
Corcoran	Dagwood	Demetrius	Donato	Durant
Elazaro	Garmund	Gaud	Giraud	Holecombe
Horacio	Hurlee	Jacopo	Janiuszck	Johnathon
Kapuki	Koenraad	Lucerne	Lucian	Mahmud
Manchu	Maury	Murray	Nikulas	Radburn
Raymund	Ruark	Sandus	Sebastiano	Shaughn
Sultan	Tommaso	Truman	Yuma	

Male 8-7-6

Once again, here is a combination that ends in a 6 and should be considered in the top 20% of the 81 possible combinations. In comparison, the 6-2-8 fits into the top 5% because the source number of 6 starts with substantial, wholesome, mature ideas and cultivates the intention to a point of fruition. The weakness of beginning with an 8 source number is that expansive, far-reaching goals are continuously upgraded before they are initiated. The challenge of the less ambitious 6 expression number is to keep up with the ever expanding goals of the 8. This pattern tends to overwhelm the 6 and frustrate the 8 who wants results relatively immediately. Even so, it should be kept in mind that the 6 demands responsibility and is determined to maintain an air of sensibility in all things. Sometimes it is overlooked that the 8 has a strong sense of balance in its own right. Hence, this combination works out much better than most and exudes an air of balance in both home and business.

Araldo	Argemone	Athanase	Boone	Boonie
Buckie	Burne	Burnie	Cadao	Chesmu
Claudianus	Culley	Cuttie	Delu	Domenico
Druce	Duffie	Dustie	Galloway	Geronimo
Humbert	Humfrey	Humphrey	Huntley	Januarius
Josecito	Kanoa	Loredo	Lorenzo	Mooney
Obadias	Oberon	Olivero	Oliviero	Othello
Purcell	Quigley	Rogerio	Ruben	Rusell
Sherburn	Sullie	Tucker	Tuckie	Tupper
Turner	Ulmer	Woolsey		

IF YOU DID NOT FIND A NAME IN THE FIRST, SECOND OR THIRD CHOICES OF NAMES, YOU HAD BEST RECONSIDER BEFORE CHOOSING ANYTHING ELSE.

IT IS A SIGNIFICANT COMPROMISE TO CHOOSE A NAME NOT IN FIRST, SECOND OR THIRD CHOICES OF NAMES.

It would be rare, but it is possible to find a name not listed in this book that has a suitable "combination". If you find a name that is not in this book, go to:

www.numbers-count.com

and use the Name Calculator to determine the combination. Next, does the combination belong to the first 3 choices of names? If it does, then use the calculator to determine *how it fits with your surname*.

If you find a name that fits the first 3 choices of names, I would be pleased if you were to send it to me via the website.

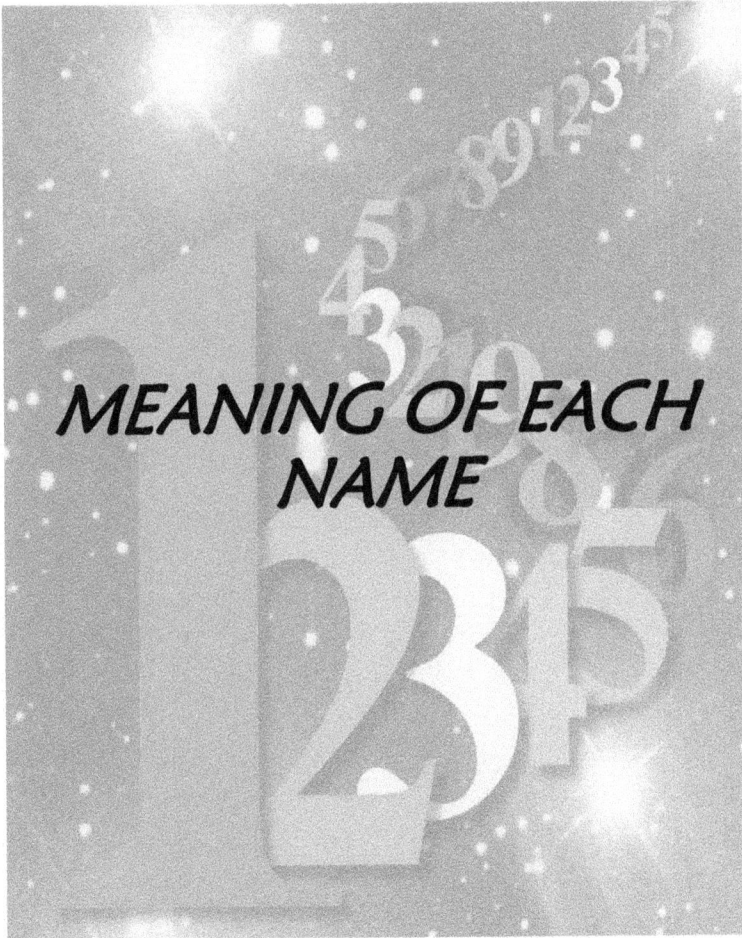

MEANING OF EACH NAME

No individual is simply one name or all of their names, although each name used will influence the overall personality and life experience as follows:

1-1-2   Ann, April, Candy, Denise, Evelyn, Gail, Kathy, Marilyn, Cary, Craig, Dylan, Hart, Joshua, Larry, Max, Walt, Zach

The cliche for this combination is "their bark is worse than their bite". The 1 source has very strong opinions and is not interested in diplomacy and tact. In contrast, the 2 expression is all about diplomacy and tact. Imagine a 1-1-2 telling a friend about how angry they are with their partner. *"When I see that so-and-so again, I'm going to tell them in no uncertain terms just what I think. They'll never push me around again. Boy, am I ever going to give them a piece of my mind."* At this moment, in walks the person in question, and the 1-1-2 says, *"Oh HI HONEY, I was just talking about you. How are you? Are you having a nice day?"* The bark was worse than the bite — lots of talk, but typically no action.

Although the 2 expression softens the 1 and offers some social skills and a sense of connection to other people, the 1 and the 2 are opposite in nature and a sense of confusion surrounds most of their activities. They can never quite decide which foot to stand on from one moment to the next. Consequently, they have difficulty achieving their goals and can appear to be shallow minded.

1-2-3   Cathy, Ellen, Esther, Liza, Marg, Mary, Nancy, Pam, Rita, Art, Delbert, Hal, Jeffrey, Lanny, Lindsay, Martin, Wendell

This is a very pleasant combination that works particularly well for women even though it begins with a 1 source number which is basic, male energy. For a woman, it fosters a definite sense of independence and strength that isn't overly masculine because the 3 expression embraces a well defined balance of feminine and masculine qualities. This combination allows people to be their own person, yet they have a cosmopolitan and gregarious personality. For the most part, they are generous, cheerful, self-contained, and consistent in their character. Surprisingly though, when they get backed into a corner, they will physically punch their contender. Why? Because the physical, confrontive 1 is living under the cover of the pleasant and bouncy 3 expression. Their weakness lies in scattering their efforts and in not completing what they start. They are pioneers at heart with good verbal skills. They can be compulsive eaters craving too many heavy, starchy foods.

1-3-4   Daisy, Gina, Kaitlin, Kathi, Linda, Michelle, Tracy, Wilma, Al, Danny, David, Dexter, Gene, Herbert, Lee, Ryan, Steven

The cliche for these people is "I'm from Missouri — don't tell me, show me". The independent, self-sufficient, persevering, practical qualities of the 1 find little relief with the analytical, intellectual, dogmatic, stubborn, dull, and plodding qualities of the 4 expression number. These individuals have to know how things work in a tangible, practical, physical sense. As children, they take everything apart to see how it works. Many accountants and lawyers are 1-3-4's. They simply don't move until they are ready to move. They can be very thick-headed.

Over a lifetime, they can accumulate a respectable estate, not out of sensitivity and responsiveness to life, but because they simply have no comprehension of when it is time to quit.

Davids are often called Dave which is a 6-8-5 combination. Whichever name is used the most frequently has the greatest impact on their personality. In comparison to David, the name Dave is exceptionally bright, insightful, and decisive. Dave functions on intuition and is impatient, not wanting to wade through endless facts. In this sense, the quick minded, decisive nature of Dave can work as a helpful complement to the obstinate nature of David.

The important point to remember here is that Davids are not your typical 1-3-4 combination if he also uses the name Dave.

1-4-5   Barb, Dee, Ethel, Fay, Gladys, Lisa, Shelley, Vivian, Bart, Clay, Frank, Lars, Lennie, Marty, Marvin, Zack

The name Frank speaks clearly for this combination which is just that, "very frank", to the point, "no muss, no fuss". The numbers 1 and 5 are similar in nature — independent, self-sufficient, determined, and initiating. They are very much their own person and will not tolerate interference in any form. The 5 expression adds an abundance of vitality to the 1 source creating a whirlwind of energy. This is not a talkative combination, but they have little trouble speaking their mind in a very blunt, critical manner. These people make great travelling salesmen where they can be on-the-go, free, independent, and promotional. They have no qualms about using high pressure tactics. Home is not where their heart lives.

1-5-6   Dawn, Fayth, Irene, Lesley, Lillian, Lydia, Sally, Traci, Bryan, Chester, Gary, Grant, Ian, Reggie, Sam, Stephen

Although this combination can be very self-centered, headstrong, and independent, they always return to an atmosphere of sensibility and congeniality. Primarily, they look out first for themselves and second, they keep an eye on the needs of their family. This combination creates a strong willed individual who knows what they want and goes straight after their desires. Their nature lends itself to being good bosses in the sense that they uphold firm convictions and are not upset by the emotional needs of others. Yet, they are sufficiently receptive to new ideas that others see them as being reasonable. These people can be very creative in a practical sense. Women with this combination are competitive and do not take a back seat to their mates at any time. These numbers are in the top 20% of the best combinations.

1-6-7   Bette, Clair, Ellie, Hilda, Jan, Kathryn, Sylvia, Yvette, Brad, Carl, Derek, Hank, Harry, Jack, Mark, Richard

The cliche for these numbers is "take it or leave it". Why? The 1 source number, which speaks directly and to the point, finds expression through the 7 which is introverted and avoids talking. When the 1 and 7 are combined, there is neither a desire nor an outlet for verbal expression, hence a personality that is reserved and not open to much discussion. These people have a way of quietly saying "no" that is so absolute and final that any further discussion would be futile. The 7 always adds a sense of dignity to any combination as it does with the 1-6-7 offering at least a limited air of grace to their rough and ready, pioneering nature. These names foster a very self-contained, private personality that prefers to live on their own. Misunderstandings and confrontation are not strangers to them.

1-7-8   Beckie, Cynthia, Fawn, Helen, Leslie, Mila, Val, Virginia, Brian, Gavin, Mac, Nat, Pierre, Randy, Ray, Sammy, Steve

This combination is interested in results — practical, tangible, physical, demonstrable results. They are not interested in stories or excuses. They operate their lives like a steamroller. If it doesn't work, get a bigger hammer. Their predisposition with material success creates an ambience of "I want what I want, and I want it now, thank you very much." Tact and patience are not among their strong points. They are self-starters, well organized, and have leadership skills.

If this combination gets lost in materiality, they can be the most ego-centric, macho combination of all because the negative side of the 8 is power-hungry, unscrupulous, domineering, oppressive, manipulative, and exploitive.

This is a most undesirable combination for a woman. If there are not offsetting qualities in other names, a woman with this combination is well described as a man in a woman's body. Women with these numbers are very prone to all manner of reproductive system disorders. It is not uncommon for them to have hysterectomies before they are 30 years of age. In addition, sexual intimacy can be extraordinary difficult for women with these numbers. Why is this so? The source number is a 1 which is male energy and the 8 is focused on material externals which is in contradiction to the internal nature of female sexuality.

Even though males with this combination have an exceptionally strong sexual focus, they seldom manifest generative disorders. They are completely preoccupied with money, sex, and power and have little or no understanding of personal intimacy.

1-8-9   Debbie, Dinah, Jennifer, Miriam, Patsy, Sandy, Tammy, Clark, Clement, Eddie, Ernest, Garth, Jay, Matt, Stan

The 9 expression is the complete opposite of the 1 source and creates a tremendous internal polarity which results in confusion and an explosive nature. The 1 source appears to be stable and dependable, yet with little warning these people can succumb to fits of anger and emotional outbursts that are very intense and unpleasant. This tendency can be well camouflaged by the inspirational, humanitarian 9 for some time but the two opposites can only survive for so long before they come unglued. This combination can suffer from nervous disorders later in life.

No individual is simply one name or all of their names, although each name used will influence the overall personality and life experience as follows:

1-9-1   Brittany, Hilary, Kay, Kimberley, Mavis, Patty, Sherrie, Barry, Dan, Ivan, Pat, Peter, Ralph, Verne, Wally, Ward

Although this combination is comprised of pure male energy, it should not be confused with the label of egocentric, macho, and chauvinistic. These people exhibit all the typical 1 qualities of being strong willed, independent, and self-sufficient. Their physical and emotional needs are basic and uncomplicated. They seldom have mood swings and are very much the same nature day in and day out. They are candid with others and appreciate the same in return. They avoid a lot of social activity and have few friends. Although they are slow to make friends, once they do, they make friends for life. On the other hand, if they ever terminate a friendship, its under exceptional and extreme circumstances and they will never reconsider their decision. They enjoy hard, physical work and can be very good with their hands. When accidents occur, their leadership skills come to the fore and they instinctively take charge and pragmatically do whatever has to be done without hesitation. Otherwise, they prefer to work on their own and avoid the public eye. Women using this combination virtually, always wear pants — skirts and dresses feel foreign to them. Both men and women with these numbers dress simply and like strong, solid colours. The 1 quality has basic material needs as described by the metaphor of the pioneer. In comparison, the 1-7-8 combination is much more prone to being materialistic and egocentric because the 8 expression focuses on external, material form.

2-1-3   Anna, Charlene, Dollie, Jocelyn, Mollie, Rose, Sandra,   Corey, Elliott, Geoff, Graham, Joe, Leroy, Ronie, Tommie

In comparison with the 2-9-2, this combination has some of the spunk of the 3 which is helpful only to a small degree. Unfortunately, the 3 expression number scatters the energy of the passive 2 and creates a combination which is very laid-back and amongst the world's great procrastinators. These people love to talk and they seem to have all day to say absolutely nothing. Imagine talking to a "good ol' Joe, easygoing Joe" and in his slow drawl he says, "Hi, how is it going? How you been lately? Garsh, darn but it's good to see you. Oh sure, I have things to do, but tell me how you are doing first." This combination typically is so "wishy-washy" and has so little substance to their personality that well-known Joes are often referred to as "Joe who?". They love to gossip and can be very graceful liars.

This combination has a very strong tendency to put on weight for a number of reasons. For one, the 2 quality dislikes saying "no" and the impulsive 3 quality adores food. That's double trouble right there. In addition, the easygoing, laid-back 2 is unwilling to exercise. They are fond of sugars and appease their emotional desires by constantly snacking.

2-2-4   Jeannie, Joyce, Kathleen, Martina, Nicole, Theresa, Allan, Christopher, Gordie, Monte, Morey, Nathan, Rodger

The easygoing 2 wants to resolve issues and remove the boundaries that separate people from one another. On the other hand, the 4 expression is completely caught in definitions and material form. The result is confusion and mental anguish between trying to dissolve boundaries while at the same time striving to establish more definition.

The passive 2 and the slow-to-decide 4 fosters a personality that is mentally slow and has very poor concentration. The 2 is interested in the emotional climate whereas the 4 is compelled to talk only of the facts of the situation. The result is a very fussy quality that is slow to change and forever lives in a great deal of emotional turmoil, personal slights, and misunderstandings. This combination is not known for their depth of mind.

The 4 is a collector and hates to let go of anything. Consequently, it creates a withholding nature, a quality of being constipated. Any combination ending in a 4 will be prone to having large hips, buttocks, and elimination problems.

The name Allen is a 6-2-8 which is very different set of qualities from Allan.

2-3-5   Abigail, Bonnie, Darlene, Lara, Melanie, Patricia, Yvonne, Boyce, Dewayne, Earle, Errol, Gregory, Leo, Wellington

In this case, the easygoing, peace loving 2 finds expression through the knife-edge, assertive, promotional, and independent 5. This doesn't work well at all because the expression number is in sharp contrast to the source number. This combination is highly sensitive, intense, and discordant.

These people suffer not only from a lot of *external* tension, but also from a great deal of *internal* tension because they can seldom graciously express what they are feeling inside. They can make a tremendous effort to be gracious and understanding, yet they simply can't leave well enough alone and insist on having the last word. No matter how hard they try to cover up their deep emotions, their expression has a sharp bite to it. As a result, their life is full of bitter experiences and misunderstandings which truly distresses their gentle inner self. Essentially, they have little control over what they say. They can suffer from intense stomach pains and from a great deal of "heart ache". This is not a healthy or a stable combination.

2-4-6   Alisa, Ava, Connie, Leanne, Lonnie, Maria, Marsha, Matilda, Devon, Fabian, Hector, Isaac, Joel, Robbie, Robert, Verdon

This is a delightful, gracious, warm, loving combination that will always go the extra mile to seek understanding. At the same time, they will not give themselves away with excessive procrastination or an inability to say no. They are a delight to be with and always find something loving and supportive to say about everyone. Their compassionate and tactful nature embraces both practical and artistic skills. They have a strong love for home and family and can also do well in the business world.

This is a desirable combination for a woman because the 2 source number is in tune with her instinctual nature. On the other hand, males using this combination can be very gentle, if not passive. Robert is often called Bob which is a 6-4-1 and affords Robert a strong measure of male energy.

2-5-7   Adrienne, Annette, Elizabeth, Martha, Tanya, Vanna, Wanda, Donnie, Georg, Gregor, Morley, Nelson, Nero, Vernon, Wolfe

This is one of the most sensitive of all the combinations because both the source and the expression numbers are gentle and vulnerable. The nurturing, loving nature of the 2 which thrives on relationships is thwarted by the 7 which prefers a great deal of privacy and alone time. The 7 isolates the 2 from the rest of the world. The result is a loving, gentle heart that never finds fulfillment. This combination finds it difficult to communicate their deep emotions and suffers from an unreasonable number of misunderstandings. Although they appear calm and refined, they are moody, jealous, easily hurt, very idealistic, and have little or no self-confidence. They can be very passive and do not like to work at anything. The extreme emotional sensitivity of this combination will reflect in poor health including very delicate lungs and weak hearts. They function on a very low level of physical energy and require a great deal of extra sleep. They take a very long time to wake-up and are definitely not morning people. These people dress with an elegant flair and can be very attractive physically.

2-6-8   Carla, Chelsea, Clara, Cleo, Danielle, Jeane, Roxie, Bobbie, Brodie, Cole, Godfrey, Leeland, Randall, Trevor

The 2-4-6 and the 2-6-8 are similar in many ways. Both are very considerate, loving, and affectionate, yet they know how to stand their ground and not give themselves away. This is a very charming personality that can do exceptionally well as a mediator or a diplomat. The 2-6-8 is much more materially oriented than is the 2-4-6 and favours business over home and family life. Like the 2-4-6, the 2-6-8 combination is very gentle for a male. These people desire quality and quantity but are short on the ambition required for the fulfilment of their dreams. They frequently fantasize about winning the lottery or inheriting money.

Although this combination creates a very pleasant ambience for a female, it is not a good combination for a woman from a health standpoint. The source number of 2 which is directly related to feminine energy is in contradiction to the 8 which is externally oriented. The contrast can manifest in reproductive system disorders.

2-7-9   Anita, Jaylene, Marcia, Marlee, Olive, Sophie, Valerie, Barnaby, Holmes, Lawrence, Ogden, Ozzie, Rodney, Roger

This is an exceptionally loving, gentle, and affectionate quality. This combination totally thrives on love, attention, acknowledgement, cuddling, and sharing everything they do with someone else. Their humanitarian ideas are exceptionally high and they seek peace at all costs, which can work to their detriment. These people can have a terrible time saying no to anyone. They have an extremely soft heart and will typically give their last dollar to a pan-handler. This combination easily becomes enmeshed in relationships where they completely lose themselves within the relationship. They are idealistic dreamers and can be deeply religious. Their emotional outbursts can be readily appeased with a few kind words and some understanding. Although this is a gentle, charming combination, these people lack self-confidence and are frequently taken advantage of by others.

2-8-1   Arlene, Elaine, Hannah, Lana, Noel, Rebecca, Sabrina, Zoe, Adam, Alan, Joey, Joseph, Leon, Lorne, Scottie, Sherlock

In this example, the desire is for peace and harmony, yet circumstances constantly dictate the need to confront issues. When these people are under pressure they tend to blurt out things which they had promised themselves not to say. Their direct manner in such situations is distressing to their desire for congenial relationships. They like knowing the details of personal confidences, but when faced with a direct question, they are compelled to tell the truth. They have a gentle heart and a direct manner of speaking. Often they feel much more than they express.

2-9-2   Catherine, Diana, Heather, Marian, Melody, Sarah, Violet, Adrian, Benoit, Dana, Desmond, Forrest, Foster, Rolfe

No other combination is purer in feminine energies than the 2-9-2. No one is more concerned with diplomacy, tact, and cooperation. Unfortunately, too much focus in one area of life creates an imbalance. These people are often known as *shrinking Violets* who avoid any and all issues at any cost. The price they pay for peace is a denial of their own personal needs resulting in a passive, impractical, indecisive, and fearful personality. In earlier years, this combination may try to compensate for their inner experience by putting on a good front, a strong offensive. Unfortunately, the less positive side will prevail in the long run. To maintain a healthy, vibrant life, this combination needs to learn how to effectively negotiate and not give themselves away. If they have integrated a sense of self-respect, their intuitive, responsive, and nurturing instincts can generate a most persuasive personality, indeed. This combination can be impossible to pin down. They can have a slippery personality that can spontaneously concoct the most frivolous, clever, unrelated excuses imaginable. When you back them into a corner to solicit a direct answer, they can be as flabbergasted at what they say as you are. They are masters at "little white lies".

The abundance of 2 in this example results in poor circulation creating a physiology vulnerable to cold weather. This combination suffers from "cold feet" both physically and psychologically. They readily retain body fluids and are prone to being overweight. They are subject to kidney trouble and weak bladders.

These people have very quick, receptive minds. Their greatest enigma is forgetting just as quickly as they learn — particularly material facts and people's names. Forgetting people's names is devastating to them because their entire sense of diplomacy and tact centers around being personal with people. Often their mind will go blank in the midst of making personal introductions to their oldest friends.

Possibly the most classic 2-9-2 name is Cinderella.

3-1-4   Bunny,   Constance,   Georgina,   Natalia, Rowena, Rusty, Ruth, Budd, Buz, Churchill, Duddy, Ludwig, Morrison, Wilbur, Yul

This combination takes the creative ability of the 3 and combines it with the precision and detailed skills of the 4. As a consequence, these people are outstanding at creating and sewing clothes and at all manner of hobbies. Their bubbly inner nature is thwarted by the placid 4, yet they always have a smile for everyone. They have a playful side but prefer the stability and tradition of home and family. They like to be productive and organized although sometimes the disorganized 3 can show itself behind cupboard doors.

3-2-5   Adelaide, Caroline, Cornelia, Joanne, Roseann, Rubi, Susi, Cyrus, Fernando, Horace, Lorance, Quintin, Rudy, Russ

These numbers have many of the contradictions of the 2-3-5 combination but they have little desire to be nice. The 3 source loves a good argument and the 5 expression has no qualms about what it has to say. There is no loss for words here, nor is there any apology for what is said. In their opinion, they like to tease others. Unfortunately, their teasing is sarcastic and hurtful. Finishing projects is the last thing on these people's minds given that neither the 3 nor the 5 has any interest in completing what they start. There is a lot of energy and power in this combination and it is hard for them to sit still. They enjoy a wide variety of experiences with the opposite sex, who are receptive to their vibrant personalities. Underlying their dashing charm is a great deal of vanity. These people are promoters who need plenty of freedom and variety to keep them busy but don't expect them to fill out any paperwork whatsoever.

3-3-6   Dorothy, Jollean, Judy, Maryanna, Rosemary, Suki, Veronica, Cameron, Dunc, Dustin, Jaromey, Leonard, Norton, Ryun, Stu

The accountable and responsible instincts of the 6 draw out the positive aspects of the 3 and create a particularly congenial and wholesome personality. People with this combination have a superb sense of humour and, at the same time, they are very clear on their direction in life and on their goals. They prefer to do business in an easygoing manner but do not hesitate to back up their smile with conviction and strength. This is a completely balanced combination that offers the best of all possible worlds. They are artistic, creative, practical, and systematic. There is little they cannot do if they set their mind to it. They have a mature, robust, and well balanced physical appearance.

3-4-7   Alanna, Amanda, Barbara, Lucy, Roberta, Rosalie, Trudy, Bronson, Burt, Colton, Connor, Dru, Kurt, Luis, Thornton

On first encounter, this combination begins with a 3 and appears to be a cheerful, gregarious, and vibrant personality expressing through the refined, poised, and dignified 7.

The second half of the story is less positive — capturing the argumentative, superficial, vain, and extravagant 3 source because the 7 expression internalizes rather than offers an outlet for the 3. Fundamentally, the energies are opposite — an extroverted source and an introverted expression. The push-pull of these opposite qualities offers a cheerful, optimistic, magnetic, and imaginative personality one moment and a superficial, vain, and whining nature in the next.

In the end, the 7 expression renders this combination very difficult to understand and hard to live with. Underneath their refined and congenial manner lives a surprisingly "tough cookie" who looks out for themselves. This can be particularly true of a Barbara if she is also called Barb which is a 1-4-5 combination. A barb is like a hook used for catching fish or hanging up meat — not a very pleasant image to identify with.

These are physically attractive people who have pleasant smiles and a difficult personality to comprehend.

3-5-8   Annemarie, Cassandra, Deborah, Georgia, Judi, Marjorie, Abraham, Aeron, Burc, Curt, Dusty, Geraldo, Guy, Kurtis

This is one of the four truly balanced combinations. The other three are 3-3-6, 6-9-6 and 6-2-8.

In this case, the magnetic, optimistic, gregarious, cosmopolitan, articulate, and imaginative 3 source finds expression through the 8 which is the number of material fruition. The 8 expression adds discrimination, balance, leadership, and efficiency to the 3 source. In other words, the 8 draws the 3 to completion and capitalizes on its imaginative, artistic, and entertaining qualities. The 8 insists on results and doesn't allow the 3 to become scattered, unfocused, or superficial.

3-6-9   Carole, Joanie, Judith, Luci, Savanna, Tamara, Wenona, Angelo, Bud, Butch, Conroy, Curtis, Hunt, Orson, Pinkus

This is a musical, expressive, artistic combination that is always looking for an opportunity to serve and entertain others. Music, dance, drama, and the arts are an integral part of their lives. They are emotional, high strung, and can talk your ear off. For the most part, they are cheerful and bubbly, yet they often fall into the depths of complete despair. Lady luck, who is related to the lucky 3, bails them out at the eleventh hour just before everything is lost. Even so, their losses are substantial.

This is a very scattered and disorganized quality that lives on inspiration. Although these people may not admit it, they love the drama of life. They have deep spiritual convictions and can verbalize their humanitarian instincts exceptionally well. They have a wonderful sense of humour and make good public speakers.

3-7-1   Joella, Loretta, Madelaine, Natasha, Rosalyne, Roxanne,   Alberto, Buck, Chuck, Gordon, Socrates, Woody, Yuri

These people have great opening lines but quickly run out of steam and haven't too much to say. They make great first impressions. They often enter business meetings with the firm resolve not to interrupt. But, if the meeting gets bogged down, the powerful 3 barges through the blunt 1, and, once again, they tread where angels fear to go. Fortunately, they are very resilient and can recover quickly from sticking their foot in their mouth.

Where the 1-2-3 is considered to be a desirable combination, the energy flow of the 3-7-1 restricts the vibrant, dynamic 3 from finding an outlet. As a result, the negative side of the 3 prevails and this combination can be very argumentative, forceful and self-centered. This combination is always starting over again from the beginning.

3-8-2   Alana, Elinora, Katharina, Leona, Lisa-Maria, Lorraine, Aristotle, Buddy, Gus, London, Murphy, Osborn, Ulrick

This is a very bubbly quality that wants to be nice to everyone. They love people, parties, social events, and talking about anything. They love to party all night and hate to get up in the morning — any morning. Although, this is truly a delightful, gracious, fun loving quality to socialize with, from a result and production point of view, this combination is easy-going Joe (2-1-3) in reverse. Joe doesn't move forward very fast at all, so you can well image how productive he is in reverse!! In their desire to resolve conflict and maintain peace, they do not hesitate to stretch the truth. They like to tease as long as no one gets hurt. This combination is never at a loss for words.

3-9-3   Carolyne, Charlotte, Katrina, Rozanne, Ruby, Sunny, Yoko, Alexander, Buzz, Judd, Justin, Monro, Quinn, Sloane, Uri

This combination is the unrestricted child running wild in the candy store. They are highly emotional and strive to appease their emotions with compulsive eating. They are wonderfully creative but seldom, if ever, complete anything. They can play music by ear and have an exceptionally strong voice that is superb for opera. This combination is the ultimate extrovert who has no idea of when or how to stop talking. They are completely unorganized and thrive on emotional drama. Life is strictly a game to be enjoyed — an excuse to have fun. They are possibly the world's worst housekeepers. These people are very subject to skin disorders such as rashes, acne, skin cancer, etc.

4-1-5   Anastassia, Georgiana, Hugette, Murielle, Prudence, Ursa, Arthur, Claud, Hagood, Horatio, Paolo, Paul, Salvatore

The analytical and intellectual qualities of the 4 are enlivened by the vibrant promotional nature of the 5. Where the 4 wants more data before making a decision, the 5 impatiently states that enough is enough and demands that a decision be made. This creates a much more progressive quality than most other combinations with a 4 source number. Unfortunately, they pay a price of internal struggle between indecision and impulsiveness. This can be an accident prone combination because the impulsive 5 wants change and travel whereas the 4 wants to stay at home and work on some organizational details. Consequently, when the 5 is speeding down the freeway and the 4 has its mind back at home, accidents happen. This combination does not accumulate many tangible results over a lifetime.

4-2-6   Audry, Faun, Joenna, Lurleen, Roseanna, Ruthann, Uta, Artur, Audy, Barnum, Dagwood, Murray, Raymund, Truman

The 4-2-6 and the 6-7-4 are amongst the better combinations, given the wholesome, congenial, and responsible influence of the 6. Wherever the 6 is found, there is a strong tendency to bring out the positive qualities of the associated number.

This combination is intellectual, honest, trustworthy, loyal, organized, and persevering. They are excellent listeners and have outstanding analytical skills. Although they are a bit on the reserved side and don't like surprises or being spontaneous, they have a maturity that is inviting. They have a very strong love for home, family, and take an interest in community affairs. They can be on the fussy side and worry a bit too much, but, all-in-all, this combination facilitates an attractive list of positives.

4-3-7   Chiquita, Jacqui, Lauri, Lucilla, Maryruth, Susann, Ula, Antonio, Dustan, Gunar, Jonathon, Orlando, Quinlan, Ronaldo

This is a very analytical combination that is extremely hard to understand or get to know. The 7 expression shuts the door on the dull, fussy, dogmatic, and sceptical 4. They easily get stuck on small facts and refuse to discuss their feelings or anything personal. They have very limited verbal skills and a very placid, dull personality. In contrast, these people can be good technical writers or excel in theoretical mathematics and physics. This is an unhealthy combination subject to cancer and growths.

4-4-8   Gertrude, Honoria, Julia, Luisa, Mauri, Mura, Suzette, Angus, Apollo, Durward, Enrique, Giuseppe, Gunthar, Saul

In this case the analytical 4 finds an effective outlet through the administrative, organized qualities of the 8 expression. The 8 and the 4 are in harmony with each other which draws out the more positive qualities of both numbers. This is a serious, hard working combination that is all business and not interested in social functions unless it will further business contacts. They are most content in the laboratory or the office, although they have an eye for good design and can enjoy a well constructed, quality home.

4-5-9   Annamaria, Juliann, Oona, Rosamond, Shaun,
            Suzan, Una, Darius, Dugal, Guntar, Gustav,
            Hercule, Stuart, Theodore

4's and 9's don't go together well at all. Here, the 4 source is
attuned to the subconscious (the underground) and is always
in search of new and more data. The 4 quality hates to let go
of anything regardless of it's obsolescence. In contrast, the 9
expression is all about letting go and surrender. Such action is
blasphemy to the 4.   This combination is exceptionally
discordant and is prone to outbursts of anger and rage. In this
example, the 9 intensifies the negative qualities of the 4. This
is one of the least desirable of all the combinations.

The only combination which ends in a 9 and is not
counterproductive is the 6-3-9. This combination functions
effectively because the exceptional qualities of the 6 are
sufficiently balanced not to be depleted by the 9 which insists
on giving everything away.

4-6-1   Cleopatra,   Georgianna,   Lucia,   Lucinda,
            Surina, Wonona, Cassius, Hercules, Juan,
            Klaus, Lukas, Rudyard, Vaughn

This is a physically strong and mechanical combination that
loves to fix things and putter with their hands. Their narrow-
minded, mechanical nature reflects in their personality which is
placid and not verbally expressive to say the least. This is a
basic bread, meat, and potatoes person who has little or no
sense of refinement. They have outstanding tenacity and
endurance. They love to complete what they start as long as
they can start over again from the beginning. In this sense,
they are excellent framers or roofers in the housing industry.

4-7-2   Bruna, Dolora, Lucienne, Murial, Pomona, Susan, Utina, Ashburn, Claus, Garwood, Gustaf, Lucas, Reuben, Sullivan

These people have some good organizational skills but tend to be impractical when it comes to interfacing with life. They get hung-up on details and are often accused of being picky. They look to others to do the job for them and continuously run into differences of opinion and emotional upsets with the very people they most desire to please. They have a pleasant manner but lack inspiration and any sense of spontaneity. They strive very hard to be socially proper and, at the same time, they are somewhat defensive.

4-8-3   Eleonor, Eunice, Juliette, Laurin, Leanora, Maud, Tatum, Aldus, Austin, Duncan, Harwood, Marcus, Tomasso, Uriah

In this example, the 3 energizes the 4 creating an inspired scientist who loves to talk about his technical insights and his latest invention. Mind you, this is the mad scientist with 10,000 incomplete inventions to his name. But he sure can tell a great story and bring a sense of vitality and aliveness to any mathematical equation. How so much technical know how and detail can live in such a messy environment is another of mother nature's mysteries. They tend to be loud both verbally and in their dress.

4-9-4   Anastasia, Aubry, Donnamarie, Julina, Romona, Rosabella, Abdul, Donovan, Faust, Huntlee, Julian, Spaulding, Thurstan

Julian Bream, one of the world's master guitarists, embodies the technical perfection of this combination. He demonstrates all the 4's positive qualities — patient, practical, disciplined, intellectual, reliable, organized, and persevering. They can have outstanding powers of concentration. Others with the same combination could just as easily embody most of the 4's negative qualities — discontent, sceptical, narrow-minded, fussy, rigid, dogmatic, stubborn, dull, slow, and unproductive. Which side of the coin is reflected will be a function of childhood conditioning and current circumstances. Typically, they will embrace one side of this coin in certain activities and the opposite side in others.

5-1-6   Christine, Ginger, Kristine, Paula, Peggy, Jeri, Shirley, Benny, Clive, Erwin, Fred, Herb, Kenny, Timmie, Vincent

This is a vibrant, alive and dynamic combination. No moss grows under the feet of the 5 who has outstanding analytical skills and a determination to move forward at every opportunity. The 6 expression offers a clear channel for the aliveness of the 5. The 6 also helps to stabilize the 5 by adding an air of caution, responsibility, and accountability. Internally, these people are intense. Externally, they are congenial and progressive. They exude a great deal of confidence and trust in their lightning fast mental abilities. They have no fear of getting backed into a corner or of being taken advantage of in any way at any time. This combination is in the top 20% of all possible combinations.

5-2-7   Cher, Fern, Jacqueline, Lynne, Meg, Nell,
                   Susannah, Teri, Erich, Glenn, Henry, Kerby,
                   Lenny, Mervyn, Seth, Willie

This is one of four particularly accident prone combinations.
The others are 7-7-5, 4-1-5, and 5-8-4.

The 7 lives in a space beyond words and is focused on the
more abstract and etherial qualities of life. Combined with the
dynamic, challenging 5 that likes to do everything fast,
including walking and driving, accidents occur because the 5
insists on fast movement and the 7 is often not focused on or
connected to their physical reality.

The reasoning is slightly different, yet similar, for the 4-1-5 and
the 5-8-4 combinations. In these cases, the 5 is always a-way-
ahead of the 4 which has one foot stuck in the mud and is
contemplating more data.

The 5-2-7 combination is exceptionally intelligent, high-strung,
and sensitive. It is impossible to pin them down. They prefer
to live alone and are very much their own person. They suffer
from nervous, tense stomachs full of butterflies. When they
visit a friend, they will rattle off a whole stream of insights and
ideas. Before you have time to respond, they have wished you
a good day and have vanished in front of your very eyes. They
love the freedom of wide open spaces, the outdoors, nature,
and travel. A fast car, a good stereo, and two weeks of non-
stop driving is their idea of a good holiday.

5-3-8   Beth, Betsy, Cheryl, Inger, Laura, Shelby, Susanna, Wendy, Bryce, Denny, Eric, Gregg, Keith, Louie, Tyler, Vince

This is a very quick, intelligent quality, that effectively achieves results. They are a bit too intense for most people, but all in all this is a respectable combination. They can be prone to stuttering because the 8 expression empowers the 5 source and then has a hard time keeping up with the thought process of the 5. This combination has a predisposition towards success and can be outstanding promoters and sales people. The 5 thrives on taking a stance for causes and the 8 is focused on justice which entices people with these names to work as lawyers or in the legal profession. These people can be gamblers because the impulsive 5 is combined with the 8 which wants the very best that money can buy.

Although this can be considered among the better combinations, the 8 expression number empowers the 5 source creating a fiery, no-nonsense personality. In comparison, the 5-1-6 combination which is similar to the 5-3-8 is more desirable because the 6 draws out the positives of the 5 in a congenial fashion creating a very wholesome, principled nature.

This combination is not recommended for a woman because it ends in an 8 which creates a strong external material focus and detracts from the inner female processes.

5-4-9   Bess, Betty, Blythe, Louise, Maura, Shelly, Tess, Vivien, Bert, Chet, Chevy, Ed, Fidel, Henri, Jeff, Les, Lyle, Red

In comparison to the 5-3-8, this combination is even more intense and, instead of culminating in success, they are plagued with personal and material losses.   Like all combinations with a 5 source number, this combination hates to be repressed and can become particularly volatile when they don't get their own way. Underlying a somewhat flamboyant exterior, they have a naive trust in people. They deeply desire to assist people and are a champion of the underdog. Unfortunately, their high ideals are a constant source of disappointment for them. Their sarcastic bite stems from an underlying insecurity and a long history of perceived betrayals by life. They are aware of their naivety and it bothers them to no end when they forgo their first impressions and once again trust people they instinctively knew they shouldn't. In such a case, they will berate themselves a thousand times over before letting it go. This is also most distressing to them because both the 9 and the 5 want desperately to move on and be done with it.

5-5-1   Becky, Christie, Edith, Meryl, Paulette, Peg, Rickie, Edwin, Desi, Gerry, Gilbert, Greg, Jed, Mitchell, Perry

The word "hell" is a 5-5-1 and aptly reflects just how difficult this combination is to endure. The enthusiastic, enterprising, freedom loving, and insightful 5 is thwarted by the 1 that is content with the basics of life. The 5 which is bursting at the seams to fly to the moon is weighted down and forced to keep both feet on the ground. Imagine a garden nozzle attached to a fire-fighting hose. The implication is a tremendous amount of pressure striving to get out of the tiny nozzle which causes the hose to be unmanageable and whip uncontrollably in all directions. This conflict is not necessarily apparent when observing people with this combination because the 1 expression always presents a solid, stable, consistent front. These people can be very creative, dynamic, and productive. These positives are sharply offset by the excessive stress that these numbers cause the physical body. This combination fosters very strong women, indeed.

5-6-2   Bev, Bridget, Debby, Kelly, Mildred, Penny, Sydney, Winnie, Dennis, Eddy, Felix, Fredrick, Glen, Mike, Ted, Telly, Wes

The promotional, versatile, self-reliant, decisive, adventurous 5 is combined with the pleasant personality of the 2 creating a vibrant, dynamic nature that has some very good people skills. The 2 helps to take the sharp edge off the decisive, knife-edge of the 5. Yet, don't be fooled, behind the understanding, friendly presentation is a very determined, critical mind that can harbour some very strong, contemptuous, and bitter resentments. This is a moody combination that easily becomes depressed and filled with a sense of despair.

The name Mike is often well complimented by the name Michael which is a 6-9-6. In addition, Mike and Michael are often interchanged in conversation, whereas Ted is not often called Edward. Besides, Edward is a 6-4-1 which is not as desirable as the completely balanced 6-9-6 combination of Michael.

5-7-3   Becki, Cicely, Del, Jillie, Laurette, Myrtle, Peri, Sherry, Ben, Gerri, Izzie, Ken, Mel, Melvin, Mickey, Reg, Shep

This is an exceptionally spontaneous nature that is never at a loss for words. The 3 loves to tease and make a game out of everything. Unfortunately, the knife-edge, critical nature of the 5 comes through and there can be a note of cruelty in their teasing. These people are outstanding promoters and always on the go. They are jacks of all trades and master of none. They seldom finish anything they start and have a hundred and one projects on the go at the same time. This is an impulsive and disorganized combination that will smile at you and do whatever they damned well please. Their creative and musical skills are outstanding.

5-8-4   Courtney, Debbi, Gwen, Jerry, Juanita, Monique, Trixie, Elvis, Jerry, Len, Lew, Merv, Neil, Percy, Sidney, Teddy

All the enthusiastic, decisive, enterprising, freedom loving qualities of the 5 are stagnated by the 4, creating a sceptical, narrow-minded, fussy, dogmatic nature that wants to get going but can't. This is a critical, moody, intolerant combination that pays the price with digestive and elimination problems. There is no real lack of intelligence here — they are simply stuck in a rut and they hate it.

5-9-5   Jenny, Kimberly, Maureen, Nelly, Sheri, Vickie, Whitney, Cecil, Drew, Jimmie, Lewis, Ned, Terry, Trent, Wilfred

This is an intense combination that is well aware of their critical, moody, chaotic, temperamental, contemptuous, bitter, intolerant, and cruel nature. Consequently, they can be very strong disciplinarians and make a great effort not to lose emotional control because once they do, they have a terrible time reversing the outpour of negative spite. If they are at peace with their negative side, they can be exceptionally versatile, self-reliant, enthusiastic, insightful, and enterprising. This is a difficult combination to live because it offers a very fine line between total transformation and utter self-destruction.

These people are often hyper-active and find it impossible to sit still for five minutes. They cannot stand to be thwarted or repressed in any manner whatsoever. Even though they are exceptionally critical of others, they detest even the smallest amount of criticism directed to them. They are keenly aware of their own shortcomings and within their own minds they are constantly berating themselves.

6-1-7   Anne, Ashley, Gale, Glenda, Grace, Harriet, Hazel, Pearl, Darrell, Harvey, Marcel, Simon, Stewart, Walter, Warren

Although the 7 restricts the verbal expression of the 6 and adds a tone of reservation and caution, the 7 expression creates a refined, poised, and dignified personality with all the positive qualities of the 6 and few of the negative qualities of the 7. They are exceptionally intelligent and capable people although they keep a formal distance in personal relationships. They hold their body a bit on the stiff side and keep their head drawn back to signal that it is inappropriate for anyone to stand too close. They play their cards close to their chests and consider their personal affairs to be very private. It is difficult to really know someone with this combination. Their intelligence and dignity creates a strong cover personality that is initially hard to identify and is ultimately impenetrable.

6-2-8   Bea, Brenda, Erika, Jasmine, Leah, Marge, Polly, Toby, Abe, Allen, Archie, Colin, Edgar, Floyd, Rob, Ross, Wallie

This is a balanced combination in the sense that the 8 expression draws the energy of the 6 to a point of completion and fruition. Material success is typically substantial given that this combination begins with the capable, intelligent, responsible qualities of the 6 and completes with the discriminating and results oriented nature of the 8. These people have a very strong sense of commitment to home, family, business, and community. They stay clear, focused, and self-contained in times of conflict. This combination fosters an exceptionally capable administrator who embraces a deep sense of concern and respect for those who he manages. On a less positive note, the 8 doesn't add much humour or relaxation to the rather serious 6.

Although this is a balanced combination, it is very results oriented and is not suitable for everyone. This is especially true for women because the external material focus of the 8 is at odds with the energy of the internal female genitals. The administrative and material gains that this combination offers are typically offset by reproductive disorders for women using these numbers.

6-3-9 Angie, Carmen, Erica, Holly, Jody, Lori, Patrice, Sheila, Charley, Earl, Gino, Keith, Harvie, Jake, Matthew, Ringo

The 9 draws out the artistic, musical, and community-minded qualities of the 6 and adds a flair of inspiration to an already wholesome and congenial nature. This combination has a strong humanitarian side that is generous, compassionate, and empathic. They have a good sense of rhythm and appreciate music. These people can have intense moments of jealousy, temper, and possessiveness which pass rather quickly. Although they can worry extensively about the welfare of family, friends, and community, they always maintain an atmosphere of responsibility. This is one of the better first name combinations.

6-4-1 Cathie, Elsa, Eva, Faye, Kate, Lois, Mae, Stacey, Vera, Alfred, Bob, Bobby, Clifford, Edward, Frankie, Robb, Rod

This is a very capable, determined, responsible combination that does not mince a lot of words with their actions. They are honest and candid. They are very clear on what they want and are quite prepared to work for their goals. They like to be in charge of small groups such as a department in their office where they can participate in a leadership role. Although they have a deep love for home and family, they run their home more like a military academy than a home. Maternal instincts are present although the focus is on action and hard work. They are perfect candidates for the rank of a sergeant. This combination can suffer from headaches.

6-5-2   Dianne, Doris, Jade, Jamie, Nadine, Paige, Robyn, Tracie, Andrew, Charlie, Cody, Gerald, Jared, John, Morris, Tony

These are very intelligent, capable, responsible people who are gracious and easygoing.   They always have something pleasant to say about everybody and are a perfect choice for giving a toast to the bride or grace at the supper table.   Their intelligence comes across in a smooth and friendly manner. They are excellent diplomats, combining a superb depth of mind with diplomacy and tact.   As delightful as they are to be with from a social standpoint, living or working with them can be another matter because, in the end, they have a very definite   tendency   to   procrastinate.   Apart   from   their procrastinating ways, these people enjoy a wholesome, well-balanced personality.

6-6-3   Alice, Allie, Bobbi, Claire, Debra, Frances, Isabel, Jackie, Jane, Jean, Jessica, Madge, Maxine, Meghan, Charles, Ethan, James, Jock, Lyndon, Sean, Tom

Like the 6-5-2 combination, these are very intelligent, capable, responsible people who have a gregarious, cosmopolitan, cheerful, optimistic, and magnetic personality.   Unfortunately, they can have an argumentative, emotional nature that is hard to pin down and can be somewhat superficial.   They love to quibble, tease, and generally argue the point.   If you state what a beautiful clear day it is, they will likely take the opposite position to see if they can get a rise out of you.   They are fun and playful but can truly be a trial to those looking for a commitment, definition, and decisions.

6-7-4   Beverley, Hayley, Karen, Marcie, Melinda, Robin, Roslyn, Albert, Blake, Bradley, Dale, Fraser, Rory, Roy, Toni

On one hand, the innate intelligence of the 6 is supported by the intellectual skills of the 4 creating an exceptionally capable analyzer who does not tend to get lost in the detail — an analyzer who actually knows when to quit. On the other hand, the 4 is not expressive or spontaneous. This combination is on the reserved side, not favouring surprises or idle talk. The 4th physical sense is hearing. These people are superb listeners who portray a most sincere desire to understand other people's point of view. They have a non-threatening style of asking questions which combined with their ability to intelligently reflect on what they have heard, offers the other person a deep sense of being understood. They strive to understand and do not confuse their convictions with the opinions of others.

6-8-5   Dolly, Eileen, Gayle, Janet, Jaye, Joy, Molly, Thelma, Bjorn, Clarke, Colt, Dave, Lloyd, Scott, Tommy, Wayne

This is a particularly vibrant and alive combination that thrives on newness, change, and travel. They are exceptionally quick of mind and could never be accused of having any grass grow under their feet. They are versatile, self-reliant, decisive, curious, enthusiastic, enterprising, freedom loving, adventurous, and very insightful. Not too many people are willing or capable of keeping up with this combination. Even so, there is a sense of sensibility infused in their character and a wholesomeness that is easy to admire. Life is not all roses for this combination given the 5 expression number which has intense likes and dislikes resulting in some bitter experiences and personal disappointments.

6-9-6   Cecilia, Diane, Edna, Flo, Helga, Janice, Kaye, Mabel, Maggie, Marnie, Petra, Rae, Shelagh, Stella, Suzu, Kory, Alex, Dean, Don, Michael, Norm, Rolf, Troy, Victor, Wade

This is one of the few completely balanced combinations. It is the only combination where the source number and the expression number are equal and the combination can be considered balanced.

This combination is responsible, accountable, sensible, paternal, maternal, affectionate, artistic, stable, wise, congenial, and wholesome of character. They are most capable of doing anything they choose to do both artistic or practical. They create a wonderful home atmosphere and participate fully in community activities, offering their wisdom and support wherever they go. Sometimes they can be a bit on the bossy side and assume that they have all of the answers which is reflected in their favourite expression of "I know". They are so used to being tuned into a global knowingness, that even when they have no idea of what they are being told, they habitually interject "I know. Yes, I know." This habit is exasperating to those close to them.

All-in-all, this is a superb combination. They certainly make excellent counsellors and educators. Their only weakness stems from assuming too much responsibility for themselves and others. As a result, they can suffer from mental stress in the form of migraine headaches.

If Don is also called Donald, the 7-7-5 combination of Donald will create a more sensitive and intense quality to the degree it is used.

7-1-8   Gloria, Jordan, Natalie, Noreen, Olga, Rosa, Sondra, Antony, Josiah, Mason, Riccardo, Rowan, Zacharie

This combination can be exceptionally shrewd in business. The 7 is superbly analytical and intuitive which, combined with the 8, moves the insights of the 7 to material success. Given that the 7 never gives anything away with facial expressions and both the 7 and 8 are very conservative with words, these people can be very active behind the scenes in the financial world and no one would ever know. If they choose to be in an administrative position, they will offer few words of advise, yet convey a strong message that no excuses will be tolerated for a lack of results.

They are clever, refined, dignified, confident, shrewd, and discriminating in everything they do. These people understand power and authority. They are completely self-contained and quite impossible to be close to, or to truly know.

Generative disorders are virtually unavoidable for a woman using this combination and are also common with males.

7-2-9   Fiona, Jeanna, Margo, Melodie, Monika, Nicola, Vanessa, Clayton, Geordie, Gerome, Hogan, Nicholas, Raymond, Waylon

A 9 expression number always intensifies the source number with which it is associated. In the case of the 7 which is already very sensitive, vulnerable, introspective, and aloof, the result is a hyper-sensitive, fearful, nervous, and very flighty personality. This combination is all ungrounded inspiration and dreams combined with humanitarian and religious ideals. They can be extremely jealous and suffer from deep, emotional mood-swings. Often they will strive to cover-up their extreme sensitivity by being talkative. Losses and misunderstandings are a constant plight of this combination. Although they appear to be much more extroverted than the 7-9-7 combination, they suffer from all of the same stress and frustrations.

7-3-1   Allison, Cora, Marjory, Maryanne, Melonie, Monica, Taylor, Arnold, Charlton, Gaylord, Jackson, Marlon, Pablo, Roland

Both the 7 and the 1 are very much their own person and not very communicative verbally. They demand a great deal of their own space and prefer to live on their own. On the other hand, the 7 loves to share moments of deep intimacy and can enjoy being very physical. When they are in such a mood, their haunting attractiveness is very alluring to the opposite sex. Given that the 1 also has a strong sex drive, this combination can find a great deal of satisfaction in sexuality. Unfortunately, exquisite moments of deep sexual union are followed by long periods of complete detachment which can leave the other party in utter confusion. Misunderstandings continuously result from the double message of "come here, go away". This is a recurring theme for most of the combinations beginning or ending in a 7. The theme is particularly strong in this example where the 7 is combined with the 1. These people are destined to lead a life of separation and detachment, only savouring the joys of relationship for brief periods. Loneliness is a familiar cry in their heart although they will not acknowledge it for long before they push forward in life ignoring their need for love and personal relationships.

7-4-2   Dora, Leanna, Lynn, Margaret, Margot, Norah, Sonya, Ursula, Adolf, Caesar, Carlton, Mario, Noah, Omar, Oscar, Sly

This combination and its mirror image, the 2-4-7, are amongst two of the most sensitive, ungrounded, and confused of the 81 possible combinations.

The 7 lives in a world of abstraction where boundaries are loosely defined and words fail to capture the essence of their experience. The 2 expression is also short on boundaries and is sensitive and impressionable. The result is a very self-conscious personality that has little or no self-esteem. These people live in a world which is truly difficult for them or anyone to define. They are constantly concerned for their sanity during both awake and sleep times. Life for them is like a dream and it is a great struggle to tell what is real and what is not.

The 7-4-2 combination is more chatty than the 2-4-7 which can be almost invisible in nature. Both qualities are aloof, striving to protect their vulnerability, and at the same time desperate for affection which is a keynote of the 2 and a strong craving of the 7. Remember that 7's are very sensual and love intimacy but only for short durations because the vulnerability quickly becomes overwhelming. This is particularly true of both the 7-4-2 and the 2-5-7 combinations. Where the 7-3-1 combination will bond strongly for short periods of time with long intervals between times of closeness, the 7-4-2 constantly lives in a push-pull struggle without relief. The physical wear of their vacillation drains their vitality and leaves them forever tired. These people are very late risers and have little desire to talk before noon.

7-5-3   Colleen, Deanna, Donna, Marianne, Nora, Pamela, Sharon, Amos, Dalton, George, Harrison, Jarod, Jerome, Norman

This numeric sequence is interesting to compare to the 3-4-7 combination in example 14. In the end, the 3-4-7 retracts upon itself and shuts the rest of the world out which leads to endless misunderstandings. In contrast, the 7-5-3 moves from introversion to extroversion. They draw from a source that is beyond words and are compelled to express what they are sensing and feeling. It's not an easy task but they give it a superb effort. *They wear their emotions on their sleeve* whereas the 3-4-7, who graciously smiles at the world, is very private and closed in the final analysis.

The 7-5-3's have their fair share of moodiness and introversion, yet they will come around in relatively short order and take another "kick at the cat" in an effort to find words for their feelings. When this quality is nervous, they will babble away to cover up their sensitivities. It's very difficult to determine how they will be from one moment to the next — one moment they will be the life of the party and the next they will go to their room and bury themselves in a book ignoring that it is their birthday party down-stairs. They have a very inquisitive nature and love to read. They can be perpetual students determined to find the answers to life, yet they are scattered in their efforts and seldom complete what they start. They bring a dramatic flair to everything they do.

Both the 7-5-3 and the 3-4-7 combinations are dealing with opposing forces and neither one is desirable for a life of harmony and nurturing relationships.

7-6-4   Angela, Candace, Carol, Joan, Lola, Oprah,
Shannon, Sonia, Carlo, Francois, Harold,
Jacob, Lealand, Thomas, Walton

This is a difficult combination to live because the 4 does not offer the etherial, aloof 7 much of an outlet except in an analytical, detailed way. Since the 7 also has strong analytical skills, this combination can be very successful in research where abstract concepts are being formulated into tangible facts. They are also clever at electronics, accounting, and mathematics.

Where the 7 is finely tuned to the gentler elements of life, the 4 is very mechanical and intellectual. The result is a personality that is inspired but comes across in a stodgy fashion. They don't flow very well and find it hard to truly connect with people. Although their verbal skills are limited, intellectually they are very capable. Physically, they are prone to illness because they frequently suffer from indigestion and constipation.

7-7-5   Amelia, Marlo, Morgan, Olivia, Rosalyn, Sonja,
Sophia, Barron, Bradford, Brandon, Carlos,
Donald, Jason, Marco

Not only is this one of the most accident prone of all the combinations, they have the weirdest accidents imaginable — a cupboard door pops open, a saucer falls out and hits the dish rack by the sink, flipping a knife off the counter into their little toe that then proceeds to become infected. Only if you have these numbers or live with someone with these numbers could you believe what happens to them.

This is an independent, very high strung combination, that runs on nervous energy and seldom sits still long enough for anyone to find out how they are. Besides, if you could physically pin them down, the etherial 7 won't have words to capture their experience anyway. This combination devours books and all manner of information. They are wonderfully vibrant and alive but these numbers do not lend themselves to intimate, long-term relationships.

Under their vibrant exterior lives bitterness, resentment, jealousy, and depression. Their sharp, intense, and often arrogant nature is easily offended. They can be very self-righteous when hurt. This combination often meets with unexpected, sudden death through freak accidents or heart failure at an early age.

When Donald is called Don at the office and Donald at home, his experience will be relative to what he is called. This is true of many names which have common abbreviations.

7-8-6   Lenore, Lisa-Marie, Lorna, Mary-Jane, Phoebe, Rhonda, Geoffrey, Harmon, Howard, Lyn, Malcolm, Mallory, Somerset

This is the only combination beginning with a 7 that has a wholesome balance to it. Why? The 7 is a very refined, delicate quality that needs a great deal of consistent support and understanding for it not to retreat inward and disconnect from the outer world. The 6 is the only number that has sufficient balance, stability, and insight to nurture the 7 into participating openly in life. The 6 draws out the philosophic, spiritual, mystical, inquisitive, refined, poised, and dignified qualities of the 7. At the same time, the 6 helps the 7 to remain practical in its inspiration rather than becoming deeply abstract and aloof. Even so, this is not an easy combination to live because the 7 is constantly striving to comprehend those qualities of life which go beyond words. They prefer a private, reserved life style. This combination is particularly astute at poetry, music, writing, and acting.

7-9-7   Carolyn, Doreen, Marion, Mona, Naomi, Norma, Victoria, Anthony, Carroll, Crawford, Randolf, Roman, Sampson, Sloan

This is one of the three most difficult of all combinations to live within our world. The other two are 7-2-9 and 9-7-7.

Not only does the 7 expression draw from the crown chakra, the spiritual connection which is beyond words, but there is no outlet for the highly sensitized, inner experience through the 7 expression number. Everything, both positive and negative, that can be said about the 7 is amplified here. Unfortunately, the negative qualities tend to overshadow the positive qualities creating a very secretive, repressed, disconnected, pessimistic, aloof, nervous, and fearful personality that is deeply introverted. Their fragile, delicate nature is hurt *extremely* easily. For example, their sensitivity can amplify the slightest indiscretion of a loved one into devastating jealousy. *Walking on egg-shells* is an apt metaphor for the experience of living with a person using a 7-9-7 combination. They are secretive and private to an extreme. The sense of butterflies in their stomach is so strong that they are often shocked to be told that other people don't have the same experience. To them, butterflies and a nervous stomach are like a heart beating — it's simply part of living. This sensation can be so intense that they can spend a lifetime trying to cure what is diagnosed as an ulcerated stomach. Other names may take the edge off the 7-9-7 but under a somewhat poised and dignified exterior is a hyper-sensitive person who is under extreme stress.

Their lungs are particularly vulnerable to pneumonia and pleurisy. The slightest upset can take their breath away and cause a great deal of difficulty breathing. They can die without supposed warning because their calm exterior and private nature offered few, if any, clues to their inner turmoil.

They find their best relief in the out-of-doors and through writing, poetry, and music.

8-1-9   Augusta, Carlotta, Johanna, Magnolia, Ruthie, Sue, Yolanda, Buddie, Cooper, Culver, Currey, Shakespeare, Woodley, Yule

This is an attractive combination in the sense that the 8 has a strong sense of justice, confidence, authority, and leadership. They have a clear perception of life and how it works. When combined with the humanitarian, and inspirational nature of the 9, the result is a strong and inviting personality that can express themselves with outstanding insight in both business and the arts. Unfortunately, where the 8 attracts superb business opportunities, the humanitarian ideals of the 9 lose or give away all of the profits earned. Combinations which *end* in a 9 also *end* in losses both personally and materially. In this case, the losses are substantial because both the 8 and the 9 have very high ideals and are striving to achieve significant goals in life.

8-2-1   Carolina, Joanna, Lurline, Rosanna, Roxana, Rubie, Susie, Burgess, Burnett, Johnathan, Montgomery, Murrey, Quentin

This is a hard-nosed business personality from the old-school

— get a bigger hammer if it doesn't work the first time. There is no lack of determination, will, and obstinance here. This self-centered personality is interested in results and has no concern for the feelings and personal needs of others. Although the tendency is to be unscrupulous, calculating, and materialistic, they can be true pioneers for justice and truth with no fear of being blunt and demanding. These people crave material success but seldom, if ever, get off the ground — they are forever pioneering new ventures and beginning once again from square one. This combination needs the support of offsetting numbers in other names to soften their hard-hitting, material focus.

8-3-2   Bunnie, Lucille, Pollyanna, Rolanda, Ronalda, Tomasina, Boothe, Currie, Elwood, Hubert, Jonathan, Rooney, Rustie

In contrast to the previous example, this very smooth business personality has excellent people skills and can readily solicit the help of others. Unfortunately, the desired results are seldom achieved because these people tend to be too trusting in others and too empathic toward their employees. They allow personal issues to be confused with business needs. These people attract excellent business opportunities but seldom are willing to work hard enough to fulfill their contractual obligations. There is always someone to blame for the loss of their material dreams. They adore all the material conveniences of modern day living and fantasise about yachts and mansions with servants and gourmet chefs.

8-4-3   Brooke, Julie, Luise, Margareta, Rosalee, Trudey, Quenby, Armando, Derwood, Gunther, Jurgen, Romeo, Roscoe, Ulysses

This strong personality can be most convincing with their verbal skills. There is a tendency to be indulgent in food, drink, and sexuality. Their appetite for both quantity and quality will show early in life around their waistline. Even so this is a cheerful, magnetic, vital combination that would do very well if they could learn not to scatter their efforts. They constantly promote their business by entertaining their clients and suppliers. They love to give extravagant parties where no expense is spared. This is a go-for-broke personality with a belief in living for today, for tomorrow you may die. They like to gamble with life. The 3 expression scatters the administrative and executive focus of the 8, limiting their accomplishments.

8-5-4   Annamarie, Isadora, Jude, Judie, Oriana, Rosemarie, Bruce, Buster, Hughe, Jules, Luke, Miguel, Theodor

This combination combines an administrative sense with a particularly good eye for facts and figures which stands them well in the business and scientific worlds. They are exceptionally patient with a strong bent for results. Although they are slow to move and decide, they are exceptionally thorough and absolute sticklers for detail. Their nature is steady, reserved, practical, and persevering. Behind their discerning, placid nature is a very self-confident identity. Their dogmatic and stubborn streak can only be appeased with solid business logic. They are tight-fisted with money and likely have been accused of being a penny pincher more than once or twice in their life. They are particularly good at mathematics and physics.

Their love of rich foods runs into difficulty with the 4 which holds onto everything creating gastro-intestinal problems. They are also very subject to gout given their liking for rich foods, poor digestion, and slow elimination.

8-6-5   Coralee, Joana, Juliet, June, Loralee, Lucie, Trudie, Duke, Ellwood, Huey, Hunter, Huxley, Tulley, Quent

This is a very strong, self-reliant, versatile combination that doesn't take no for an answer from anyone. This quality wants results and they want them now. They are not much fun to live with when they don't get what they want. When their callous and bitter side comes out, they have little trouble telling people what they think or feel or where to go in no uncertain terms. They are inclined to be impatient and know-it-alls. They are often accused of having very thick skin. In their own minds, they do not see themselves as defiant and head-strong as people perceive them to be.

They have an abundance of energy and have a hard time sitting still. They love change and travel especially when they can go first class. Their impulsive nature undermines their innate business sense.

Women with this combination have difficulty with personal relationships because they are forever trying to control the relationship and be the boss. A woman with these numbers would always wear the pants in her home.

8-7-6   Antoinette,   Morgana,   Muriel,   Pandora,
Roxanna, Susen, Boone, Dustie, Humphrey,
Huntley, Purcell, Ruben, Tucker

Once again, here is a combination that ends in a 6 and should
be considered in the top 20% of the 81 possible combinations.
In comparison, the 6-2-8 fits into the top 5% because the
source number of 6 starts with substantial, wholesome, mature
ideas and cultivates the intention to a point of fruition.   The
weakness of beginning with an 8 source number is that
expansive, far-reaching goals are continuously upgraded
before they are initiated. The challenge of the less ambitious 6
expression number is to keep up with the ever expanding goals
of the 8. This pattern tends to overwhelm the 6 and frustrate
the 8 who wants results relatively immediately.   Even so, it
should be kept in mind that the 6 demands responsibility and is
determined to maintain an air of sensibility in all things.
Sometimes it is overlooked that the 8 has a strong sense of
balance in its own right.   Hence, this combination works out
much better than most and exudes an air of balance in both
home and business.

8-8-7   Carlota, Darla-Jo, Dolores, Eleanor, Elenora,
Lavonna, Buckley, Edmund, Guthrie, Leopold,
Redmund, Russell

In this example, all the positive qualities of the 8 are kept in
close check by the 7 expression number which plays its cards
close to the chest. As a result, this can be a very shrewd
business combination that attracts excellent opportunities but
never experiences complete success in anything they do.
They can come within a hair's breath of success but somehow
they can never quite close that final, small gap. Why? It's the
nature of the 7 to discover the secrets of life but it takes the 8

to make the theory practical and material. Because the energy flow goes from the 8 to the 7, goals are never fully realized. When a combination ends in an 8, goals and objectives flourish and grow to fruition — material and spiritual success.

8-9-8   Alexandra, Georgetta, Justine, Ramona, Rosalina, Suzie, Dudley, Julien, Monroe, Rupert, Sherwood, Woodie, Zeus

On the surface, this may appear to be the ultimate business combination, yet this is another example where too much of a good thing is not healthy.

This combination attracts huge business opportunities where the game rules are centered around shrewd materiality and power. They love the world of high finance, banking, economics, and politics. These people play for keeps and will not hesitate to unscrupulously exercise obscure options found in the fine print of contracts. Manipulation and exploitation are common bed partners of these numbers. Take heed and do not be tempted to use this combination for a business name.

These people love quality and quantity to the extreme and suffers from a constant diet of rich, gourmet foods. They are prime candidates for gout, which is excruciatingly painful.

9-1-1   Cindy, Christin, Iris, Kirstin, Kristin, Nicki, Suzanne, Claude, Gil, Irwin, Nick, Phillip, Skip, Timmi, Wilt

These people have high ideals and wonderful intentions but lack outlets for their dreams. The humanitarian, universal ideals of the 9 are tapered down to the single, independent, detached reality of the 1. The result is tension in the head, throat, and nervous system which gives way to confusion, dizziness, frustration, and fits of temper. The metaphor of a huge fire hose with a garden nozzle outlined in Example 37, is also applicable to this combination. The extreme polarity difference between the 9 and the 1 will eventually take its toll on health and personal success.

9-2-2   Audrey, Ivy, Liz, Mindy, Phyllis, Raquel, Sue-Ann, Trish, Beau, Doug, Guido, Kirby, Maurey, Rich, Saunders, Will

In comparison to the 2-9-2 in Example 10, this combination is more lively and willing to participate in life. Yet, the universal ideals of the 9 find little tenacity in the 2 expression, resulting in a very easy going, laid back, likable personality. It is very difficult for them to say no to anyone asking for help. They are emotional, gentle dreamers who lack will power to follow through with their intentions. They are lost outside of relationship and always seek the approval of others. The 2 quality always has a tendency to turn food into fluids which results in overweight, even on a conservative diet.

9-3-3   Christy, Cindi, Eugenie, Jacquie, Kris, Kristy, Laurie, Chris, Eugene, Laurier, Leonardo, Lou, Ricky, Willis

This is a very inspired personality that can talk a mile a minute. They are full of fun, laughter, optimism, and imagination. They can play music by ear and have a strong, melodious lilt to their voice. They have a magnetic personality that loves to tease and is hard to resist. Their weakness lies in being too fun-loving. They tend to scatter their efforts and have an extremely hard time organizing themselves let alone others. They are never on time and will somehow manage to be late for their own funeral. Underlying their bubbly nature is a very spiritual focus with exceptionally high humanitarian ideals. They can suffer from extreme mood swings. The best way to get them out of the depths of depression and despair is with love, affection, and any old corny joke.

9-4-4   Beulah, Bibi, Kitty, Lily, Missy, Sybil, Vi, Winny, Audie, Clint, Cyril, Jacques, Julio, Kirk, Louis, Rudolf

This combination becomes ecstatic when they see a spiritual idea manifest in physical reality. They will often skip and dance about when such events occur which is quite in contrast to their otherwise stodgy personality. Unfortunately, this is a difficult combination to live because the idealistic, unconditional 9 is forced to express through the placid, intellectual 4 that is never quite ready to make a decision. This robs the 9 of its spontaneity and destroys many inspired dreams. The frustration of the 9 compounds the overall problem and the 4 degenerates into being fussy, stubborn, and unproductive. Once the catch-22 cycle starts it becomes exceptionally difficult to break. These people can be extreme perfectionists regarding the smallest of details. This is one of the least desirable combinations and is not offering any favours for those who choose to use it.

9-5-5   Beula, Gigi, Glynis, Julianne, Kristi, Liby, Mitzi, Ricki, Bing, Jim, Flin, Philipp, Rick, Sid, Virgil, Wilf, Woodrow

The inspired 9 and the versatile and impulsive 5 create a medium to large tornado of activity around these people. There is a great deal of impatience and intensity here which can be exhausting for those living with them. Seldom are they overweight because they run on nervous energy even when they are sitting still. Don't cross these people because they will seek revenge. They can be very strong disciplinarians in an effort to avoid their contemptuous and cruel streak that can express when they lose control. They attract many bitter experiences in life which is difficult for them to understand given the humanitarian ideals of their hearts. This is a high strung, self-reliant, promotional nature which starts a thousand and one projects and never finishes any. There is no lack of mental agility here.

The name Jim is offset by the name James, 6-6-3, to the degree Jim is also called James.

9-6-6   Claudine, Ginny, Kim, Laurel, Lil, Pauline, Tilly, Trixy, Billy, Britt, Dirk, Griffin, Hugo, Skippy, Tim, Vik

This is one of the more delightful and wholesome combinations available. It is referred to in Chapter 23 in the discussion of destiny combinations. This combination offers the best of many worlds because the accountable, responsible, and sensible 6 draws out all of the positive qualities of the 9. In this case, the humanitarian and altruistic nature of the 9 finds expression in unconditional love, forgiveness, compassion, empathy, and tolerance. Plus all the intuitive, musical, artistic, and visionary qualities of the 9 are enhanced by the 6 expression. The result is a well balanced, affectionate, artistic, stable, wise and congenial nature that embraces life and achieves their goals.

9-7-7   Guinevere, Ingrid, Jill, Lilly, Liv, Mimsy, Nikky, Vicky, Bruno, Irving, Jimmy, Kin, Maurice, Philip, Smitty, Vic

Once again, this is one of the most difficult of all combinations to live. Two other very similar combinations are the 7-2-9 and the 7-9-7. In this example, the 7 restricts the expression of the 9 offering little or no outlet for the inspiration and enthusiasm of the source number. The 9 which is high-strung and somewhat nervous to begin with is not well complimented by the 7 which is sensitive, delicate, and vulnerable to all the subtle energies of life. These people have much to offer but it is difficult for them to feel safe enough to share what they feel. They have a tendency to be somewhat tight-lipped. They enjoy expressing themselves in art, music, and writing. When they get a common cold, it settles immediately in their lungs and care must be taken that it doesn't turn into pneumonia. In addition, this combination can suffer from nervous disorders, given the high level of sensitivity of both the 9 and the 7. These people crave affection and understanding, yet are forced to live a very lonely life. They are intelligent and well read with exceptional writing skills.

9-8-8   Kristyn, Lauren, Lizzy, Maude, Milly, Mimi, Trixi, Vikki, Bill, Dwight, Lauren, Mitch, Samuel, Skipp, Slim, Timmy

The universal ideals of the 9 strive to find expression through

---

the 8 in the material world. Ask these people how they are doing and they will tell you about the big business deal that didn't quite make it. But there is one cooking now that will be "the big one", putting them on easy street for the rest of their lives. The 9 quality is inspired and visionary but lacks the practicality to put their ideals into action. The 8 expression helps this process considerably. Unfortunately, the 8 also has huge plans for material success and between the two of them, they get carried away with schemes to become billionaires. They want immediate results and lack the patience and willingness to make the effort required to achieve their goals. Remember, the 8 is an administrator and not the worker. These people can have an air of being pompous and good-natured at the same time.

Although this is not a recommended combination for a first name, it does work effectively for a destiny combination as discussed in Chapter 23. To work towards and include significant humanitarian and material goals in one's life is unquestionably desirable as long as such goals are not all consuming to the exclusion of personal and family needs.

9-9-9   Jacquelyn, Laurell, Luella, Lilli, Micki, Nikki, Vicki, Chip, Cliff, Dick, Dougy, Duane, Gib, Mick, Phil, Willy

In this example, all the qualities of the 9 are embraced in full force. As humanitarian, loving, and altruistic as these people are, they can be equally as possessive, jealous, selfish, and unforgiving. They can change from moment to moment, swinging from the heights of inspiration to the depths of self-pity and vile temper. This combination is dramatically influenced by the other names with which it associates. These people usually specialize in professional careers and can be extreme perfectionists. They tend to seek careers where they can fulfill their humanitarian ideals and serve people.

The lesson of the 9 is to let-go, surrender, and forgive. If they make any effort to hold onto loved ones or material things, they are taken from them or they lose them. They must walk a fine line of detachment which is extremely exasperating because they love so dearly and deeply. This apparent contradiction results in a sense that life is unfair. They can find it particularly difficult to understand how their love for their family is seen as smothering and possessive.

ALPHABETIC INDEX of ALL NAMES

with

REFERENCE

NUMBERS

HOW TO USE THIS SECTION

This section alphabetically lists more than 18,000 names. Following each name is a 3 digit number which is the numerological combination of the name. Look up the combination in the preceding section of this book, "What Each Name Means", to read about the qualities of the name that interests you.

Although you may find a name that you like and it's a great combination, make sure it fits correctly with your surname to create a desireable "destiny" for your child. A superb name and an undesirable destiny is not going to server your child.

If you need help, email me at:

lance@numbers-count.com

FEMALE NAMES WITH REFERENCE NUMBERS

Aaren	753	Aarika	325	Ab	123
Abagael	832	Abagail	336	Abbe	641
Abbey	628	Abbi	145	Abbie	641
Abby	123	Abbye	628	Abdel	696
Abella	786	Abena	775	Abeni	674
Aberah	718	Abi	123	Abie	628
Abigail	235	Abigaile	731	Abigale	731
Abina	279	Abiona	876	Abira	224
Abra	224	Acacia	369	Acantha	393
Ada	246	Adabel	797	Adabela	898
Adabella	832	Adabelle	336	Adah	235
Adal	279	Adala	371	Adali	279
Adalia	371	Adalie	775	Adalin	235
Adaline	731	Adamina	347	Adamma	336
Adan	292	Adar	246	Adara	347
Adda	281	Addi	189	Addia	281
Addie	685	Addy	167	Adel	674
Adela	775	Adelaida	821	Adelaide	325
Adele	279	Adelfia	742	Adelheid	213
Adelia	775	Adelice	213	Adelina	731
Adelind	674	Adeline	235	Adelise	281
Adella	718	Adelle	213	Adelma	729
Adelmo	325	Adelpha	742	Adelphe	246
Adelphia	742	Adena	797	Aderes	257
Aderes	268	Adesina	718	Adey	628
Adi	145	Adie	641	Adiea	742
Adiel	674	Adila	279	Adina	292
Adine	696	Adira	246	Adlee	279
Adlen	639	Adli	178	Adoette	887
Adolfa	843	Adolphina	898	Adolphine	393
Adonia	898	Adora	843	Adorabella	538
Adoree	843	Adorjan	819	Adorna	898
Adrea	742	Adria	246	Adriaen	797
Adrian	292	Adriana	393	Adriane	797
Adriann	257	Adriann	268	Adrianna	358
Adrianne	753	Adriano	898	Adrien	696
Adriena	797	Adriene	292	Adrienne	257
Adrienne	268	Adya	224	Aelda	775
Aeldra	775	Aeldrida	729	Aelfreda	347
Aeriel	235	Aeriela	336	Africa	292
Africah	281	Afrika	281	Afrikah	279
Afton	742	Ag	178	Agace	718

Agacia	314	Agata	393	Agate	797
Agatha	382	Agathe	786	Agave	729
Aggi	156	Aggie	652	Aggy	134
Agla	213	Agna	235	Agnella	797
Agnes	641	Agnesa	742	Agnese	246
Agnessa	753	Agnesse	257	Agnesse	268
Agneta	753	Agni	134	Agnita	257
Agnita	268	Agnola	865	Agnus	448
Agnya	213	Agueda	123	Ahimsa	246
Ahira	281	Aida	246	Aidan	292
Aiden	696	Aigneis	641	Aijondeta	437
Aila	235	Ailee	235	Aileen	281
Ailene	281	Ailey	617	Aili	134
Ailie	639	Ailis	145	Aimee	246
Aimil	178	Aindrea	797	Aine	652
Ainslee	292	Ainsley	674	Ainslie	696
Airleas	742	Aisha	292	Aisleen	292
Aislinn	156	Aithne	663	Aiyanna	382
Aja	213	Ajame	753	Ajiyi	189
Ajlette	281	Akasma	371	Akela	753
Akeyla	731	Akeylah	729	Akili	156
Akira	224	Akoni	775	Akosua	235
Alain	281	Alaine	786	Alameda	821
Alana	382	Alanah	371	Alane	786
Alanna	347	Alannah	336	Alarica	369
Alarice	764	Alarise	742	Alathia	347
Alayne	764	Alba	257	Alba	268
Albane	718	Alberga	731	Alberta	775
Albertina	731	Albertine	235	Albina	213
Albine	617	Albinia	213	Alcina	224
Alcine	628	Alcinia	224	Alda	279
Aldora	876	Alecia	764	Aleda	775
Aleece	764	Aleen	281	Aleeza	325
Alein	685	Alejandra	843	Alejandrina	898
Alejia	742	Aleka	753	Aleksey	246
Alena	786	Alene	281	Aleria	731
Alesia	742	Alessandra	854	Aleta	753
Aletea	358	Aletha	742	Alethe	246
Alethea	347	Alethia	742	Aletia	753
Alette	279	Alex	696	Alexa	797
Alexandra	898	Alexandre	393	Alexandretta	448
Alexandrette	843	Alexandria	898	Alexandrina	854
Alexandrine	358	Alexena	358	Alexi	696
Alexia	797	Alexina	753	Alexine	257

Alexine	268	Alexis	617	Aleyde	257
Aleyde	268	Alfi	191	Alfie	696
Alfina	257	Alfina	268	Alfonsine	325
Alfreda	742	Alfy	178	Alhena	775
Ali	134	Alia	235	Alice	663
Alicea	764	Alida	279	Alidia	279
Alie	639	Aliette	279	Alika	257
Alika	268	Alike	652	Alikee	257
Alikee	268	Alile	663	Alim	178
Alima	279	Alina	281	Aline	685
Alis	145	Alisa	246	Alischer	663
Alisen	696	Alisha	235	Alison	797
Aliss	156	Alissa	257	Alissa	268
Alisz	134	Alita	257	Alita	268
Alithea	742	Alithia	246	Alitza	246
Alitzah	235	Alix	191	Aliz	123
Aliza	224	Alizag	292	Alizka	246
Alka	257	Alka	268	Allain	224
Allana	325	Alleen	224	Allegra	742
Allegri	641	Allene	224	Alli	167
Allie	663	Allina	224	Allis	178
Allison	731	Allix	134	Alloula	292
Allson	731	Allsun	437	Allula	595
Ally	145	Allyce	674	Allyn	191
Allys	156	Allyson	718	Alma	279
Almeda	729	Almeira	775	Almeria	775
Almeta	797	Almira	279	Almire	674
Almiron	731	Aloha	821	Aloisa	843
Aloise	347	Aloisia	843	Alona	887
Alonza	876	Aloysia	821	Alpha	292
Alphonsina	821	Alphonsine	325	Alta	257
Alta	268	Althea	742	Althee	246
Altheta	764	Aludra	573	Alula	562
Aluma	573	Alumice	911	Alura	538
Alva	279	Alveria	775	Alverta	797
Alvina	235	Alvine	639	Alvinia	235
Aly	112	Alya	213	Alyce	641
Alyda	257	Alyda	268	Alys	123
Alysa	224	Alyse	628	Alysia	224
Alyson	775	Alyss	134	Alyssa	235
Alzena	775	Ama	246	Amabel	797
Amabella	832	Amabelle	336	Amadea	887
Amadika	314	Amajeta	876	Amalea	876
Amalee	371	Amaleta	898	Amalia	371

Amalie	775	Amalinda	371	Amalita	393
Amaliya	358	Amanda	347	Amandi	246
Amandie	742	Amandine	797	Amando	843
Amandy	224	Amara	347	Amarah	336
Amarantha	415	Amargo	821	Amaris	257
Amaris	268	Amarrah	336	Amaryllis	292
Amata	369	Amber	663	Amberly	674
Ambrosia	876	Ambrosina	832	Ambrosine	336
Ambur	461	Ame	641	Amealia	876
Amecia	775	Amedee	786	Amelea	371
Amelia	775	Amelie	279	Amelina	731
Amelinda	775	Amelinde	279	Ameline	235
Amelita	797	Amena	797	Amethyst	663
Ami	145	Amice	674	Amicia	279
Amie	641	Amii	145	Amilda	224
Amina	292	Amine	696	Amineh	685
Aminta	224	Amintha	213	Aminthe	617
Amira	246	Amirali	279	Amity	145
Amma	281	Amsey	639	Amy	123
Amye	628	An	156	Ana	257
Ana	268	Anaba	371	Anabel	718
Anabella	843	Anabelle	347	Anala	382
Analiese	393	Analise	797	Ananda	358
Anane	718	Anastasia	494	Anastasie	898
Anastassia	415	Anatola	911	Anatolia	911
Anatolie	415	Anda	292	Andee	292
Anderea	393	Andi	191	Andie	696
Andra	292	Andre	696	Andrea	797
Andreana	854	Andree	292	Andrel	639
Andria	292	Andriana	358	Andy	178
Ane	652	Anela	786	Anemone	854
Anestassia	819	Anet	674	Aneta	775
Anett	696	Anetta	797	Anette	292
Ange	639	Angel	663	Angela	764
Angelica	797	Angelien	224	Angelika	786
Angeliki	685	Angelina	729	Angeline	224
Angelique	551	Angelita	786	Angelle	292
Angeni	685	Angie	639	Angil	167
Angy	112	Ani	156	Ania	257
Ania	268	Anibal	213	Anica	281
Anicka	213	Aniela	786	Anikke	696
Anila	281	Anissa	279	Anita	279
Anitra	279	Aniveta	729	Anjali	292
Anjanette	369	Ankie	674	Ann	112

Ann Louise	652	Anna	213	Anna Louise	753
Annabal	369	Annabel	764	Annabell	797
Annabella	898	Annabelle	393	Annabla	369
Annable	764	Annaliese	358	Annalise	753
Annamaria	459	Annamarie	854	Anne	617
Anne Louise	257	Anne Louise	268	Anneliese	753
Annelise	257	Annelise	268	Annemarie	358
Annes	628	Annetta	753	Annette	257
Annette	268	Anni	112	Annice	641
Annie	617	Annis	123	Annise	628
Annissa	235	Annmaria	358	Annona	865
Annonciade	448	Annora	819	Annunciata	628
Anny	189	Annys	191	Annze	696
Anoki	775	Anona	819	Anora	854
Anouchka	292	Anouck	112	Anselma	742
Anselme	246	Ansis	178	Ansley	674
Anstace	729	Anstance	775	Anstice	628
Anthe	663	Anthea	764	Anthonia	821
Antoinette	876	Antoinietta	472	Antonetta	472
Antoni	731	Antonia	832	Antonie	336
Antonietta	472	Antonina	887	Anula	584
Anuska	584	Anya	235	Aolani	887
Apangela	843	Apara	371	Aphrodite	336
Apolline	393	April	112	Aprile	617
Aprilette	257	Aprilette	268	Aquene	549
Ara	292	Arabel	753	Arabela	854
Arabele	358	Arabella	887	Arabelle	382
Arah	281	Araminta	325	Ararita	325
Araxie	764	Arbel	652	Arbelia	753
Arbelie	257	Arbelie	268	Arbell	685
Arda	246	Ardath	257	Ardath	268
Ardatha	358	Ardean	797	Ardeea	347
Ardeen	292	Ardele	279	Ardelia	775
Ardelis	685	Ardell	617	Ardella	718
Ardelle	213	Arden	696	Ardena	797
Ardene	292	Ardenia	797	Ardere	246
Ardia	246	Ardilla	213	Ardine	696
Ardis	156	Ardith	156	Ardlee	279
Ardra	246	Ardyce	652	Ardys	134
Ardyth	134	Arela	731	Areli	639
Arella	764	Aren	652	Areta	729
Arete	224	Aretha	718	Aretta	742
Arette	246	Argenta	753	Argente	257
Argente	268	Argentia	753	Aria	292

Ariadna	393	Ariadne	797	Ariana	358
Ariane	753	Arianie	753	Arianna	314
Aridatha	358	Ariel	639	Ariela	731
Ariella	764	Arista	235	Arita	224
Ariza	281	Arlana	382	Arlanna	347
Arlee	235	Arleen	281	Arleigh	696
Arlen	685	Arlena	786	Arlene	281
Arleta	753	Arletta	775	Arlette	279
Arlie	639	Arliene	281	Arlina	281
Arlinda	235	Arline	685	Arluene	584
Arly	112	Arlyn	167	Arlyne	663
Armande	742	Armandine	797	Armela	775
Armida	281	Armilla	213	Armina	292
Armine	696	Arminia	292	Arna	257
Arna	268	Arnalda	336	Arnette	292
Arnice	685	Arnina	213	Arria	292
Arselma	786	Artha	213	Arva	246
Arvella	718	Aryn	134	Arzice	628
Asa	213	Asadel	786	Asber	639
Asela	742	Asenka	786	Asger	685
Asha	292	Ashe	696	Ashely	617
Ashia	292	Ashla	235	Ashlan	281
Ashlee	235	Ashleigh	696	Ashlen	685
Ashley	617	Ashli	134	Ashly	112
Asia	213	Asisa	224	Asiza	292
Asoka	832	Aspasia	393	Asta	235
Astera	731	Asteria	731	Astra	235
Astraea	832	Astrea	731	Astred	674
Astrid	178	Asvina	213	Asya	281
Atalanta	437	Atalante	832	Atalaya	437
Atalia	358	Atalie	753	Atalya	336
Atara	325	Athalea	843	Athalee	347
Athalia	347	Athalie	742	Athena	764
Athenee	764	Athie	617	Atira	224
Atlanta	336	Atlante	731	Attalie	775
Attie	641	Aubane	178	Auberta	145
Aubierge	595	Aubina	573	Aubine	977
Aubree	527	Aubrette	562	Aubrey	999
Aubrie	922	Aubry	494	Audi	448
Audie	944	Audra	549	Audre	944
Audrey	922	Audrie	944	Audry	426
Audrye	922	Augusta	819	Auguste	314
Augustina	865	Augustine	369	Auita	527
Aundrea	191	Aura	595	Aure	999

Aurea	191	Aurel	933	Aurelea	639
Aurelia	134	Aurelie	538	Aurelle	562
Auri	494	Auria	595	Aurie	999
Aurilia	538	Auriol	134	Aurora	292
Aurore	696	Austin	483	Austina	584
Austine	988	Autum	764	Autumn	729
Ava	246	Avasa	358	Aveline	235
Avelsa	786	Avena	797	Avene	292
Avera	742	Averi	641	Averil	674
Averilia	775	Averill	617	Averilla	718
Avery	628	Averyl	652	Avi	145
Avice	674	Avida	281	Aviela	775
Avira	246	Avirice	674	Avis	156
Avisa	257	Avisa	268	Aviva	281
Avivah	279	Avivi	189	Avril	178
Avrilla	213	Avrit	167	Avvy	167
Avyril	156	Awanata	437	Awandella	821
Awendela	382	Awenita	731	Axelle	235
Ayasha	371	Ayelet	235	Ayita	292
Ayla	213	Aymee	224	Ayoka	898
Ayondela	415	Ayril	112	Azalee	325
Azalia	325	Azaliea	821	Azelia	729
Aziza	279	Azize	674	Azizi	178
Azriela	729	Azura	584	Bab	145
Babara	347	Babb	167	Babbie	663
Babette	281	Babie	641	Babs	156
Balbina	235	Balbine	639	Balbinia	235
Bambi	189	Bambie	685	Bamby	167
Baptista	257	Baptista	268	Baptiste	652
Baptistine	617	Bar	123	Bara	224
Barb	145	Barbara	347	Barbarah	336
Barbe	641	Barbee	246	Barberine	292
Barbette	281	Barbey	628	Barbi	145
Barbie	641	Barbra	246	Barbro	742
Barby	123	Bari	123	Barra	224
Barrie	628	Bas	134	Basilie	663
Bathia	235	Bathilda	213	Bathilde	617
Bathsheba	753	Batilda	224	Batilde	628
Batista	279	Batsheva	786	Battista	292
Batyah	213	Bautista	573	Bea	628
Beata	742	Beatrias	753	Beatrice	279
Beatrisa	753	Beatrix	617	Beatriz	639
Bebe	145	Bebhinn	549	Becca	685
Becka	674	Becki	573	Beckie	178

Becky	551	Beda	663	Bee	123
Beitris	551	Bekki	562	Bekky	549
Bel	551	Bela	652	Belatha	764
Belia	652	Belicia	685	Belinda	652
Belita	674	Bell	584	Bella	685
Bellanca	775	Bellance	279	Belle	189
Bellina	641	Belloma	336	Belva	696
Belvia	696	Bena	674	Bendite	145
Benedetta	764	Benedicta	279	Benedicte	674
Benetta	224	Benigma	696	Benigna	617
Benita	696	Benni	538	Bennie	134
Benny	516	Benoite	797	Beppi	573
Berdine	123	Berdy	549	Berengaria	358
Berengere	257	Berengere	268	Berenia	279
Berenice	617	Beret	145	Berget	123
Bergetta	246	Bergette	641	Bergitte	145
Beril	551	Berna	674	Bernadene	775
Bernadetta	369	Bernadette	764	Bernadina	775
Bernadine	279	Bernadotta	461	Bernardina	775
Bernardine	279	Bernelle	641	Berneta	292
Bernetta	224	Bernette	628	Berney	156
Berni	573	Bernia	674	Bernice	112
Bernie	178	Bernita	696	Berny	551
Berri	527	Berrie	123	Berry	595
Bert	549	Berta	641	Berte	145
Bertha	639	Berthe	134	Berthilda	617
Berthilde	112	Berti	549	Bertie	145
Bertilda	628	Bertilde	123	Bertille	112
Bertina	696	Bertine	191	Bertrada	786
Bertrade	281	Bertrande	246	Berty	527
Berura	922	Beryl	538	Beryle	134
Bess	549	Besse	145	Bessie	145
Bessy	527	Beta	641	Beth	538
Bethany	663	Bethel	167	Bethena	281
Bethesda	281	Bethia	639	Bethiah	628
Bethina	685	Bethseda	281	Beti	549
Betica	674	Betina	696	Betsey	134
Betsy	538	Betta	663	Bette	167
Betti	562	Bettina	628	Bettine	123
Bettrys	551	Betty	549	Betula	977
Beula	955	Beulah	944	Bev	562
Beverle	696	Beverlee	292	Beverley	674
Beverlie	696	Beverly	178	Bevin	527
Bevvy	584	Bharbara	336	Bian	178

Bianca	213	Biancha	292	Bianche	696
Bibi	944	Bibiane	696	Biddie	516
Biddy	988	Bill	988	Bille	584
Billi	988	Billie	584	Billy	966
Bina	178	Binah	167	Binga	156
Binni	933	Binnie	538	Binny	911
Binti	999	Bird	966	Birdella	639
Birdelle	134	Birdena	628	Birdie	562
Birgit	922	Birgitta	145	Birthe	538
Bitki	966	Bitney	573	Bittee	167
Blaine	617	Blair	156	Blaire	652
Blake	674	Blakelee	718	Blakeley	281
Blanca	246	Blanch	134	Blanche	639
Blanchette	279	Blandine	617	Blane	617
Blanka	235	Blayne	685	Blaze	641
Blessin	538	Blessing	516	Blinne	562
Blinni	966	Blinnie	562	Blinny	944
Bliss	977	Blisse	573	Blita	178
Blitha	167	Blithe	562	Blondell	224
Blondelle	729	Blondie	257	Blondie	268
Blondy	639	Blossom	325	Bluinse	821
Bluma	494	Blyth	764	Blythe	549
Bo	628	Bobbee	764	Bobbette	718
Bobbi	663	Bobby	641	Bobbye	246
Bobette	786	Bobina	797	Bobine	292
Bobinette	742	Bohdana	819	Bona	775
Bonamy	797	Boni	674	Bonita	797
Bonitta	729	Bonne	235	Bonnee	731
Bonni	639	Bonnibelle	729	Bonnie	235
Bonnilyn	696	Bonnilyne	292	Bonnilynne	257
Bonnilynne	268	Bonny	617	Bradlee	292
Bradleigh	663	Bradley	674	Bradly	178
Brana	279	Branca	213	Brandais	235
Brande	628	Brandea	729	Brandeis	639
Brandi	123	Brandice	652	Brandie	628
Brandy	191	Branna	235	Branwen	685
Breana	775	Breanne	235	Brear	628
Bree	123	Breen	178	Breena	279
Breita	641	Bren	573	Brencis	527
Brenda	628	Brene	178	Brenn	538
Brenna	639	Brett	562	Brey	595
Bria	123	Briana	279	Brianna	235
Brianne	639	Bride	562	Bridey	549
Bridget	562	Bridgette	189	Bridgid	988

Name	No.	Name	No.	Name	No.
Bridie	562	Brie	527	Brier	527
Brieta	641	Brietta	663	Brigette	145
Brigid	944	Brigida	145	Brigido	641
Brigit	922	Brigitta	145	Brigitte	549
Brigitto	641	Brina	178	Brindle	551
Briney	551	Brinn	933	Brinna	134
Briny	955	Briseida	674	Brit	944
Brita	145	Britney	573	Britni	999
Britt	966	Britta	167	Brittan	123
Brittaney	696	Brittani	123	Brittany	191
Britteny	595	Brittnee	123	Brittney	595
Brittni	922	Brittny	999	Brona	775
Bronnee	731	Bronnie	235	Bronny	617
Bronwen	281	Bronwyn	663	Brook	347
Brooke	843	Brooks	358	Brucie	854
Bruella	988	Bruelle	483	Bruna	472
Brundhild	382	Brunehilda	944	Brunehilde	448
Brunella	944	Brunelle	448	Brunetta	922
Brunhild	347	Brunhilda	448	Brunhilde	843
Bryana	257	Bryana	268	Bryanna	213
Brydee	145	Brydie	549	Bryn	775
Bryna	156	Brynhild	922	Brynley	562
Brynn	731	Brynna	112	Brynne	516
Buena	977	Buffy	336	Buna	472
Bunni	336	Bunnie	832	Bunny	314
Buona	178	Burdeen	426	Burdene	426
Burnhild	347	Burnia	472	Burnice	819
Cabby	156	Cabriona	819	Cacie	663
Cacilia	292	Cacilie	696	Caddy	191
Cadena	731	Cadenza	729	Cai	134
Cailin	123	Caimile	617	Caire	639
Caitlin	145	Caitrin	112	Cal	167
Calandra	369	Calandre	764	Calandria	369
Calantha	336	Calanthe	731	Caldwell	639
Caleah	753	Caledonia	461	Caledonie	865
Calesta	797	Calida	213	Calista	292
Calisto	797	Calla	292	Calle	696
Calley	674	Calli	191	Callida	246
Callie	696	Callista	235	Callula	538
Cally	178	Caltha	279	Calypso	731
Calysta	279	Cam	178	Camala	314
Camel	617	Camelia	718	Camella	742
Camellia	742	Cameo	371	Cami	178
Camila	213	Camile	617	Camilla	246

Camille	641	Camillo	742	Cammi	123
Cammie	628	Cammy	191	Canace	729
Candace	764	Candi	134	Candice	663
Candida	279	Candide	674	Candido	775
Candie	639	Candima	279	Candis	145
Candra	235	Candre	639	Candy	112
Cannie	641	Capee	213	Cappi	189
Capri	112	Capriccia	279	Caprice	641
Capucine	999	Cara	235	Caralie	764
Carel	663	Caren	685	Carena	786
Caresa	742	Caressa	753	Caresse	257
Caresse	268	Carey	617	Cari	134
Caria	235	Cariad	279	Carie	639
Carilla	292	Carin	189	Carina	281
Carine	685	Carissa	257	Carissa	268
Carisse	652	Carita	257	Carita	268
Caritta	279	Carleen	224	Carlen	628
Carlene	224	Carley	641	Carleyne	292
Carli	167	Carlie	663	Carlin	123
Carlina	224	Carline	628	Carlino	729
Carliss	189	Carlissa	281	Carlita	281
Carlota	887	Carlotta	819	Carly	145
Carlye	641	Carlyn	191	Carlynn	156
Carlynne	652	Carlysle	685	Carma	279
Carmacita	336	Carman	235	Carmel	617
Carmela	718	Carmelina	764	Carmelita	731
Carmella	742	Carmelo	314	Carmen	639
Carmena	731	Carmencita	786	Carmene	235
Carmi	178	Carmia	279	Carmie	674
Carmilla	246	Carmina	235	Carmine	639
Carmita	292	Carna	281	Carnation	865
Carneen	246	Carnene	246	Carniela	729
Carniella	753	Caro	731	Carol	764
Carola	865	Carole	369	Carolin	729
Carolina	821	Caroline	325	Carolle	393
Carolus	178	Carolyn	797	Carolyne	393
Carolynn	753	Carolynne	358	Caron	786
Carree	235	Carressa	753	Carri	134
Carrie	639	Carrie-Ann	742	Carrissa	257
Carrissa	268	Carrol	764	Carroll	797
Carrolle	393	Carry	112	Cary	112
Caryl	145	Caryn	167	Casandra	347
Casey	628	Casia	246	Casie	641
Casmira	281	Cass	156	Cassandra	358

Cassandre	753	Cassandry	235	Cassaundra	652
Cassey	639	Cassi	156	Cassie	652
Cassondra	854	Cassy	134	Caste	663
Catalin	246	Catalina	347	Catarina	314
Catarine	718	Cate	652	Caterina	718
Catha	246	Cathal	279	Catharina	393
Catharine	797	Cathay	224	Cathe	641
Cathee	246	Catherin	696	Catherina	797
Catherine	292	Cathi	145	Cathie	641
Cathlaina	336	Cathleen	235	Cathlene	235
Cathreine	292	Cathrine	696	Cathryn	178
Cathy	123	Cathyleen	213	Cati	156
Catie	652	Catina	213	Catlaina	347
Catlee	281	Catlin	145	Catrina	213
Catrine	617	Catriona	819	Caty	134
Caye	617	Cayla	246	Ceara	731
Cecelia	292	Cecil	595	Cecile	191
Cecilia	696	Cecilla	639	Cecily	573
Cedena	235	Cedy	551	Ceepa	213
Ceil	562	Celah	652	Celandine	224
Celandon	325	Cele	167	Celene	628
Celesta	292	Celeste	696	Celestia	292
Celestin	156	Celestina	257	Celestina	268
Celestine	652	Celestyn	134	Celestyna	235
Celia	663	Celie	167	Celina	628
Celinda	663	Celine	123	Celinka	641
Celisse	189	Celka	685	Cella	696
Celosia	371	Cenydd	551	Cerealia	369
Cerelie	663	Cerella	292	Cerellia	292
Cerise	145	Ceryl	549	Cesarine	292
Cesya	628	Chaireen	279	Chairene	279
Chaitra	246	Chanda	224	Chandal	257
Chandal	268	Chandi	123	Chandra	224
Chandre	628	Channa	235	Chantal	235
Chantalle	764	Chara	224	Charen	674
Charena	775	Charil	156	Charin	178
Charis	134	Charissa	246	Charita	246
Charity	123	Charla	257	Charla	268
Charlach	279	Charlaine	718	Charleen	213
Charlena	718	Charlene	213	Charlie	652
Charline	617	Charlot	775	Charlotta	898
Charlotte	393	Charlsey	641	Charmain	224
Charmaine	729	Charmane	729	Charmell	639
Charmian	224	Charmine	628	Charmion	729

Charo	729	Charolotte	999	Charris	134
Charry	191	Chartsie	652	Charyl	134
Chastity	156	Chattie	663	Chauncey	988
Chaya	292	Chea	628	Chee	123
Chela	652	Chelsey	145	Chelsie	167
Chelsy	549	Chenoa	371	Chepito	224
Cher	527	Cheran	674	Chere	123
Cheren	178	Cherena	279	Cherey	191
Cheri	527	Cherianne	235	Cherice	156
Cherida	663	Cherie	123	Cherilyn	584
Cherilynn	549	Cherin	573	Cherise	134
Cherish	527	Cherlyn	584	Cherolyn	281
Cherolyne	786	Cherolynn	246	Cherolynne	742
Cherri	527	Cherrie	123	Cherrita	641
Cherry	595	Chery	595	Cherye	191
Cheryl	538	Cheryle	134	Cheryleen	685
Cherylene	685	Cheslie	167	Chesna	685
Chessa	641	Chessy	527	Chiah	112
Chiara	224	Chiarra	224	Chickie	573
Chicky	955	Chika	145	Chilali	189
Childe	595	Chimene	123	Chiquita	437
Chiriga	191	Chistabelle	246	Chita	145
Chitsa	156	Chlarimonda	898	Chlarimonde	393
Chlarinda	257	Chlarinda	268	Chlaris	167
Chloe	257	Chloe	268	Chlorinda	753
Chlorinde	257	Chlorinde	268	Chloris	663
Cholly	663	Choomia	461	Chris	933
Chriselda	617	Chrissie	549	Chrissy	922
Christa	156	Christabel	617	Christabella	742
Christabelle	246	Christal	189	Christalle	628
Christan	112	Christean	617	Christel	584
Christelle	123	Christen	516	Christia	156
Christian	112	Christiana	213	Christiane	617
Christie	551	Christilla	123	Christin	911
Christina	112	Christine	516	Christle	584
Christmas	112	Christopher	224	Christy	933
Christye	538	Christyna	189	Chrysa	112
Chryseida	652	Chryseis	527	Chrystal	167
Chryste	538	Chrystod	674	Chyna	156
Chynna	112	Cicely	573	Cicily	977
Cid	977	Ciel	562	Cilehe	156
Cilka	189	Cilla	191	Cimmie	527
Cinda	134	Cindee	134	Cinderella	292
Cindi	933	Cindie	538	Cindy	911

Cinna	145	Cinofila	786	Cipressa	639
Ciri	933	Cirila	167	Cirilla	191
Cissie	551	Cissy	933	Clair	167
Claire	663	Clairette	213	Clar	167
Clarabell	753	Clarabella	854	Clarabelle	358
Claramae	819	Claramay	382	Clare	663
Clarence	257	Clarence	268	Claresta	797
Clareta	786	Claretta	718	Clarette	213
Clarey	641	Clari	167	Claribel	628
Clarice	696	Clarie	663	Clarimond	718
Clarimonda	819	Clarimonde	314	Clarinde	663
Clarine	628	Clarisa	279	Clarise	674
Clariss	189	Clarissa	281	Clarisse	685
Clarista	292	Clarita	281	Clarrie	663
Clary	145	Claude	911	Claudeen	562
Claudelle	573	Claudene	562	Claudetta	156
Claudette	551	Claudia	516	Claudian	562
Claudie	911	Claudina	562	Claudine	966
Claudy	483	Cleantha	731	Cleanthe	235
Clem	516	Clematis	641	Clemence	696
Clemency	178	Clementia	281	Clementina	246
Clementine	641	Clemmi	551	Clemmie	156
Clemmy	538	Cleopatra	461	Clerissa	685
Cleva	617	Cliantha	235	Clianthe	639
Clio	663	Clo	663	Clodagh	775
Clodia	718	Clodie	213	Clorinda	764
Cloris	674	Clothilda	753	Clothilde	257
Clothilde	268	Clotilda	764	Clover	213
Clovie	213	Clovis	628	Clydette	134
Clymene	145	Clytie	562	Cobina	718
Cocheta	371	Codee	775	Codi	674
Codie	279	Cody	652	Coelina	325
Cohila	753	Coleen	729	Colene	729
Colet	281	Coletta	314	Colette	718
Coline	224	Colinette	764	Colleen	753
Collete	729	Collett	246	Collette	742
Colley	279	Collie	292	Colline	257
Colline	268	Colly	674	Colomba	437
Colombe	832	Colombina	483	Columba	134
Columbia	134	Columbine	584	Comfort	369
Con	685	Concepcion	887	Conceptia	325
Conception	876	Concha	718	Conchetta	358
Conchita	731	Concordia	461	Concordie	865
Concordina	426	Concordy	347	Conni	641

Connie	246	Conny	628	Conrada	832
Conradina	887	Conradine	382	Consolata	551
Consolation	112	Constance	314	Constancia	819
Constancy	786	Constanta	898	Constantia	898
Constantina	854	Constantine	358	Constanza	865
Consuela	639	Consuelo	235	Cora	731
Corabel	382	Corabella	426	Corabelle	821
Corah	729	Coral	764	Corale	369
Coralee	865	Coralen	325	Coralie	369
Coraline	325	Corall	797	Corbina	718
Corbinna	764	Cordeilla	347	Cordelia	314
Cordelie	718	Cordella	347	Cordey	257
Cordey	268	Cordi	674	Cordie	279
Cordula	112	Cordy	652	Coreen	786
Corella	393	Corena	382	Corenda	336
Corene	786	Corentine	764	Corett	279
Coretta	371	Corette	775	Corey	213
Cori	639	Corie	235	Corilea	369
Corilee	764	Corileen	729	Corilla	797
Corin	685	Corina	786	Corine	281
Corinna	742	Corinne	246	Coriss	652
Corissa	753	Corisse	257	Corisse	268
Corliss	685	Corlissa	786	Corly	641
Cornela	325	Cornelia	325	Cornelie	729
Cornelle	753	Cornie	281	Corny	663
Coro	336	Corona	483	Coronie	887
Correna	382	Correy	213	Corri	639
Corrianne	347	Corrie	235	Corrina	786
Corrine	281	Corrinne	246	Corry	617
Cortney	281	Cory	617	Cosetta	382
Cosette	786	Cosima	786	Cosina	797
Courtenay	685	Courtnay	189	Courtney	584
Crescent	156	Crescenta	257	Crescenta	268
Crescente	652	Crescentia	257	Crescentia	268
Cressid	595	Cressida	696	Cressy	538
Creva	674	Cris	944	Crisela	674
Criseyde	167	Crispina	178	Crispine	573
Crissie	551	Crissy	933	Crista	167
Cristabel	628	Cristal	191	Cristen	527
Cristi	966	Cristie	562	Cristin	922
Cristina	123	Cristine	527	Cristiona	729
Cristy	944	Crysta	145	Crystal	178
Crystie	549	Cunegonde	167	Cybele	167
Cybella	696	Cybil	966	Cybill	999

Cyd	775	Cydni	911	Cydnie	516
Cyma	156	Cymbre	573	Cyn	786
Cynde	516	Cyndee	112	Cyndi	911
Cyndia	112	Cyndie	516	Cynth	797
Cynthea	674	Cynthia	178	Cynthie	573
Cynthin	933	Cynthis	988	Cynthy	595
Cypres	595	Cypressa	617	Cypris	999
Cyra	112	Cyrena	663	Cyrenia	663
Cyrilla	178	Cyrille	573	Cythera	628
Cytherea	224	Cytherere	628	Cytheria	628
Cytherine	178	Dabney	696	Dacey	652
Dacia	279	Dacie	674	Dacy	156
Dael	674	Daffi	178	Daffie	674
Daffodil	753	Daffy	156	Dagania	371
Dagney	652	Dagny	156	Dail	178
Daile	674	Daisey	639	Daisi	156
Daisie	652	Daisy	134	Dalan	235
Dale	674	Daleen	235	Dalene	235
Dalenna	786	Dalia	279	Dalic	112
Dalien	639	Dalila	213	Dalilah	292
Dalita	292	Dallas	224	Damara	382
Damaris	292	Damita	213	Dammara	336
Dana	292	Danae	797	Danee	292
Danella	764	Danette	246	Dani	191
Dania	292	Danica	235	Danice	639
Daniela	731	Daniele	235	Danielea	336
Daniella	764	Danika	224	Danila	235
Danit	123	Danita	224	Danitza	213
Danlei	639	Danna	257	Danna	268
Danni	156	Dannie	652	Danny	134
Dannye	639	Danya	279	Danyelle	246
Daphie	617	Daphne	663	Dara	246
Darb	167	Darbie	663	Darby	145
Darcee	279	Darcey	652	Darci	178
Darcie	674	Darcy	156	Darda	281
Dareen	292	Darel	674	Darelle	213
Daren	696	Dari	145	Daria	246
Darice	674	Darilye	652	Darilyn	112
Darla	279	Darla-Jo	887	Darlean	731
Darleen	235	Darlene	235	Darline	639
Darlo	775	Daron	797	Darrah	235
Darree	246	Darrelle	213	Darry	123
Darryl	156	Darsey	639	Darya	224
Daryl	156	Dasha	246	Dashnis	112

Dasi	156	Dasie	652	Dasya	235
Datha	257	Datha	268	Dathi	156
Daudi	483	Dauna	595	Daveen	246
Daveta	718	Davida	235	Davina	246
Davine	641	Davita	213	Dawn	156
Dawna	257	Dawna	268	Dawnn	112
Day	123	Dayan	279	Dayana	371
Dayle	652	Dayleen	213	Dayna	279
Deana	797	Deane	292	Deanna	753
Deanne	257	Deanne	268	Deardre	281
Deb	562	Debbee	685	Debbi	584
Debbie	189	Debborah	371	Debby	562
Debbye	167	Debi	562	Debora	369
Deborah	358	Deboreah	854	Debra	663
Decima	628	Dede	189	Dedi	584
Dedie	189	Dedra	685	Dee	145
Dee Ann	257	Dee Ann	268	Dee Dee	281
Deedee	281	Deel	178	Deena	292
Deerdre	685	Deeya	224	Deeyn	178
Dehlia	663	Deidre	189	Deira	641
Deirdre	189	Deire	145	Del	573
Dela	674	Delaney	213	Delanie	235
Delcina	663	Delcine	167	Delfeena	797
Delfine	191	Delia	674	Delicia	617
Delight	562	Delila	617	Delilah	696
Delina	639	Delinda	674	Dell	516
Della	617	Dellas	628	Delly	584
Delma	628	Delmar	628	Delmare	224
Delora	371	Delores	786	Deloria	371
Deloris	281	Delorita	393	Delphina	696
Delphine	191	Delphinia	696	Delta	696
Demeter	617	Demetra	213	Demetria	213
Demetris	123	Dena	696	Denae	292
Dene	191	Deni	595	Denice	134
Denise	112	Denna	652	Denni	551
Dennie	156	Denny	538	Denya	674
Denys	584	Denyse	189	Deonne	753
Derdre	189	Derinda	641	Derora	347
Derorah	336	Derori	246	Derorice	775
Desa	652	Desdemona	898	Desirae	257
Desirae	268	Desire	156	Desiree	652
Desiren	112	Desiri	551	Desma	696
Desmona	358	Dessa	663	Desta	674
Deste	178	Deva	685	Devan	641

Devi	584	Devin	549	Devina	641
Devinne	191	Devon	246	Devona	347
Devonda	382	Devondra	382	Devonna	393
Devonne	797	Devora	382	Dextra	639
Dezba	652	Dhorea	336	Di	944
Dia	145	Diahane	786	Diahann	246
Diamanta	369	Dian	191	Diana	292
Diandra	246	Diandre	641	Diane	696
Diann	156	Dianna	257	Dianna	268
Dianne	652	Diantha	213	Dianthe	617
Dianthia	213	Dickie	595	Dickla	134
Dicky	977	Dida	189	Didi	988
Diedra	685	Diedrah	674	Dierdre	189
Diklici	933	Dilys	966	Dina	191
Dinah	189	Dinanth	167	Dini	999
Dinnie	551	Dinny	933	Dion	696
Dione	292	Dionis	617	Dionne	257
Dionne	268	Diota	764	Disa	156
Dita	167	Dix	911	Dixey	584
Dixie	516	Dixil	944	Dixy	988
Doane	393	Doanna	854	Docie	279
Docila	718	Doda	786	Dode	281
Dodi	685	Dodie	281	Dodo	382
Dody	663	Doe	246	Doll	617
Dolley	281	Dolli	617	Dollie	213
Dolly	685	Dolora	472	Dolores	887
Dolorita	494	Doloritas	415	Dolyeen	718
Dolyene	718	Domenica	371	Domeniga	325
Domina	742	Dominga	729	Domingue	527
Domini	641	Dominica	775	Dominique	538
Domita	718	Domitille	279	Dona	797
Donalda	876	Donata	821	Donatienne	832
Dondi	641	Doneal	336	Donella	369
Donelle	764	Donetta	347	Donia	797
Donica	731	Donielle	764	Donna	753
Donna Lynne	371	Donnell	224	Donni	652
Donnie	257	Donnie	268	Donny	639
Dooriya	426	Dooya	426	Dora	742
Doralia	876	Doralin	731	Doralyn	718
Doralynn	764	Doralynne	369	Dorcas	786
Dore	246	Dorean	393	Doreen	797
Dorelia	371	Dorella	314	Dorelle	718
Dorena	393	Dorene	797	Doretta	382
Dorette	786	Dorey	224	Dori	641

Doria	742	Dorian	797	Dorice	279
Dorie	246	Dorinda	742	Dorine	292
Doris	652	Dorisa	753	Dorise	257
Dorise	268	Dorita	764	Dorlisa	786
Dormie	281	Doro	347	Dorolice	819
Dorolise	887	Dorotea	966	Doroteya	944
Dorothe	854	Dorothea	955	Dorothee	459
Dorothi	358	Dorothy	336	Dorree	742
Dorri	641	Dorrie	246	Dorris	652
Dorry	628	Dorthea	358	Dorthi	652
Dorthy	639	Dory	628	Dosi	652
Dot	663	Dotti	685	Dottie	281
Dotty	663	Dove	281	Dowsabel	369
Doxie	213	Doxy	685	Draga	224
Draja	257	Draja	268	Drew	595
Drina	191	Drisa	156	Drisana	213
Dru	347	Druci	371	Drucie	876
Drucill	347	Drucilla	448	Drucy	358
Druella	911	Druilla	415	Drus	358
Drusi	358	Drusie	854	Drusilla	426
Drusy	336	Dua	448	Duana	595
Duci	371	Dudee	483	Duena	999
Duenna	955	Dulce	819	Dulcea	911
Dulci	314	Dulcia	415	Dulciana	562
Dulcibella	999	Dulcibelle	494	Dulcie	819
Dulcine	865	Dulcinea	966	Dulcy	382
Dulsea	988	Duna	494	Duomi	988
Dupetta	966	Dupette	461	Durene	494
Durva	483	Dusan	415	Dusana	516
Duscha	472	Dushina	494	Dustee	472
Dustie	876	Dusty	358	Dusya	437
Dwana	257	Dwana	268	Dyami	167
Dyan	178	Dyana	279	Dyane	674
Dyani	178	Dyann	134	Dyanna	235
Dyanne	639	Dyas	134	Dyel	551
Dylana	213	Dylane	617	Dymphna	189
Dyna	178	Dynah	167	Eada	742
Eadie	246	Eadith	652	Eadrea	347
Eadwina	753	Eadwine	257	Eadwine	268
Eady	628	Eala	731	Earla	731
Earleen	786	Earlene	786	Earley	213
Earlie	235	Earline	281	Eartha	718
Easter	235	Eastre	235	Eba	628
Ebba	641	Ebonee	371	Ebony	257

Ebony	268	Echo	224	Ed	549
Eda	641	Edana	797	Edda	685
Eddi	584	Eddie	189	Eddy	562
Ede	145	Edela	279	Edele	674
Edelina	235	Edeline	639	Eden	191
Edena	292	EDi	549	Edie	145
Edin	595	Edina	696	Edine	191
Edita	663	Edith	551	Editha	652
Edithe	156	Ediva	685	Edlyn	516
Edlyne	112	Edlynn	562	Edma	685
Edmee	685	Edmonda	382	Edmonde	786
Edmunda	988	Edna	696	Edny	573
Edouardine	246	Edra	641	Edrea	246
Edwardina	797	Edwardine	292	Edwige	178
Edwina	652	Edwine	156	Edwyna	639
Edy	527	Edyth	538	Edythe	134
Eeli	134	Effi	538	Effia	639
Effie	134	Effra	639	Effy	516
Ega	674	Egberta	224	Egberte	628
Egbertha	213	Egberthe	617	Egbertina	279
Egbertine	674	Eglantina	742	Eglantine	246
Eglentyne	628	Eglintyne	123	Eglyntine	123
Eida	641	Eidann	652	Eileen	685
Eilene	685	Eilidh	562	Eilis	549
Eily	516	Eimile	178	Eir	595
Eireen	652	Eirena	257	Eirena	268
Eirene	652	Eiric	538	Eister	134
Eithne	167	Ekaterina	393	Ela	639
Elain	685	Elaina	786	Elaine	281
Elaise	246	Elan	685	Elana	786
Elane	281	Elata	753	Elberta	279
Elbertina	235	Elbertine	639	Elda	674
Eldora	371	Eldoree	371	Eldoria	371
Eldrida	628	Eleanor	887	Eleanora	988
Eleanore	483	Electra	281	Eleen	685
Elena	281	Elene	685	Eleni	189
Elenitsa	224	Elenor	786	Elenora	887
Elenore	382	Eleonor	483	Eleonora	584
Eleonore	988	Eleora	832	Elese	641
Elexa	292	Elfie	191	Elfreda	246
Elfreida	246	Elfrida	641	Elfried	145
Elfrieda	246	Elga	617	Eliane	281
Elianor	382	Elianora	483	Elianore	887
Elicia	663	Elidi	573	Elie	134

Eliette	674	Elina	685	Elinor	281
Elinora	382	Elinore	786	Eliora	336
Elisa	641	Elisabet	281	Elisabeth	279
Elisabetha	371	Elisabetta	314	Elise	145
Elisha	639	Elisheba	257	Elisheba	268
Eliska	663	Elissa	652	Elita	652
Eliva	674	Eliza	628	Elizabeta	369
Elizabeth	257	Elizabeth	268	Elizabetha	358
Elizabets	279	Elizsa	639	Elje	145
Elka	652	Elke	156	Ella	663
Ellaline	257	Ellaline	268	Ellama	718
Elle	167	Ellen	123	Ellene	628
Ellenita	246	Ellette	617	Elli	562
Ellice	191	Ellie	167	Ellis	573
Ellissa	685	Elly	549	Ellyn	595
Ellyne	191	Elma	674	Elmina	639
Elmira	674	Elna	685	Elnna	641
Elnora	382	Elnore	786	Elodie	775
Eloisa	347	Eloise	742	Elona	382
Elora	336	Elrica	663	Elsa	641
Elsbeth	178	Else	145	Elsey	123
Elsi	549	Elsie	145	Elsleoa	876
Elspet	145	Elspeth	134	Elspie	123
Elsy	527	Elva	674	Elvada	729
Elvera	279	Elvia	674	Elvie	178
Elvina	639	Elvira	674	Elwilda	663
Elwira	685	Elyette	652	Elyn	562
Elysa	628	Elyse	123	Elysha	617
Elysia	628	Elyssa	639	Elza	628
Em	549	Ema	641	Emalaina	832
Emalee	775	Emalia	775	Emdeline	674
Emelda	224	Emelia	279	Emelie	674
Emelina	235	Emeline	639	Emelita	292
Emelyan	213	Emelye	652	Emelyne	617
Emera	246	Emerald	224	Emerant	224
Emeraude	189	Emila	674	Emile	178
Emilee	674	Emili	573	Emilia	674
Emilie	178	Emilien	134	Emilienne	685
Emiline	134	Emily	551	Emina	696
Emlyn	516	Emlyne	112	Emlynn	562
Emlynne	167	Emm	584	Emma	685
Emmalee	729	Emmaline	279	Emmalyn	652
Emmalynn	617	Emmalynne	213	Emmanuelle	112
Emmeline	674	Emmey	167	Emmi	584

Emmie	189	Emmott	235	Emmy	562
Emmye	167	Emogene	371	Emuna	999
Emunah	988	Emyle	156	Emylee	652
Ena	652	Engelbert	617	Engelberta	718
Engelbertha	797	Engelberthe	292	Engracia	764
Enid	595	Enli	584	Enola	382
Enrica	685	Enrichetta	224	Enrika	674
Enriqueta	562	Eolande	832	Eostre	731
Eppie	156	Eran	652	Erda	641
Erecka	257	Erecka	268	Erena	257
Erena	268	Erica	639	Ericha	628
Ericka	652	Erika	628	Erin	551
Erina	652	Erine	156	Erinn	516
Erinna	617	Erlene	685	Erlina	685
Erline	189	Erma	641	Erme	145
Ermin	595	Ermina	696	Ermine	191
Erminia	696	Erminie	191	Erna	652
Ernaline	246	Ernesta	281	Ernestine	641
Eroca	336	Ertha	617	Erva	641
Ervina	696	Ervinia	696	Erwina	617
Eryn	538	Erzbet	134	Esma	652
Esmaria	753	Esme	156	Esmeralda	336
Esmeraldah	325	Esmeralde	731	Essa	628
Essie	123	Essy	595	Esta	639
Estee	639	Estel	167	Estele	663
Estell	191	Estella	292	Estelle	696
Ester	134	Esther	123	Estienne	641
Estonia	382	Estrelita	281	Estrella	292
Estrellita	224	Etana	775	Etenia	279
Ethel	145	Ethelda	281	Etheldred	639
Etheldrede	235	Ethelin	191	Ethelinda	246
Etheline	696	Etheljean	718	Ethelred	685
Ethelreda	786	Ethelyn	178	Ethered	652
Ethyl	527	Ethylyn	551	Etiennette	279
Etta	641	Etti	549	Ettie	145
Etty	527	Euclea	562	Eudice	472
Eudocia	674	Eudokia	663	Eudora	641
Eudore	145	Eudosia	652	Eudoxia	617
Eufemia	516	Eugena	538	Eugenia	538
Eugenie	933	Eula	933	Eulalee	167
Eulalia	167	Eulalie	562	Eunice	483
Eupheme	911	Euphemia	516	Euphemie	911
Eurica	933	Euridice	472	Eurydice	459
Eusebie	933	Eustacia	167	Eustacie	562

Eva	641	Evadne	246	Evaleen	731
Evalyn	617	Evalynn	663	Evanessa	325
Evangelia	314	Evangelina	369	Evangeline	764
Evangelista	347	Evania	797	Evanne	257
Evanne	268	Eve	145	Eveleen	235
Evelene	235	Evelina	235	Eveline	639
Eveling	112	Evelyn	112	Evelyne	617
Evetta	281	Evette	685	Evey	123
Evi	549	Evie	145	Evinrude	448
Evita	663	Evonne	753	Evvie	189
Evvy	562	Evy	527	Ewa	652
Ewalt	617	Eyde	123	Eydie	123
Eysllt	573	Ezera	281	Ezmeralda	314
Ezraela	325	Ezraella	358	Ezreta	213
Fabia	281	Fabiana	347	Fabianna	393
Fabienne	292	Fabiola	821	Fac	191
Fadeyushka	112	Fae	663	Faina	224
Fairlee	292	Fairlie	696	Faith	178
Falda	246	Faleyka	797	Faline	652
Fallon	786	Falma	246	Fan	123
Fanchette	281	Fanchon	797	Fancie	652
Fancy	134	Fanechka	764	Fania	224
Fanni	178	Fannie	674	Fanny	156
Fanya	292	Farah	257	Farah	268
Farica	292	Farida	213	Farlee	292
Farrah	257	Farrah	268	Farren	628
Fath	178	Fatima	235	Fatimah	224
Fatina	246	Fatma	235	Faun	426
Faunia	527	Fausta	595	Faustina	551
Faustine	955	Fauve	911	Favor	718
Favora	819	Fawn	178	Fawne	674
Fawnia	279	Fay	145	Fayanne	753
Faydra	281	Faye	641	Fayette	281
Fayina	292	Fayme	685	Fayola	876
Fayre	641	Fayth	156	Faythe	652
Feadora	415	Feadore	819	Fealty	696
Federica	246	Fedora	314	Fedore	718
Fedya	685	Fela	696	Felcia	639
Felda	641	Felecia	235	Felice	134
Felicia	639	Felicidad	628	Felicie	134
Felicitas	663	Felicite	156	Felicity	538
Felipa	674	Felis	516	Felise	112
Felisha	696	Felita	628	Feliza	685
Felka	628	Felma	641	Femi	516

Fenelia	257	Fenelia	268	Fenella	281
Fenix	584	Feodora	911	Feodore	415
Ferdinanda	764	Fern	527	Fernanda	729
Fernande	224	Fernandina	775	Ferne	123
Ferran	628	Fey	549	Fidela	641
Fidele	145	Fidelia	641	Fidelity	549
Fiemi	516	Fifi	933	Fifine	584
Filana	257	Filana	268	Filberta	641
Filberte	145	Filbertha	639	Filberthe	134
Filia	191	Filida	145	Filide	549
Filipa	178	Filippa	156	Filis	911
Fillida	178	Fillis	944	Filma	145
Filomena	393	Fina	123	Finella	685
Finola	753	Fiona	729	Fionn	674
Fionna	775	Fionnula	112	Fiora	764
Fiorenza	314	Flan	156	Flann	112
Flanna	213	Flannery	685	Flavia	246
Flavie	641	Flavienne	257	Flavienne	268
Fleta	628	Fleur	898	Fleurette	944
Flo	696	Flor	696	Flora	797
Florance	382	Flore	292	Florella	369
Florence	786	Florencia	382	Florentia	371
Florenza	347	Florette	742	Flori	696
Floria	797	Florida	742	Floridia	742
Florie	292	Florina	753	Florinda	797
Florine	257	Florine	268	Floris	617
Florri	696	Florrie	292	Florry	674
Floss	628	Flossi	628	Flossie	224
Flossy	696	Flower	257	Flower	268
Fonda	764	Fondea	369	Fortuna	145
Fortune	549	Fotina	742	Fran	123
France	652	Franceline	246	Francene	213
Frances	663	Francesca	797	Francette	292
Franci	156	Francie	652	Francine	617
Francisca	292	Franciska	281	Francoise	369
Francy	134	Francyne	685	Frani	123
Frank	145	Franke	641	Frankie	641
Frankisca	281	Franky	123	Franni	178
Frannie	674	Franny	156	Fraya	246
Frayda	281	Fred	516	Freda	617
Freddi	551	Freddie	156	Freddy	538
Fredella	279	Frederica	246	Frederika	235
Frederique	999	Fredi	516	Fredia	617
Fredra	617	Fredrika	639	Freedja	224

Freela	292	Freida	617	Frerika	685
Frerike	189	Freya	641	Freyja	652
Frida	112	Frieda	617	Friederik	134
Friederike	639	Friedie	112	Fritzi	977
Frodis	628	Frond	663	Fulvia	448
Fynnia	156	Gabbe	628	Gabbey	696
Gabbi	123	Gabbie	628	Gabey	674
Gabi	191	Gabie	696	Gabriel	639
Gabriela	731	Gabriele	235	Gabriell	663
Gabriella	764	Gabriellia	764	Gabrila	235
Gaby	178	Gada	224	Gadi	123
Gae	674	Gaea	775	Gael	617
Gaetane	358	Gai	178	Gaia	279
Gail	112	Gaile	617	Gailea	718
Gala	213	Galatea	832	Gale	617
Gali	112	Galiana	369	Galice	641
Galiena	764	Galinka	281	Galita	235
Gallie	641	Galya	281	Ganesa	742
Ganice	663	Ganya	213	Garai	279
Garda	224	Gardenia	775	Gardie	628
Garland	213	Garnet	652	Garnette	279
Gartred	641	Garunda	573	Gaudeline	516
Gavilla	281	Gavra	224	Gavriella	786
Gavrielle	281	Gavrila	257	Gavrila	268
Gavrilla	281	Gay	156	Gaye	652
Gayel	685	Gayfreyd	641	Gayl	189
Gayla	281	Gayle	685	Gayleen	246
Gaylene	246	Gayleyn	628	Gaynor	718
Gazella	731	Geela	213	Gelasia	729
Gelasie	224	Gelsey	191	Gelya	685
Gemina	674	Gemini	573	Geminine	134
Gemma	663	Gemmel	191	Gen	538
Gena	639	Genda	674	Gene	134
Genele	663	Geneva	279	Genevieve	224
Genevra	279	Genevre	674	Genia	639
Genie	134	Genna	685	Genni	584
Gennie	189	Gennifer	156	Genny	562
Genovera	876	Genoveva	821	Genvra	674
Georgana	415	George	753	Georgeanna	966
Georgeanne	461	Georgee	358	Georgena	819
Georgene	314	Georgetta	898	Georgette	393
Georgi	257	Georgi	268	Georgia	358
Georgiana	415	Georgianna	461	Georgianne	865
Georgie	753	Georgina	314	Georgine	718

Georgy	235	Geralda	753	Geraldina	718
Geraldine	213	Geranium	977	Gerardine	279
Gerda	628	Gerdee	628	Gerdi	527
Geri	573	Gerianna	786	Gerianne	281
Gerilee	617	Gerlinda	617	Gerlinde	112
Germain	674	Germaine	279	Germana	775
Geromina	371	Gerri	573	Gerrie	178
Gerry	551	Gert	595	Gerta	696
Gerti	595	Gertie	191	Gertrud	843
Gertruda	944	Gertrude	448	Gertrudis	854
Gerty	573	Gervaise	235	Gery	551
Geva	628	Geziena	224	Ghaly	178
Gia	178	Giacinta	281	Giamo	729
Gian	134	Giana	235	Gianina	281
Gianna	281	Gigi	955	Gila	112
Gilada	257	Gilada	268	Gilah	191
Gilberta	652	Gilberte	156	Gilbertha	641
Gilberthe	145	Gilbertina	617	Gilbertine	112
Gilda	156	Gildas	167	Gili	911
Gilia	112	Gilian	167	Gilji	922
Gill	944	Gillane	696	Gillean	696
Gilleon	292	Gillette	189	Gilli	944
Gillian	191	Gillie	549	Gilly	922
Gimia	123	Gina	134	Ginelle	191
Ginerva	674	Ginette	178	Ginevra	674
Ginger	516	Gini	933	Ginneh	573
Ginni	988	Ginnie	584	Ginnifer	551
Ginny	966	Giorgia	753	Giovanna	832
Gipsy	944	Giralda	257	Giralda	268
Girisa	189	Girosal	729	Gisa	189
Gisela	628	Gisele	123	Gisella	652
Giselle	156	Gita	191	Gitana	257
Gitana	268	Githa	189	Giuditta	461
Giulia	415	Giulietta	955	Giustina	461
Gizal	191	Gizale	696	Gizela	696
Gizi	966	Gizike	584	Glad	156
Gladdie	696	Gladdy	178	Gladi	156
Gladine	617	Gladis	167	Gladys	145
Gleda	652	Glen	562	Glena	663
Glenda	617	Glenice	191	Glenine	123
Glenn	527	Glenna	628	Glennie	123
Glennis	538	Gloire	213	Glori	617
Gloria	718	Gloriana	865	Gloriane	369
Glorianna	821	Glorianne	325	Glory	685

Glyn	764	Glynis	955	Glynna	191
Glynnis	911	Goda	729	Godgifu	966
Godina	775	Godiva	764	Golda	753
Goldarina	819	Goldi	652	Goldia	753
Goldie	257	Goldie	268	Goldina	718
Goldy	639	Goranna	887	Gorgene	718
Grace	617	Gracia	213	Gracie	617
Gracye	685	Grata	292	Gratia	292
Gratiana	358	Gratie	696	Gray	156
Grayce	685	Graziella	731	Greer	178
Greeta	292	Gregoria	358	Grenta	652
Gressa	696	Greta	696	Gretal	639
Gretchen	178	Grete	191	Gretel	134
Grethal	628	Grethe	189	Grethel	123
Gretna	652	Gretta	628	Grier	573
Griselda	663	Griselde	167	Griseldi	562
Griseldis	573	Grishelda	652	Grishelde	156
Grishilda	156	Grishilde	551	Grissel	538
Grizel	595	Grizela	696	Grizelda	641
Grizella	639	Grizema	617	Grizemalie	246
Grizzell	527	Grocea	314	Grocenea	865
Groeneia	832	Guadalupe	437	Guda	426
Gudren	876	Gudrin	371	Gudrun	674
Guendolen	167	Guenever	977	Guenevere	573
Guenna	988	Guida	426	Guilla	448
Guin	336	Guinevere	977	Guinivere	472
Guinna	483	Gunda	472	Gunhilda	494
Gunhilde	898	Guriona	134	Gurisina	448
Gurisyna	426	Gurisyne	821	Gurisynna	472
Gurisynne	876	Guriszea	977	Gus	382
Gussi	393	Gussie	898	Gussy	371
Gusta	415	Gustava	551	Gustave	955
Gusti	314	Gustie	819	Gusty	382
Guyonne	562	Gwen	584	Gwenda	639
Gwendolen	729	Gwendolene	325	Gwendolin	224
Gwendoline	729	Gwendolyn	292	Gwendolyne	797
Gwenette	639	Gwenhwyvar	652	Gwenn	549
Gwenne	145	Gwenni	549	Gwennie	145
Gwenny	527	Gwenora	382	Gwenore	786
Gwillym	922	Gwladys	191	Gwyladys	178
Gwyn	786	Gwyneth	573	Gwynn	742
Gwynna	123	Gwynne	527	Gwynnie	527
Gyan	112	Gyasi	167	Gyna	112
Gypsy	562	Gytha	167	Hadria	235

Hadwisa	292	Hafia	257	Hafia	268
Hahdee	224	Haidee	235	Haidie	639
Hailee	224	Hailey	696	Haily	191
Halcyon	786	Halcyone	382	Haldana	325
Halee	224	Haleen	279	Haleena	371
Haleigh	685	Halen	674	Haley	696
Halfreida	731	Halfrida	235	Halfrieda	731
Hali	123	Halian	279	Halicia	257
Halicia	268	Halie	628	Halimeda	718
Halla	257	Halla	268	Halley	639
Halli	156	Hallie	652	Hally	134
Halona	876	Halsey	617	Hama	235
Hana	246	Hanae	742	Hanako	865
Hanan	292	Hanice	674	Haniya	224
Hanna	292	Hannah	281	Hanne	696
Hannele	235	Hanni	191	Hannie	696
Hannis	112	Hanny	178	Happi	145
Happy	123	Hara	281	Haracia	325
Haralda	369	Haraldina	325	Harlene	279
Harley	696	Harli	123	Harlie	628
Harmonia	887	Harmonie	382	Harmony	764
Harolda	865	Haroldina	821	Harri	189
Harrie	685	Harriet	617	Harrietta	731
Harriette	235	Harriot	718	Harriott	731
Harriotte	336	Hasana	358	Hasina	257
Hasina	268	Hatawa	369	Hateya	786
Hatti	134	Hattie	639	Hatty	112
Haydee	213	Hayley	674	Hazel	617
Hazle	617	Heath	696	Heather	292
Hebe	112	Hectorine	797	Heda	639
Hedda	674	Heddi	573	Heddie	178
Heddy	551	Hedi	538	Hedia	639
Hedvig	551	Hedvige	156	Hedvika	696
Hedwig	562	Hedwiga	663	Hedwige	167
Hedy	516	Hedya	617	Heida	639
Heidi	538	Heidie	134	Hela	628
Helaina	775	Hele	123	Helen	178
Helena	279	Helene	674	Helenka	292
Helga	696	Helice	156	Heliena	279
Helixa	685	Hellen	112	Helli	551
Helline	112	Helma	663	Helmine	123
Heloise	731	Helsa	639	Heluska	955
Helyette	641	Helyn	551	Hendrika	617
Henia	641	Heniuta	966	Henka	663

Henne	191	Henni	595	Hennie	191
Henrie	145	Henrietta	281	Henriette	685
Henrika	663	Hera	685	Herma	639
Hermance	224	Hermia	639	Hermina	685
Hermine	189	Herminia	685	Herminie	189
Herminone	742	Hermione	786	Hermosa	347
Herta	617	Hertha	696	Herzl	516
Hesper	178	Hespera	279	Hesperia	279
Hester	123	Hesther	112	Hestia	628
Heta	617	Hetti	538	Hettie	134
Hetty	516	Hiberna	663	Hibiscus	369
Hiedy	516	Hilaire	628	Hilaria	224
Hilary	191	Hild	966	Hilda	167
Hildagard	281	Hildagarde	786	Hilde	562
Hildegaard	786	Hildegard	685	Hildegarde	281
Hildemar	617	Hildie	562	Hildred	516
Hildreta	685	Hildreth	573	Hildretha	674
Hildy	944	Hillary	134	Hilliary	134
Hilma	167	Hinda	189	Hirsuma	448
Hisa	191	Hisoka	729	Hitty	911
Hoa	786	Hola	729	Holda	764
Holle	257	Holle	268	Hollea	358
Holli	652	Hollie	257	Hollie	268
Holly	639	Hondia	786	Hondra	786
Honey	224	Honna	797	Honnet	224
Honor	347	Honora	448	Honore	843
Honori	347	Honoria	448	Honorine	898
Honour	641	Horacia	821	Horatia	819
Hortense	775	Hortensia	371	Hoshi	685
Huberta	933	Huberte	437	Hubertha	922
Huberthe	426	Huetta	933	Huette	437
Hugete	483	Hugette	415	Huguette	718
Hulda	461	Humita	459	Humphrey	876
Huseina	955	Hwyana	279	Hyacineth	663
Hyacinth	167	Hyacinthe	663	Hyacinthie	663
Hydie	516	Hyland	191	Hymiena	663
Hynda	167	Ian	156	Ianthe	663
Ianthina	224	Ib	922	Ibbey	527
Ibbie	549	Ibby	922	Ica	134
Ida	145	Idalia	279	Idalina	235
Idaline	639	Idalla	213	Idalle	617
Idebet	189	Idelea	279	Idelia	674
Idell	516	Idella	617	Idelle	112
Iden	595	Idette	189	Idonia	797

Idonie	292	Idris	955	Iduna	494
Ierne	156	Ignatia	257	Ignatia	268
Ignatzia	246	Ila	134	Ilana	281
Ilanna	246	Ilda	178	Ilde	573
Ileana	786	Ileane	281	Ileen	189
Ileene	685	Ilena	685	Ilene	189
Ilia	134	Iline	584	Ilise	549
Iljabeth	674	Iljabetha	775	Ilka	156
Ilke	551	Illeana	729	Illeen	123
Illene	123	Illona	729	Illone	224
Ilmari	178	Ilnaha	279	Ilona	786
Ilonka	718	Ilsa	145	Ilsabeth	674
Ilsabetha	775	Ilse	549	Ilu	336
Iluska	461	Ilya	112	Ilysa	123
Ilyse	527	Ilyssa	134	Imala	279
Imena	696	Imma	189	Imogen	279
Imogene	775	Imogine	279	Imojean	314
Imperia	628	Imperial	652	Imy	922
Ina	156	Inalani	246	Indira	191
Indra	191	Ines	562	Inesita	685
Inessa	674	Inez	549	Inga	134
Ingaberg	639	Ingabert	674	Ingaborg	731
Ingar	134	Inge	538	Ingeberg	134
Ingebiorg	235	Ingeborg	235	Inger	538
Ingibiorg	639	Ingrid	977	Ingunna	448
Inia	156	Inje	562	Innis	922
Innogen	246	Inoa	753	Ioannis	729
Iodie	246	Iola	731	Iolande	336
Iolanthe	393	Iole	235	Iona	753
Ione	257	Ione	268	Ionia	753
Iov	641	Ira	191	Ireen	156
Ireene	652	Irena	652	Irene	156
Irenee	652	Irenna	617	Irenne	112
Ireta	628	Irete	123	Iretta	641
Irette	145	Irina	156	Iris	911
Irisa	112	Irita	123	Irma	145
Irme	549	Irmina	191	Irmine	595
Irvetta	685	Irvette	189	Isa	112
Isabeau	134	Isabel	663	Isabelita	786
Isabella	797	Isabelle	292	Isadora	854
Isadore	358	Isak	134	Isas	123
Isbel	562	Iseabail	764	Iseabal	764
Iseult	865	Ishbel	551	Ishi	999
Ishie	595	Isidora	753	Isidore	257

Isidore	268	Isis	922	Isleen	191
Isobella	393	Isoda	753	Isol	641
Isola	742	Isolabella	437	Isolabelle	832
Isold	685	Isolda	786	Isolde	281
Isolt	663	Issi	922	Issie	527
Issy	999	Ita	123	Ite	527
Iuana	551	Iunis	369	Iva	145
Ivana	292	Ivanna	257	Ivanna	268
Ivanne	652	Ivett	584	Ivette	189
Ivica	178	Ivie	549	Ivonna	753
Ivonne	257	Ivonne	268	Ivory	628
Ivria	145	Ivy	922	Iwilla	123
Iye	573	Iza	189	Izabel	641
Izabella	775	Izusa	494	Izzy	955
Jacenta	729	Jacey	628	Jacie	641
Jacinda	246	Jacinta	224	Jacinth	112
Jacintha	213	Jacinthe	617	Jacinthia	213
Jackeline	257	Jackeline	268	Jackelyn	639
Jacketta	718	Jacki	167	Jackie	663
Jacklin	156	Jacklyn	134	Jackquelin	944
Jackqueline	549	Jacky	145	Jaclin	134
Jaclyn	112	Jaclyne	617	Jaclynn	167
Jacoba	865	Jacobina	821	Jacobine	325
Jacqeleen	729	Jacqelene	729	Jacqueleen	123
Jacqueleine	123	Jacquelene	123	Jacquelin	922
Jacqueline	527	Jacquelyn	999	Jacquelyne	595
Jacquelynn	955	Jacquenetta	639	Jacquenette	134
Jacquetta	178	Jacquette	573	Jacqui	437
Jacquie	933	Jacquine	988	Jacquotte	674
Jacy	123	Jacynth	189	Jade	652
Jadeen	213	Jadeena	314	Jadine	617
Jae	617	Jaemi	652	Jaemie	257
Jaemie	268	Jaime	652	Jaimie	652
Jaimy	134	Jaine	663	Jakie	639
Jaleen	292	Jalene	292	Jamesina	729
Jamesy	641	Jamey	639	Jami	156
Jamie	652	Jamila	281	Jamilla	224
Jamille	628	Jamima	292	Jamina	213
Jammie	696	Jan	167	Janaya	347
Janaye	742	Jandy	189	Jane	663
Janean	729	Janeczka	718	Janeen	224
Janeet	281	Janek	685	Janel	696
Janela	797	Janella	731	Janelle	235
Janene	224	Janessa	786	Janet	685

Janett	617	Janetta	718	Janette	213
Janeva	718	Janey	641	Jani	167
Janice	696	Janie	663	Janifer	639
Janina	224	Janine	628	Janis	178
Janissa	281	Janit	189	Janith	178
Janitt	112	Janitta	213	Janitte	617
Janiusz	461	Janiuszck	426	Janka	281
Janna	224	Jannel	652	Jannelle	281
Jannet	641	Jannett	663	Janot	786
Janthina	235	Janthine	639	January	549
Jany	145	Janyte	663	Jaquelin	988
Jaquelyn	966	Jaquenetta	696	Jaquenette	191
Jaquinth	461	Jardena	718	Jaretta	753
Jarietta	753	Jarita	235	Jarmine	617
Jaromey	336	Jarona	865	Jarvia	257
Jarvia	268	Jaryeen	246	Jaryene	246
Jascha	246	Jasia	224	Jasisa	235
Jasmin	123	Jasmina	224	Jasmine	628
Jasvinder	663	Javida	292	Javina	213
Javine	617	Jay	189	Jaycee	224
Jaye	685	Jaylene	279	Jayme	639
Jaymee	235	Jaymie	639	Jayne	641
Jaynell	617	Jaynet	663	Jaynett	685
Jaynetta	786	Jaynette	281	Jayney	628
Jayson	753	Jaz	191	Jazmin	191
Jean	663	Jeana	764	Jeanelle	731
Jeanenne	775	Jeanette	718	Jeani	663
Jeanine	224	Jeanna	729	Jeanne	224
Jeannette	764	Jeannie	224	Jeannine	279
Jeannot	347	Jehane	257	Jehane	268
Jehanne	213	Jelena	292	Jelene	696
Jelenna	257	Jelenna	268	Jelenne	652
Jeljen	112	Jem	551	Jemie	156
Jemima	696	Jemimah	685	Jemina	617
Jeminah	696	Jemma	696	Jemmie	191
Jemmy	573	Jen	562	Jena	663
Jenafor	336	Jenda	617	Jenette	617
Jeni	562	Jenica	696	Jenifer	134
Jeniffer	191	Jenilee	696	Jenn	527
Jenna	628	Jennee	628	Jennette	663
Jenni	527	Jennica	652	Jennie	123
Jennifer	189	Jennilee	652	Jennine	178
Jenny	595	Jensine	134	Jeraldine	246
Jeralee	742	Jere	112	Jeremia	257

Jeremia	268	Jeremiah	246	Jeremy	134
Jeri	516	Jerilee	641	Jeri-Lee	641
Jerilynn	538	Jeritza	628	Jermaine	213
Jeroldine	742	Jerri	516	Jerrie	112
Jerrilee	641	Jerrine	167	Jerry	584
Jerrylee	628	Jersey	191	Jerusha	911
Jery	584	Jerzy	573	Jeska	641
Jess	538	Jessa	639	Jessabell	224
Jessalin	628	Jessalyn	696	Jessalynn	652
Jessalynne	257	Jessalynne	268	Jessamie	279
Jessamine	235	Jessamy	652	Jessamyn	617
Jesse	134	Jesselyn	191	Jesselynn	156
Jesselynne	652	Jessi	538	Jessica	663
Jessie	134	Jessika	652	Jessy	516
Jesusa	933	Jetta	652	Jewel	191
Jewell	134	Jewelle	639	Jeysoca	336
Jezabel	257	Jezabel	268	Jezabella	382
Jezabelle	786	Jezebel	652	Jezebella	786
Jhande	696	Jhandie	696	Jhanett	696
Jhenda	696	Ji	911	Jill	977
Jillana	235	Jillane	639	Jillayne	617
Jilleen	134	Jillene	134	Jilli	977
Jillian	134	Jillie	573	Jilly	955
Jina	167	Jinny	999	Jiri	911
Jivanta	235	Jivella	628	Jivvella	663
Jo	617	Jo Ann	729	Joachima	876
Joakima	876	Joan	764	Joana	865
Joane	369	Joanie	369	Joanka	887
Joann	729	Jo-Ann	729	Joanna	821
Joanne	325	Joano	461	Joaquima	246
Joasia	821	Jobey	213	Jobi	639
Jobie	235	Jobina	786	Joby	617
Jobye	213	Jobyna	764	Jocasta	876
Joccoaa	573	Jocelan	336	Jocelin	235
Joceline	731	Jocelyn	213	Jocelyne	718
Jodee	753	Jodi	652	Jodie	257
Jodie	268	Jody	639	Joeann	325
Joeanna	426	Joeanne	821	Joela	347
Joell	279	Joella	371	Joelle	775
Joellen	731	Joelly	257	Joelly	268
Joelyn	279	Joelynn	235	Joelynne	731
Joergee	382	Joette	753	Joey	281
Johana	854	Johane	358	Johanna	819
Johannah	898	Johanne	314	Johna	753

Johnath	764	Johnna	718	Joice	246
Joicelin	235	Joicelyn	213	Joisse	235
Joji	628	Jola	742	Jolanda	843
Jolanta	821	Jolee	742	Joleen	797
Jolene	797	Joletta	382	Joli	641
Jolie	246	Joliee	742	Joline	292
Jollean	336	Jollena	336	Joly	628
Jolyn	674	Jomi	652	Jomina	718
Jona	764	Jonalee	898	Jonalen	358
Jonanna	876	Jonanne	371	Jonati	786
Jonatia	887	Jonell	235	Jonette	718
Joni	663	Jonia	764	Jonica	797
Joniki	685	Jonilla	731	Jonina	729
Jonine	224	Jonis	674	Jonisa	775
Jonit	685	Jonithea	371	Jonitsa	797
Jonitta	718	Jonitte	213	Jonny	696
Jonsy	652	Jonya	742	Jora	718
Jorah	797	Jordain	718	Jordan	718
Jordana	819	Jordanna	865	Jorey	281
Jorgee	786	Jorgena	347	Jori	617
Jorie	213	Joris	628	Jorrie	213
Jory	685	Josana	876	Josane	371
Josann	731	Josanne	336	Joscelie	786
Joscelin	246	Josceline	742	Joscelyn	224
Joscelyne	729	Josee	729	Josefa	382
Josefina	347	Josefine	742	Josel	257
Josel	268	Joselen	718	Joselene	314
Joselin	213	Joseline	718	Josella	382
Joselle	786	Joselyn	281	Joselyne	786
Josepha	382	Josephe	786	Josephina	347
Josephine	742	Josetta	369	Josette	764
Josey	292	Josi	628	Josiane	371
Josie	224	Josilen	213	Josilene	718
Josilin	617	Josiline	213	Josilyn	685
Josilyne	281	Joslin	617	Josline	213
Joslyn	685	Joslynn	641	Josse	235
Josseline	729	Josselyn	292	Jossey	213
Josy	696	Jourdan	112	Joveen	718
Joveena	819	Jovine	213	Jovita	775
Joy	685	Joya	786	Joyan	742
Joyann	797	Joyce	224	Joycelin	213
Joycelyn	281	Joye	281	Joyita	718
Joylee	729	Joyleen	775	Joylene	775
Joylie	224	Joylin	674	Joylyn	652

Joylyne	257	Joylyne	268	Joylynn	617
Joyous	696	Joys	696	Juana	562
Juanita	584	Jude	854	Judi	358
Judie	854	Judilah	472	Judith	369
Juditha	461	Judy	336	Judye	832
Juhiel	832	Juhli	336	Jule	843
Julee	448	Julena	999	Julenne	459
Juley	821	Juli	347	Julia	448
Juliana	595	Juliane	999	Juliann	459
Julianna	551	Julianne	955	Julie	843
Julienne	459	Juliet	865	Julieta	966
Julietta	988	Juliette	483	Julina	494
Juline	898	Julissa	461	Julita	461
July	325	Julyanna	538	Julyanne	933
Juma	459	Jumana	516	Juna	461
June	865	Junella	933	Junemarie	516
Junette	415	Junia	461	Juniata	584
Junie	865	Junieta	988	Junina	426
Junine	821	Juno	966	Juritas	448
Justeena	595	Justie	843	Justina	494
Justine	898	Justinn	358	Jutta	459
Kacey	639	Kachina	292	Kachine	696
Kacie	652	Kacy	134	Kaela	753
Kafryna	224	Kagami	246	Kai	123
Kaia	224	Kaie	628	Kaila	257
Kaila	268	Kaile	652	Kailey	639
Kaili	156	Kailie	652	Kaimi	167
Kaimie	663	Kairl	156	Kaitlin	134
Kaitlyn	112	Kaitlynn	167	Kaitlynne	663
Kaja	235	Kajsa	246	Kakalina	336
Kala	257	Kala	268	Kalah	246
Kalama	393	Kalantha	325	Kalanthe	729
Kaleah	742	Kaleena	314	Kalere	257
Kalere	268	Kali	156	Kalica	281
Kalika	279	Kalila	281	Kalilah	279
Kalina	213	Kalinda	257	Kalinda	268
Kalindi	156	Kaliska	281	Kalki	178
Kalle	685	Kalli	189	Kallie	685
Kallista	224	Kallisto	729	Kally	167
Kaly	134	Kalypso	729	Kamali	292
Kamara	369	Kamarah	358	Kamaria	369
Kamata	382	Kameko	382	Kami	167
Kamika	281	Kamil	191	Kamila	292
Kamilah	281	Kamile	696	Kamilka	224

Kamilla	235	Kamillah	224	Kamille	639
Kanaka	393	Kanake	797	Kandace	753
Kandee	224	Kandice	652	Kandie	628
Kandy	191	Kaneen	235	Kanene	235
Kania	279	Kaniel	617	Kanika	292
Kanya	257	Kanya	268	Kapera	797
Kapila	235	Kapua	595	Kar Lai	257
Kar Lai	268	Kara	224	Karal	257
Karal	268	Karalai	358	Karalee	358
Karan	279	Karayan	358	Kardal	292
Karee	224	Kareen	279	Karel	652
Karell	685	Karen	674	Karena	775
Karene	279	Karesi	639	Karey	696
Kari	123	Karie	628	Kariline	617
Karilla	281	Karilyn	189	Karilyne	685
Karilynn	145	Karilynne	641	Karim	167
Karin	178	Karina	279	Karine	674
Karisa	235	Karissa	246	Karita	246
Karjin	189	Karla	257	Karla	268
Karlana	314	Karlanah	393	Karlee	257
Karlee	268	Karleen	213	Karlen	617
Karlene	213	Karli	156	Karlie	652
Karlotta	898	Karlotte	393	Karly	134
Karmel	696	Karmella	731	Karmen	628
Karmili	191	Karna	279	Karol	753
Karola	854	Karole	358	Karolina	819
Karoline	314	Karolle	382	Karoly	731
Karolyn	786	Karolyne	382	Karolynn	742
Karolynne	347	Karon	775	Karosi	731
Karotine	393	Karrah	213	Karrell	685
Karrie	628	Karsti	156	Karstie	652
Karyl	134	Karyn	156	Karyne	652
Kasa	235	Kasandra	336	Kasey	617
Kasi	134	Kasia	235	Kasienka	718
Kasim	178	Kasinda	235	Kasmira	279
Kass	145	Kassandra	347	Kassey	628
Kassi	145	Kassia	246	Kassie	641
Kata	246	Katalin	235	Katannia	358
Katannya	336	Katarina	393	Katarine	797
Kate	641	Katee	246	Katel	674
Katerina	797	Katerine	292	Kateryn	674
Katey	628	Kath	134	Katha	235
Katharina	382	Katharine	786	Kathe	639
Katherina	786	Katherine	281	Kathern	685

Katheryn	663	Kathi	134	Kathi Lea	764
Kathie	639	Kathie Lea	369	Kathie Lee	764
Kathleen	224	Kathlene	224	Kathlin	123
Kathline	628	Kathreen	281	Kathrine	685
Kathryn	167	Kathryne	663	Kathy	112
Kathy Lea	742	Kathy Lee	246	Kathye	617
Kati	145	Katia	246	Katie	641
Katina	292	Katine	696	Katinka	224
Katleen	235	Katlin	134	Katline	639
Katrin	191	Katrina	292	Katrine	696
Katrinka	224	Katrya	224	Katryn	178
Katsuyo	134	Katti	167	Kattie	663
Katty	145	Katura	549	Katuscha	573
Katushka	562	Katy	123	Katya	224
Katyra	224	Kaula	551	Kavindre	663
Kawa	279	Kay	191	Kaya	292
Kaycee	235	Kaye	696	Kayla	235
Kayle	639	Kaylee	235	Kayley	617
Kaylil	167	Kaylyn	167	Kaylynn	123
Kaylynne	628	Kaz	112	Kea	628
Keady	641	Keahi	617	Kealoha	448
Keddie	112	Kedma	617	Keeley	639
Keelia	257	Keelia	268	Keely	134
Keena	279	Keeree	224	Keeren	674
Kefira	685	Kei	527	Keiki	549
Keiko	246	Keitha	639	Kejin	584
Kekoa	347	Kekona	393	Kelcey	167
Kelci	584	Kelcie	189	Kelcy	562
Kelda	696	Kele	156	Kelee	652
Keleen	617	Kelene	617	Kelia	652
Kelii	551	Kelila	685	Kelle	189
Kellen	145	Kelley	167	Kelli	584
Kellia	685	Kellie	189	Kellie-Ann	292
Kellie-Anne	797	Kellina	641	Kellsie	191
Kelly	562	Kelly-Ann	674	Kelly-Anne	279
Kelosia	369	Kelsey	145	Kelsi	562
Kelsie	167	Kelsy	549	Kelula	988
Kelvina	652	Kenda	628	Kendra	628
Kendre	123	Kenna	639	Kennda	674
Kenzie	167	Keoma	369	Keran	674
Kerani	674	Keree	628	Kerel	156
Kerem	167	Keren	178	Kerey	191
Keri	527	Keriann	639	Kerianne	235
Kerral	652	Kerri	527	Kerri-Ann	639

Kerri-Anne	235	Kerrie	123	Kerrie-Ann	235
Kerrie-Anne	731	Kerril	551	Kerrin	573
Kerry	595	Kerry-Ann	617	Kerry-Anne	213
Kersen	189	Kersti	551	Kerstie	156
Kerstin	516	Kersty	538	Kerwina	639
Keryl	538	Keryle	134	Kerylen	189
Kesava	775	Kesi	538	Kesia	639
Kesin	584	Kesley	145	Keslie	167
Kessiah	639	Kessie	145	Kester	156
Kettey	145	Ketti	562	Kettie	167
Ketty	549	Ketura	944	Ketzia	639
Keva	663	Kevin	527	Kevina	628
Kevyn	595	Keziah	696	Khaleel	279
Kherun	865	Ki	922	Kiah	112
Kial	156	Kibbe	562	Kichi	944
Kiele	156	Kieran	674	Kiersten	112
Kiery	595	Kija	134	Kijhi	922
Kikelia	674	Kiki	944	Kikilia	178
Kilesa	663	Kiley	538	Kim	966
Kimama	213	Kimball	156	Kimber	584
Kimberlee	628	Kimberley	191	Kimberli	527
Kimberlie	123	Kimberly	595	Kimberlyn	551
Kimberlynn	516	Kimberlynne	112	Kimbra	189
Kimi	966	Kimie	562	Kimmi	911
Kimmie	516	Kimmy	988	Kindie	527
Kindy	999	Kineta	696	Kini	977
Kinna	134	Kiona	775	Kip	999
Kipp	977	Kippie	573	Kippy	955
Kira	123	Kiral	156	Kiran	178
Kirbee	145	Kirbie	549	Kirby	922
Kiri	922	Kiril	955	Kirila	156
Kirill	988	Kirima	167	Kirimia	167
Kirin	977	Kirinna	134	Kirsi	933
Kirstee	156	Kirsten	516	Kirsteni	516
Kirsti	955	Kirstie	551	Kirstin	911
Kirstina	112	Kirsty	933	Kirva	167
Kirwa	178	Kiryl	933	Kirylee	134
Kirylen	584	Kirylena	685	Kisa	134
Kishi	922	Kiska	156	Kismet	595
Kissa	145	Kissee	145	Kissie	549
Kistna	112	Kit	944	Kita	145
Kitti	966	Kittie	562	Kitty	944
Kiva	167	Kivi	966	Kizza	191
Kizzee	191	Kizzie	595	Klair	156

Klara	257	Klara	268	Klare	652
Klarika	279	Klementina	235	Klesa	663
Kloe	257	Kloe	268	Koko	347
Kokudza	178	Kola	753	Kolina	718
Kolmie	292	Kolya	731	Koma	764
Kona	775	Konana	832	Konni	639
Konstance	393	Konstanze	358	Kora	729
Koral	753	Koraley	336	Koralie	358
Kordula	191	Kore	224	Koree	729
Koreel	753	Koreen	775	Korella	382
Koren	279	Koresa	336	Koressa	347
Kori	628	Kori Anne	336	Korianne	336
Kori-Anne	336	Korie	224	Korlahne	393
Korlane	314	Korney	257	Korney	268
Korrie	224	Korry	696	Kory	696
Kosma	775	Krima	167	Kris	933
Krishan	178	Krishna	178	Kriss	944
Krissie	549	Krissy	922	Krista	156
Kristabel	617	Kristabella	742	Kristabelle	246
Kristae	652	Kristal	189	Kristan	112
Kristea	652	Kristee	156	Kristel	584
Kristen	516	Kristi	955	Kristie	551
Kristin	911	Kristina	112	Kristine	516
Kristsan	123	Kristy	933	Kristyn	988
Kristyna	189	Kristyne	584	Krysia	112
Krysta	134	Krystal	167	Krystalle	696
Krystha	123	Krystie	538	Krystin	988
Krystle	562	Krystyna	167	Krystyne	562
Krystynna	123	Kuleea	551	Kulya	437
Kumi	369	Kuni	371	Kuri	325
Kurma	461	Kusa	437	Kveta	685
Kvetia	685	Kwame	628	Kwamina	279
Kwanita	257	Kwanita	268	Kyla	134
Kyle	538	Kylen	584	Kylie	538
Kylila	167	Kylyn	516	Kylynn	562
Kylynne	527	Kym	764	Kymberlee	696
Kymberley	178	Kymberlie	191	Kyna	156
Kynthia	167	Kyra	191	Kyrena	652
Kyrene	156	Kyrenia	652	La Reina	786
La Roux	191	La Verne	235	Laara	336
Lacey	641	Lacie	663	Ladell	641
Ladonna	887	Laetita	775	Laetitia	775
Lahela	753	Laili	167	Lailie	663
Laina	281	Laine	685	Lainey	663

Lainie	685	Lais	145	Laka	257
Laka	268	Lakya	235	Lalasa	371
Lalena	729	Lalita	281	Lallie	696
Lana	281	Lanae	786	Lancey	696
Landa	235	Lane	685	Lanetta	731
Lanette	235	Laney	663	Lani	189
Lanie	685	Lanier	685	Lanita	213
Laniuma	538	Lanna	246	Lannah	235
Lanni	145	Lannie	641	Lanny	123
Lao	731	Laole	369	Lara	235
Laraine	786	Larancy	292	Larayne	764
Larell	696	Lari	134	Larina	281
Larine	685	Larisa	246	Larissa	257
Larissa	268	Lark	156	Larke	652
Larli	167	Larochka	876	Larousse	652
Larraine	786	Laryssa	235	Lasca	279
Lashi	134	Lassie	652	Latashia	358
Latia	257	Latia	268	Latisha	257
Latisha	268	Latitia	279	Latonia	819
LaToya	832	Latreece	786	Latreese	764
Latreshia	753	Latrice	685	Latricia	281
Latta	279	Lauchie	955	Laura	538
Lauralee	663	Laure	933	Lauree	538
Laureen	584	Laurel	966	Laurell	999
Laurella	191	Lauren	988	Laurena	189
Laurencia	123	Laurene	584	Laurentine	562
Lauretta	178	Laurette	573	Lauri	437
Laurice	966	Laurie	933	Laurin	483
Laurine	988	Laurissa	551	Laurna	584
Lauryn	461	Lauryne	966	Lavana	336
Laveda	729	Lavella	742	Lavelle	246
Lavena	731	Lavender	279	Laverna	731
Laverne	235	Lavetta	729	Lavette	224
Lavi	178	Lavina	235	Lavinia	235
Lavinie	639	Lavon	731	Lavone	336
Lavonna	887	Lavvie	628	Lawree	281
Lawrence	279	Lawrie	685	Lawrine	641
Layla	246	Laylie	641	Layne	663
Layney	641	Lazla	257	Lazla	268
Lea	639	Leagh	696	Leah	628
Leala	764	Leana	786	Leandra	731
Leane	281	Leann	641	Leanna	742
Leanne	246	Leanor	382	Leanora	483
Leatrice	281	Leatrix	628	Leda	674

Ledah	663	Lee	134	Lee Ann	246
LeeAnn	246	Leeanna	347	Leeanne	742
Leeba	257	Leeba	268	Leelah	257
Leelah	268	Leena	281	Leesa	246
Leeza	224	Legra	617	Lehua	922
Lei	538	Leia	639	Leiani	685
Leiann	641	Leianna	742	Leianne	246
Leigh	595	Leigha	696	Leila	663
Leilah	652	Leilani	628	Leilia	663
Leinaeh	279	Leisha	639	Leith	549
Leithia	641	Lel	562	Lela	663
Lelah	652	Leland	663	Lelani	628
Lelia	663	Lella	696	Lemar	674
Lemi	573	Lemuela	516	Lemuella	549
Lena	685	Lencay	696	Lenci	527
Lene	189	Lenee	685	Leneta	213
Lenetta	235	Lenette	639	Lenis	595
Lenita	617	Lenka	617	Lenna	641
Lenni	549	Lennie	145	Lenny	527
Lenora	382	Lenore	786	Lenos	292
Lenta	617	Lenusya	977	Leocadie	819
Leoda	371	Leodora	977	Leoine	786
Leola	369	Leolie	764	Leoline	729
Leoma	371	Leona	382	Leonanie	843
Leonarda	437	Leonarde	832	Leonardina	483
Leonardine	887	Leonda	336	Leondra	336
Leone	786	Leonelle	358	Leonete	314
Leoni	281	Leonidisa	347	Leonie	786
Leonn	246	Leonor	887	Leonora	988
Leonore	483	Leontina	369	Leontine	764
Leontyne	742	Leopolda	988	Leopoldina	944
Leopoldine	448	Leora	336	Leota	358
Leotie	753	Lerinda	639	Lerona	382
Lerone	786	Les	549	Leshia	639
Leska	663	Leslee	674	Lesley	156
Lesli	573	Leslie	178	Lesly	551
Lesya	628	Let	551	Leta	652
Letha	641	Lethia	641	Lethita	663
Leticia	685	Letilia	685	Letisha	652
Letita	674	Letitia	674	Letizia	641
Letreece	281	Letrice	189	Letta	674
Letti	573	Lettia	674	Lettice	112
Lettie	178	Letty	551	Leva	674
Levana	731	Levane	235	Levania	731

Levanna	786	Levashka	797	Leverna	235
Levey	156	Levi	573	Levia	674
Levina	639	Levka	696	Levona	336
Levy	551	Lewanna	797	Lewanne	292
Lexa	696	Lexi	595	Lexie	191
Lexine	156	Lexy	573	Leya	617
Leyla	641	Lezlie	156	Lia	134
Liam	178	Lian	189	Liana	281
Liane	685	Liang	167	Lianna	246
Lianne	641	Lib	955	Libbey	551
Libbi	977	Libbie	573	Libby	955
Licha	156	Lici	966	Liciena	628
Lida	178	Liddy	999	Lidia	178
Lidie	573	Lidiya	156	Lidochka	729
Lieda	674	Liene	189	Liesa	641
Liese	145	Liesel	178	Liesse	156
Lihwa	178	Lijette	189	Liko	652
Lil	966	Lila	167	Lilac	191
Lilah	156	Lilais	178	Lilas	178
Lileye	145	Lili	966	Lilia	167
Lilian	123	Liliana	224	Liliane	628
Lilianne	674	Lilias	178	Lilika	189
Lilith	977	Lilja	178	Liljana	235
Lilka	189	Lill	999	Lilla	191
Lillani	156	Lilli	999	Lillian	156
Lilliana	257	Lilliana	268	Lilliane	652
Lillias	112	Lillie	595	Lillis	911
Lilly	977	Lillyan	134	Lily	944
Lilyan	191	Lilyane	696	Lilyanne	652
Lin	988	Lina	189	Lind	933
Linda	134	Linde	538	Lindee	134
Lindey	516	Lindi	933	Lindie	538
Lindoro	336	Lindsay	123	Lindsey	527
Lindsy	922	Lindy	911	Line	584
Linea	685	Linell	551	Linet	516
Linetta	639	Linette	134	Linn	944
Linnea	641	Linnell	516	Linnet	562
Linnett	584	Linnetta	685	Linnette	189
Linnie	549	Linnzi	933	Linsay	178
Linsey	573	Linzy	955	Liolya	742
Liona	786	Lionnette	786	Lioree	731
Lira	134	Lirann	145	Liranna	246
Liranne	641	Lireen	189	Lireena	281
Lirisa	145	Lirissa	156	Lirone	281

Lisa	145	Lisa Maria	382	Lisa Marie	786
Lisabet	685	Lisabeta	786	Lisabeth	674
Lisandra	246	Lisbet	584	Lisbeth	573
Lise	549	Liseli	573	Liseta	663
Lisetta	685	Lisette	189	Lisha	134
Lishe	538	Lisli	977	Lissa	156
Lissi	955	Lissie	551	Lissilma	134
Lissy	933	Lisy	922	Lita	156
Litlit	911	Litonya	786	Litsa	167
Liuka	459	Liusade	988	Liv	977
Liva	178	Livana	235	Livanga	213
Livanna	281	Livanne	685	Livi	977
Livia	178	Livie	573	Liviya	156
Livona	731	Livvi	922	Livvie	527
Livvy	999	Liwanu	448	Liz	922
Liza	123	Lizabeta	764	Lizabeth	652
Lizanka	292	Lizaveta	786	Lizbeth	551
Lizette	167	Lizina	178	Lizite	549
Lizzie	516	Lizzy	988	Lodema	325
Lodie	279	Loella	393	Loiree	731
Loireena	887	Loiren	281	Lois	641
Loise	246	Lokelani	347	Lokni	617
Lola	764	Loleta	382	Lolita	786
Lollie	292	Lolly	674	Lolotea	988
Lom	674	Lona	786	Lonee	786
Loneta	314	Loni	685	Lonna	742
Lonni	641	Lonnie	246	Lonya	764
Lora	731	Lorain	786	Loraine	382
Lorainne	347	Loral	764	Loralee	865
Loraleen	821	Loraleigh	336	Loralie	369
Loralyn	797	Loralynn	753	Loralynne	358
Lore	235	Lorea	336	Loreca	369
Loree	731	Loreen	786	Lorelei	764
Lorelia	369	Lorelie	764	Lorell	292
Lorelle	797	Loren	281	Lorena	382
Lorenda	336	Lorene	786	Lorenza	371
Loretta	371	Lorette	775	Lori	639
Loria	731	Lorianna	843	Lorianne	347
Lorie	235	Loriennah	336	Lorihanne	336
Lorilee	764	Lorill	696	Lorilyn	696
Lorilynn	652	Lorilynne	257	Lorilynne	268
Lorinda	731	Lorine	281	Loring	663
Loris	641	Lorita	753	Lorna	786
Lorrain	786	Lorraine	382	Lorrainne	347

Lorrayne	369	Lorrell	292	Lorri	639
Lorrie	235	Lorrin	685	Lorris	641
Lorry	617	Lory	617	Lota	753
Lotta	775	Lotte	279	Lotti	674
Lottie	279	Lotty	652	Lotus	966
Lou	933	Louane	685	Louanna	246
Louanne	641	Louella	696	Louisa	145
Louise	549	Louisette	189	Louisitte	584
Loukas	167	Loula	167	Loulou	966
Loutitia	178	Love	279	Lovella	347
Loyal	742	Loyce	246	Lu	336
Luana	584	Luane	988	Luann	448
Luanna	549	Luanni	448	Lucasta	595
Luce	865	Lucelle	437	Lucerne	426
Lucette	415	Luci	369	Lucia	461
Luciana	527	Lucianna	573	Lucianus	731
Lucie	865	Lucienne	472	Lucila	494
Lucile	898	Lucill	336	Lucilla	437
Lucille	832	Lucina	426	Lucinda	461
Lucine	821	Lucita	483	Lucky	369
Lucrece	494	Lucrecia	999	Lucretia	988
Lucrezia	955	Lucy	347	Ludella	944
Ludie	876	Ludmila	459	Ludmilla	483
Ludovika	145	Ludwika	459	Luela	966
Luella	999	Luelle	494	Luicime	819
Luisa	448	Luise	843	Luka	459
Lukina	415	Lukyann	448	Lula	461
Lulani	426	Lulita	483	Lullani	459
Lulu	663	Luna	483	Luneta	911
Lunetta	933	Lunette	437	Lunneta	966
Lunnete	461	Lupe	819	Lupita	437
Lura	437	Lurette	472	Lurleen	426
Lurlene	426	Lurlette	415	Lurlina	426
Lurline	821	Lusa	448	Lusati	461
Lusela	977	Lusella	911	Lusita	461
Luva	472	Luvena	933	Luwana	549
Luwanna	595	Luwanne	999	Luyriner	865
Luyu	617	Luz	325	Lya	112
Lyaksandr	246	Lyda	156	Lydda	191
Lydell	527	Lydia	156	Lydiane	617
Lydie	551	Lyeea	213	Lyena	663
Lykka	156	Lyn	786	Lynd	731
Lynda	112	Lynde	516	Lyndee	112
Lyndel	549	Lyndell	573	Lyndha	191

Lyndsay	191	Lyndsey	595	Lyndsie	527
Lyndy	538	Lynea	663	Lynelle	134
Lynette	112	Lynn	742	Lynna	123
Lynne	527	Lynnea	628	Lynnell	584
Lynnelle	189	Lynnet	549	Lynnett	562
Lynnette	167	Lynsey	551	Lyova	753
Lyra	112	Lyris	922	Lysandra	224
Lysbet	562	Lysbeth	551	Lyse	527
Lysett	562	Lyssa	134	Lystra	145
Mab	167	Mabel	696	Mabella	731
Mabelle	235	Mable	696	Mabs	178
Machi	167	Mackenzie	246	Mada	281
Madalaine	876	Madaleine	371	Madalena	876
Madaline	775	Madalyn	257	Madalyn	268
Madalyna	358	Madalynn	213	Madalynne	718
Maddalena	821	Maddalene	325	Maddi	134
Maddie	639	Maddy	112	Madel	628
Madelaine	371	Madeleine	775	Madelena	371
Madelene	775	Madelia	729	Madelina	775
Madeline	279	Madella	753	Madelle	257
Madelle	268	Madelon	371	Madelyn	652
Madelynn	617	Madelynne	213	Madge	663
Madia	281	Madleine	279	Madlen	674
Madlin	178	Madoline	371	Madora	887
Madra	281	Madrue	988	Mady	167
Mae	641	Maecy	652	Maegan	775
Maelle	213	Maeve	281	Maewina	753
Maewine	257	Maewine	268	Mag	123
Magdala	393	Magdalane	854	Magdaleen	358
Magdalen	753	Magdalena	854	Magdalene	358
Magdalyn	235	Magdi	167	Magen	674
Magena	775	Maggee	292	Maggi	191
Maggie	696	Maggy	178	Magha	213
Magnhilda	246	Magnhilde	641	Magnilda	257
Magnilda	268	Magnilde	652	Magnolia	819
Mahala	369	Mahalah	358	Mahalia	369
Mahara	336	Mahesa	742	Mahina	281
Mahira	235	Mai	145	Maia	246
Maiah	235	Maible	696	Maida	281
Maidel	628	Maidie	685	Maidy	167
Maiga	224	Mair	145	Maire	641
Mairee	246	Mairen	696	Mairi	145
Mairin	191	Mairles	685	Maisey	639
Maisie	652	Maite	663	Maitilde	641

Maiya	224	Majesta	786	Makadisa	325
Makana	325	Makane	729	Makara	369
Mala	279	Malan	235	Malanie	731
Malena	731	Malia	279	Malila	213
Malina	235	Malinda	279	Malinde	674
Malissa	292	Malitta	224	Maliya	257
Maliya	268	Malka	292	Malkah	281
Malla	213	Mallissa	235	Mallorie	314
Mallory	786	Malonie	336	Malorie	371
Malory	753	Malsha	279	Malva	224
Malverna	775	Malvie	628	Malvina	279
Malynda	257	Malynda	268	Mame	685
Mamie	685	Mana	292	Manaba	325
Mancy	112	Manda	246	Mandara	347
Mande	641	Mandi	145	Mandie	641
Mandisa	257	Mandisa	268	Mandlie	674
Mandlin	134	Mandy	123	Manette	246
Mangena	731	Mani	191	Manidatta	382
Manie	696	Manipi	178	Manja	213
Mankalita	371	Mannie	652	Manny	134
Manon	753	Mansa	213	Mansi	112
Mansy	189	Manuela	134	Manuella	167
Manuelle	562	Manya	279	Mapila	257
Mapila	268	Mara	246	Marabel	797
Maralah	369	Maralda	325	Maraline	731
Maralyn	213	Maralyne	718	Maralynne	764
Mararah	336	Marceane	336	Marcela	718
Marcelia	718	Marcella	742	Marcelle	246
Marcellia	742	Marcellina	797	Marcelline	292
Marchella	731	Marchelle	235	Marchita	281
Marci	178	Marcia	279	Marcie	674
Marcile	617	Marcilka	235	Marcilki	134
Marcille	641	Marcina	235	Marcine	639
Marcsa	281	Marcy	156	Mardi	189
Mardie	685	Marea	742	Mareah	731
Marelda	729	Marelee	775	Marelen	235
Marelena	336	Marelene	731	Marella	718
Marelle	213	Maren	696	Marena	797
Maressa	764	Maretta	786	Marette	281
Marfot	731	Marg	123	Marga	224
Margalit	279	Margalo	854	Marganit	292
Margao	821	Margaret	742	Margareta	843
Margarete	347	Margaretha	832	Margarethe	336
Margaretta	865	Margarette	369	Margarita	347

Margary	292	Margaux	584	Marge	628
Margeaux	189	Margerie	224	Margerita	742
Margery	696	Marget	641	Margethe	235
Margetta	764	Margharita	336	Margi	123
Margie	628	Margisa	235	Margisea	731
Margit	145	Margo	729	Margorie	325
Margory	797	Margot	742	Margret	641
Marguerita	145	Marguerite	549	Margueritta	167
Margy	191	Mari	145	Maria	246
Mariam	281	Mariamne	742	Marian	292
Mariana	393	Mariann	257	Mariann	268
Marianna	358	Marianne	753	Maribel	696
Maribelle	235	Maribeth	674	Marica	279
Marice	674	Maridel	628	Marie	641
Mariee	246	Mariel	674	Mariele	279
Marielle	213	Marien	696	Marieta	764
Marietta	786	Mariette	281	Marigold	797
Marihannah	336	Marija	257	Marija	268
Marijan	213	Mari-Jane	718	Marijke	674
Marijo	753	Marilda	224	Marilee	279
Marilen	639	Marilin	134	Marilla	213
Marillyn	145	Marilyn	112	Marilyne	617
Marilynn	167	Marilynne	663	Marima	281
Marin	191	Marina	292	Marinda	246
Marine	696	Marinette	246	Maring	178
Marini	191	Marinie	696	Marinita	224
Marinna	257	Marinna	268	Mariom	786
Marion	797	Mariquilla	595	Maris	156
Marisa	257	Marisa	268	Marisha	246
Mariska	279	Marisol	786	Maritsa	279
Mariya	224	Marja	257	Marja	268
Marjan	213	Marje	652	Marjery	639
Marji	156	Marjie	652	Marjo	753
Marjolaine	448	Marjorie	358	Marjory	731
Marjorye	336	Marjy	134	Marketa	786
Markie	663	Marla	279	Marlais	281
Marlane	731	Marlanna	382	Marle	674
Marleah	764	Marlee	279	Marleen	235
Marlena	731	Marlene	235	Marlenny	663
Marley	652	Marleyne	213	Marli	178
Marlie	674	Marline	639	Marlisa	281
Marlise	685	Marlissa	292	Marlo	775
Marlona	832	Marlowe	336	Marlyn	112
Marna	292	Marne	696	Marnee	292

Marnett	641	Marnette	246	Marney	674
Marni	191	Marnia	292	Marnie	696
Marno	797	Marona	898	Marquita	551
Marren	696	Marriam	281	Marrilee	279
Marrim	189	Marris	156	Marrona	898
Marsha	246	Marsi	156	Marsie	652
Marsiella	729	Marteen	224	Martel	696
Martela	797	Martella	731	Martelle	235
Martene	224	Marteyna	797	Marteyne	292
Martha	257	Martha	268	Marthe	652
Marthena	718	Marti	167	Martie	663
Martika	281	Martina	224	Martine	628
Martinka	246	Martita	281	Martitia	281
Marty	145	Martyna	292	Martyne	696
Martynna	257	Martynna	268	Martynne	652
Marusya	538	Marva	281	Marvel	628
Marvela	729	Marvella	753	Marvelle	257
Marvelle	268	Marvenna	797	Mary	123
Mary Ann	235	Mary Anna	336	Mary Anne	731
Mary Beth	652	Mary Ellen	246	Mary Jane	786
Mary Jo	731	Mary Lou	156	Mary Louise	663
Marya	224	Maryan	279	Maryann	235
Maryanna	336	Maryanne	731	Marybelle	213
Marybeth	652	Marye	628	Maryellen	246
Marygold	775	Mary-Jane	786	Maryjo	731
Maryl	156	Marylee	257	Marylee	268
Marylin	112	Maryline	617	Marylise	663
Marylou	156	Marylyn	189	Maryon	775
Maryruth	437	Marys	134	Marysa	235
Maryse	639	Maryvonne	371	Marzia	235
Masha	246	Masika	279	Matana	325
Matanna	371	Matelda	742	Mathea	753
Mathia	257	Mathia	268	Mathilda	235
Mathilde	639	Matilda	246	Matilde	641
Matrika	281	Matta	281	Mattea	786
Matthea	775	Matthia	279	Matti	189
Mattie	685	Matty	167	Matyash	246
Maud	483	Maude	988	Maudie	988
Maudina	549	Maudine	944	Maura	549
Maure	944	Mauree	549	Maureen	595
Maurene	595	Maurey	922	Mauri	448
Mauricea	178	Mauricette	527	Maurine	999
Maurise	955	Maurita	562	Maurizia	538
Mauve	988	Mave	685	Mavis	191

Mavra	281	Max	112	Maxey	685
Maxi	112	Maxie	617	Maxima	257
Maxima	268	Maxime	652	Maxine	663
Maxy	189	May	123	Maya	224
Maybelle	213	Mayde	663	Maydena	729
Maye	628	Mayme	663	Mazell	696
Mea	641	Mead	685	Meade	281
Meagan	775	Meaghan	764	Meara	742
Mearl	674	Mearr	641	Meave	281
Mechelle	639	Meda	685	Medea	281
Media	685	Medill	551	Medora	382
Meg	527	Mega	628	Megan	674
Megen	178	Meggi	595	Meggie	191
Meggy	573	Meghan	663	Meghann	628
Mehatabel	314	Mehetabel	718	Mehetabelle	347
Mehetabie	775	Mehira	639	Mehitabel	213
Mehitabelle	742	Mehitable	213	Mei	549
Meira	641	Mel	573	Mela	674
Melady	696	Melan	639	Melane	235
Melanee	731	Melania	731	Melanie	235
Melanne	281	Melantha	742	Melanthe	246
Melany	617	Melba	696	Melda	628
Melenee	235	Melenie	639	Melesa	281
Melessa	292	Meli	573	Melia	674
Melicent	189	Melie	178	Melina	639
Melinda	674	Melinde	178	Melisa	685
Melisanda	786	Melisande	281	Melisandra	786
Melise	189	Melisenda	281	Melisende	685
Melisent	167	Melissa	696	Melisse	191
Melita	696	Melitta	628	Melka	696
Mell	516	Mella	617	Melli	516
Mellicent	123	Mellie	112	Mellisa	628
Mellisent	191	Melloney	742	Mellony	246
Melly	584	Melodia	325	Melodie	729
Melody	292	Meloney	718	Melonie	731
Melony	213	Melosa	382	Melta	696
Melva	628	Melvena	279	Melville	189
Melvina	674	Melvine	178	Memdi	538
Memtba	639	Mena	696	Mendeley	652
Mendi	549	Menora	393	Menorah	382
Menta	628	Menzies	191	Meralon	336
Mercedes	639	Merci	573	Mercia	674
Mercie	178	Mercy	551	Merdy	562
Merdyce	191	Mere	145	Meredeth	696

Meredith	191	Meredithe	696	Meredyth	178
Meri	549	Merida	685	Meridel	123
Merideth	191	Meridith	595	Meridyth	573
Meriel	178	Merilee	674	Merilen	134
Merilenna	281	Merilyn	516	Merilyne	112
Merilynn	562	Meris	551	Merissa	663
Merit	562	Meritta	685	Meriwa	696
Merja	652	Merl	573	Merla	674
Merle	178	Merleen	639	Merleena	731
Merlene	639	Merli	573	Merlina	639
Merline	134	Merna	696	Merola	371
Merri	549	Merride	189	Merridie	189
Merrie	145	Merrielle	617	Merrile	178
Merrilee	674	Merrilen	134	Merrili	573
Merrily	551	Merrit	562	Merritt	584
Merritta	685	Merry	527	Mersey	134
Merta	663	Mertah	652	Mertice	191
Mertle	191	Mertyce	178	Meryem	167
Meryl	551	Meryle	156	Mesha	641
Messalina	753	Messina	628	Meta	663
Metabel	224	Metis	573	Metta	685
Metys	551	Mia	145	Miada	281
Miakoda	819	Mica	178	Micada	224
Micaela	718	Micah	167	Micajah	279
Michael	696	Michaela	797	Michaelina	753
Michaeline	257	Michaeline	268	Michaella	731
Michal	191	Miche	562	Micheal	696
Michel	595	Michele	191	Michelina	652
Micheline	156	Michell	538	Michella	639
Michelle	134	Michelline	189	Michi	966
Michiko	685	Micka	191	Mickey	573
Micki	999	Mickie	595	Micky	977
Midge	562	Midori	685	Mieze	134
Migdala	292	Migina	178	Mignon	639
Mignonette	775	Miguela	955	Miguelita	977
Mijota	775	Mijra	156	Mika	167
Mikaela	797	Mikal	191	Miki	966
Mil	977	Mila	178	Milada	224
Mildred	562	Mildrid	966	Milena	639
Milene	134	Mili	977	Miliama	224
Milica	112	Milicent	584	Milijda	134
Milisent	562	Milissent	573	Milka	191
Mill	911	Millee	112	Milli	911
Millicent	527	Millie	516	Millisent	595

Milly	988	Milree	178	Milzie	562
Mimi	988	Mimie	584	Mimosa	797
Mimsy	977	Min	999	Mina	191
Minchen	573	Minda	145	Mindee	145
Mindera	641	Mindi	944	Mindie	549
Mindy	922	Minerva	641	Minetta	641
Minette	145	Mingan	134	Minima	145
Minna	156	Minne	551	Minnette	191
Minni	955	Minnie	551	Minny	933
Minowa	753	Minta	123	Mintha	112
Minthe	516	Miquela	966	Mira	145
Mirabel	696	Mirabella	731	Mirabelle	235
Mirable	696	Miralim	123	Miran	191
Miranda	246	Mirean	696	Mireille	112
Mirella	617	Mirelle	112	Miri	944
Miriam	189	Mirielle	112	Miriem	584
Mirilla	112	Mirja	156	Mirjam	191
Mirle	573	Mirna	191	Miroa	742
Mirtle	595	Mirza	134	Mischa	178
Misha	145	Mishi	944	Missie	562
Missy	944	Misti	977	Misty	955
Misu	358	Mita	167	Mitena	628
Mithuna	415	Mitia	167	Mitra	167
Mituna	426	Mitzi	955	Mitzie	551
Mizella	696	Mo	641	Moana	898
Modesta	325	Modeste	729	Modestia	325
Modestine	775	Modesty	292	Moe	246
Moina	797	Moira	742	Moire	246
Moll	617	Mollee	718	Molli	617
Mollie	213	Molly	685	Mona	797
Monah	786	Monca	731	Moneca	336
Moneka	325	Monela	336	Moneria	393
Monerra	393	Monic	639	Monica	731
Monika	729	Monique	584	Monnitta	797
Monoka	426	Mora	742	Morann	753
Moranna	854	Moranne	358	Morargi	729
Morasha	843	Moraszu	145	Moreah	336
Moreea	843	Moreen	797	Morela	371
Morelda	325	Morena	393	Morene	797
Morgan	775	Morgana	876	Morganica	819
Morganna	832	Morganne	336	Morgen	279
Morgenna	336	Mori	641	Moria	742
Moriah	731	Morie	246	Morissa	764
Morlaine	336	Morna	797	Mornea	393

Name	No.	Name	No.	Name	No.
Morri	641	Morrie	246	Morry	628
Mortina	729	Morvena	347	Morwenna	314
Mosella	325	Moselle	729	Moura	145
Moureen	191	Mourene	191	Mourie	549
Mourina	191	Mourine	595	Moya	729
Moyna	775	Moyra	729	Mozella	393
Mozelle	797	Muguette	764	Muira	448
Muire	843	Mulanna	584	Muliya	459
Muna	494	Munda	448	Mundanna	551
Muneva	944	Mura	448	Muraco	178
Murdena	944	Murial	472	Muriel	876
Muriell	819	Murielle	415	Murrell	819
Musetta	999	Musette	494	Musidora	191
Mya	123	Mycah	145	Mychael	674
Mychal	178	Myfanwy	178	Myleen	112
Mylene	112	Myna	178	Myolean	314
Myoleen	718	Myolena	314	Myolene	718
Myra	123	Myraddin	167	Myrale	652
Myranda	224	Myriam	167	Myrile	551
Myrilla	189	Myrlann	167	Myrle	551
Myrlene	112	Myrna	178	Myrt	764
Myrta	145	Myrtia	145	Myrtice	573
Myrtie	549	Myrtilla	112	Myrtille	516
Myrtis	955	Myrtle	573	Na	156
Nada	292	Nadean	753	Nadeen	257
Nadeen	268	Nadege	279	Nadena	753
Nadene	257	Nadene	268	Nadenka	775
Nadette	246	Nadia	292	Nadine	652
Nadiya	279	Nady	178	Nadya	279
Nadyusha	573	Nadzia	281	Nagida	279
Nahele	279	Naiada	393	Naida	292
Nairne	617	Nalani	246	Nama	292
Namia	292	Namie	696	Nan	112
Nana	213	Nance	641	Nancee	246
Nancey	628	Nanci	145	Nancie	641
Nancy	123	Nandi	156	Nandie	652
Nanete	235	Nanetta	753	Nanette	257
Nanette	268	Nanettja	764	Nani	112
Nanice	641	Nanine	663	Nanni	167
Nannie	663	Nannim	112	Nanny	145
Nanon	764	Naoma	898	Naomal	832
Naomi	797	Napaea	832	Napea	731
Napia	235	Nara	257	Nara	268
Narain	213	Narda	292	Nari	156

Narie	652	Nariko	775	Narilla	224
Narinda	257	Narinda	268	Nasha	257
Nasha	268	Nashie	652	Nashira	257
Nashira	268	Nashota	876	Nastassia	314
Nasya	246	Nat	178	Nata	279
Natacha	393	Natala	314	Natale	718
Natalee	314	Natalia	314	Natalie	718
Natalina	369	Nataline	764	Natalya	382
Natasha	371	Natelee	718	Natene	235
Natesa	786	Nathalia	393	Nathalie	797
Nathanaelle	483	Nathane	729	Nathania	325
Nathene	224	Nathi	167	Nathollie	336
Natica	213	Natie	674	Natika	292
Natike	696	Natividad	213	Natka	292
Nattanya	336	Nattie	696	Natty	178
Navella	764	Nayati	257	Nayati	268
Nazele	279	Nazlee	279	Neala	786
Neale	281	Nebula	911	Neci	584
Neda	696	Nedda	641	Neddy	527
Nedi	595	Nedia	696	Nediva	641
Neely	167	Neema	292	Neenah	292
Neety	156	Neida	696	Neila	685
Neile	189	Neilla	628	Neille	123
Neinah	696	Neisha	652	Nel	584
Nela	685	Nelda	639	Nele	189
Neli	584	Nelia	685	Nelie	189
Nelka	617	Nell	527	Nella	628
Nelli	527	Nellie	123	Nellwyn	516
Nelly	595	Nemia	696	Nenah	696
Neola	382	Neoma	393	Neona	314
Nepa	639	Nera	652	Nerice	189
Nerima	696	Nerine	112	Nerissa	674
Nerita	674	Nessa	674	Nessi	573
Nessia	674	Nessie	178	Nessy	551
Nesta	685	Netalae	314	Netia	674
Netie	178	Netika	696	Netka	696
Netta	696	Netti	595	Nettie	191
Netty	573	Neva	696	Nevada	742
Nevan	652	Nevin	551	Nevsa	617
Neya	639	Neysa	641	Neza	641
Nezia	641	Nezza	639	Niabi	178
Niaoima	898	Niccola	753	Niccole	257
Niccole	268	Nichol	617	Nichola	718
Nichole	213	Nicholina	764	Nicholle	246

Nicki	911	Nickie	516	Nicky	988
Nicol	628	Nicola	729	Nicole	224
Nicolea	325	Nicoletta	369	Nicolette	764
Nicoli	628	Nicolina	775	Nicoline	279
Nicolle	257	Nicolle	268	Nicollette	797
Nida	191	Nidea	696	Nieda	696
Nienah	696	Nika	178	Nike	573
Niki	977	Nikki	999	Nikky	977
Nikola	718	Nikoletta	358	Nikolia	718
Nila	189	Nilda	134	Nili	988
Nillie	527	Nima	191	Nina	112
Nineta	639	Ninetta	652	Ninette	156
Ninita	134	Ninnetta	617	Ninnette	112
Ninon	663	Niobe	279	Nipa	134
Nipsey	527	Nishera	652	Nishi	955
Niss	977	Nissa	178	Nisse	573
Nissie	573	Nissim	922	Nissy	955
Nita	178	Nitara	279	Nitsa	189
Nituna	437	Nixie	527	Niya	134
Niyann	145	Niyanna	246	Niyanne	641
Niza	145	Nizana	292	Noami	797
Nodie	292	Noel	281	Noela	382
Noelani	347	Noelie	786	Noell	224
Noella	325	Noelle	729	Noelly	292
Noellyn	257	Noellyn	268	Noelyn	224
Noemi	292	Noemie	797	Noga	731
Nohma	786	Nokomis	336	Nola	786
Nolae	382	Nolana	843	Nolcha	718
Noleta	314	Nolie	281	Nolita	718
Nollie	224	Nolly	696	Nolwenn	257
Nolwenn	268	Nomi	696	Nomida	742
Nomie	292	Nona	718	Nonah	797
Noni	617	Nonie	213	Nonna	764
Nonnah	753	Noor	358	Noorali	483
Nora	753	Norah	742	Norberta	393
Norberte	797	Norbertha	382	Norberthe	786
Nordica	731	Nordika	729	Norea	358
Noreen	718	Norene	718	Nori	652
Norina	718	Norine	213	Norita	775
Norma	797	Normi	696	Normie	292
Norna	718	Norrey	235	Norri	652
Norrie	257	Norrie	268	Norry	639
Noura	156	Nova	797	Novak	729
Novelia	336	Novella	369	Novena	358

Novia	797	Nuala	584	Numa	494
Numidia	448	Nuna	415	Nunki	336
Nuralee	584	Nuralie	988	Nuria	459
Nurianna	562	Nurianne	966	Nuriel	887
Nusi	369	Nydia	178	Nyssa	156
Nyura	437	Nyusha	437	Nyx	729
Oana	854	Obelia	358	Octavia	898
Octavie	393	October	876	Odel	279
Odele	775	Odelet	797	Odelette	325
Odelia	371	Odelie	775	Odelinda	371
Odella	314	Odelle	718	Odena	393
Odera	347	Odessa	369	Odetta	382
Odette	786	Odila	775	Odile	279
Odilia	775	Odilla	718	Odille	213
Odissan	729	Oethe	718	Ofelia	393
Ofilia	797	Okalani	819	Oko	325
Okrika	742	Ola	731	Olathe	347
Olayinka	887	Olena	382	Olenka	314
Olesia	347	Olesya	325	Oleta	358
Olethea	843	Olga	718	Olia	731
Oliana	887	Olija	742	Olimpia	753
Olimpie	257	Olimpie	268	Olinda	731
Olisa	742	Olive	279	Olivette	729
Olivia	775	Olly	641	Olva	775
Olympe	235	Olympia	731	Olympie	235
Oma	742	Ombeline	753	Omena	393
Omusa	156	Ona	753	Onani	718
Onawa	819	Ondine	257	Ondine	268
Ondrea	393	Oneida	393	Onele	786
Onella	325	Oni	652	Onida	797
Onita	775	Oola	437	Oona	459
Oonagh	426	Opal	718	Opalina	865
Opaline	369	Ophelia	393	Ophelie	797
Oprah	764	Ora	797	Orabel	358
Orabella	483	Orabelle	887	Orah	786
Oral	731	Oralee	832	Oralia	832
Oralie	336	Ordeen	797	Ordelia	371
Ordella	314	Ordene	797	Orea	393
Oredola	977	Orel	235	Orela	336
Orelee	336	Orelia	336	Orelie	731
Orenda	393	Ori	696	Oriana	854
Oriane	358	Orianna	819	Orianne	314
Orie	292	Oriel	235	Oriole	832
Orji	617	Orla	731	Orlanda	832

Orlande	336	Orlann	742	Orlanna	843
Orlea	336	Orleen	786	Orlena	382
Orlenda	336	Orlene	786	Orlina	786
Orna	753	Ornice	281	Ornita	775
Orpah	764	Orsa	718	Orsola	448
Ortensia	382	Orva	742	Osanna	821
Osanya	843	Ossama	865	Otha	718
Othelia	347	Othilia	742	Othilla	775
Otila	753	Ottavia	887	Ottavie	382
Ottilee	775	Ottilia	775	Ottilie	279
Ouida	145	Ovila	775	Oya	775
Ozora	483	Page	652	Paige	652
Paka	292	Palika	235	Palila	246
Pallas	257	Pallas	268	Palma	257
Palma	268	Palmela	786	Palmer	652
Palmira	257	Palmira	268	Paloma	854
Palometa	472	Palomita	876	Palona	865
Pam	123	Pamela	753	Pamelina	718
Pamella	786	Pamelyn	685	Pammi	167
Pammie	663	Pammy	145	Pamphila	224
Pamphile	628	Panchito	775	Pandita	292
Pandora	876	Pani	134	Pansie	641
Pansy	123	Panthea	742	Panthia	246
Panya	213	Paola	819	Paolina	865
Papina	213	Paquerette	112	Paquita	584
Paquito	189	Park	191	Parke	696
Parnella	797	Parnelle	292	Parthenia	742
Pascale	753	Pascaline	718	Pat	191
Pati	191	Patia	292	Patience	281
Patienza	742	Patrica	235	Patrice	639
Patricia	235	Patricio	731	Patrina	257
Patrina	268	Patrizia	281	Patsie	617
Patsy	189	Patte	628	Pattee	224
Patti	123	Pattie	628	Patty	191
Paula	516	Paule	911	Pauleen	562
Paulene	562	Pauletta	156	Paulette	551
Pauletto	652	Pauli	415	Paulie	911
Paulin	461	Paulina	562	Pauline	966
Paulita	538	Pauly	483	Pavela	753
Pavia	224	Pavla	257	Pavla	268
Pavlina	213	Paylee	281	Payleesa	393
Paz	167	Pazice	696	Pazit	189
Peace	213	Pearl	617	Pearla	718
Pearlamina	819	Pearle	213	Pearlie	213

Pedzie	112	Peg	551	Pegeen	617
Pegene	617	Peggi	538	Peggie	134
Peggy	516	Pelage	281	Pelagia	786
Pelcia	641	Pelipa	685	Pemba	641
Pen	538	Penda	674	Penelopa	843
Penelope	347	Peni	538	Penina	685
Penne	189	Penni	584	Pennie	189
Penny	562	Penta	652	Penthea	246
Penthia	641	Peny	516	Peony	213
Pepi	551	Pepillo	224	Pepita	674
Peppi	538	Perdita	641	Perfecta	292
Peri	573	Peria	674	Perl	516
Perla	617	Perle	112	Perlette	652
Perlie	112	Perlina	663	Perline	167
Permilla	685	Pernella	292	Pernelle	696
Peroline	764	Perpetua	573	Perrette	628
Perri	573	Perrine	134	Perry	551
Persephone	314	Persis	595	Pet	595
Peta	696	Petra	696	Petrina	652
Petrine	156	Petronella	821	Petronelle	325
Petronia	358	Petronilla	325	Petronille	729
Petula	933	Petulah	922	Petunia	955
Phaedra	718	Phaidra	213	Phebe	189
Phedra	617	Phedre	112	Phelia	696
Phemie	112	Phil	999	Phila	191
Philana	257	Philana	268	Philanthe	663
Philberta	641	Philbertha	639	Philberthe	134
Philiberte	145	Philien	551	Philina	156
Philine	551	Philipa	178	Philippa	156
Philippe	551	Philippine	516	Philis	911
Phillane	685	Phillida	178	Phillie	538
Phillipa	112	Phillippa	189	Phillis	944
Philly	911	Philmen	595	Philomela	371
Philomena	393	Philomene	797	Phoebe	786
Phoenix	281	Pholma	742	Phyl	797
Phylis	988	Phyllida	156	Phyllis	922
Phyllita	134	Phyllys	549	Pia	178
Pier	573	Pierette	628	Pierrette	628
Pietra	696	Pilan	167	Pilanna	224
Pilar	112	Pili	911	Pilisi	922
Pinga	112	Piper	551	Pippa	134
Pippi	933	Pippy	911	Pita	191
Placida	281	Placidia	281	Platona	887
Pollete	764	Pollie	246	Polly	628

Polly Ann	731	Polly Anna	832	Polly Anne	336
Pollyann	731	Pollyanna	832	Pomona	472
Poni	639	Poppaca	865	Poppy	617
Porcia	718	Portia	797	Posala	821
Powa	731	Prima	123	Primalia	257
Primalia	268	Primavera	764	Primmie	562
Primrose	235	Primula	459	Prior	674
Pris	988	Prisca	123	Priscella	685
Priscilla	189	Prisilla	156	Prissie	595
Prissy	977	Prospera	369	Pru	371
Prud	325	Prudence	415	Prudentia	999
Prudi	325	Prudie	821	Prudy	393
Prue	876	Prunella	999	Prunelle	494
Pryor	652	Psyche	584	Pualani	562
Pulcherie	437	Purity	371	Pyrena	617
Pyrenia	617	Pythea	663	Pythia	167
Queena	549	Queenee	549	Queenie	944
Quenby	843	Quenlia	977	Quenna	999
Quennie	494	Quentin	821	Querida	933
Questa	922	Quinn	393	Quinta	461
Quintana	527	Quintessa	988	Quintie	865
Quintilla	437	Quintina	426	Quiterie	415
Rabi	123	Rabiah	213	Rachael	753
Rachel	652	Rachele	257	Rachele	268
Rachelle	281	Rachie	628	Rachilde	696
Racine	685	Radella	718	Radenka	729
Radinka	224	Radmilla	257	Radmilla	268
Rae	696	Raeann	718	Rafaela	898
Rafaelia	898	Rafaella	832	Rahel	628
Rahela	729	Rain	156	Raina	257
Raina	268	Raine	652	Rainey	639
Raini	156	Raisa	213	Raissa	224
Raisse	628	Raizel	628	Rakel	652
Ralina	281	Ralphina	257	Ralphina	268
Rama	246	Ramona	898	Ramonda	843
Rana	257	Rana	268	Ranalda	336
Randa	292	Rande	696	Randee	292
Randene	257	Randene	268	Randi	191
Randie	696	Randy	178	Ranee	257
Ranee	268	Ranetta	797	Rani	156
Rania	257	Rania	268	Ranice	685
Ranique	944	Ranit	178	Ranita	279
Ranite	674	Ranitta	292	Ranitte	696
Ranna	213	Raphaela	898	Raphaelle	336

Raquel	922	Raquela	123	Rashida	246
Rashidi	145	Rasia	213	Raven	696
Ravida	281	Ray	178	Rayana	336
Raychel	639	Rayella	742	Rayelle	246
Rayette	224	Rayjie	685	Raylynn	191
Raylynne	696	Raymona	876	Raymonda	821
Raymonde	325	Rayna	235	Raynell	696
Rayshell	641	Raz	189	Razela	729
Razell	652	Raziel	628	Razilee	224
Razilen	674	Rea	696	Reba	628
Rebeca	257	Rebeca	268	Rebecca	281
Rebecka	279	Rebeka	246	Rebekah	235
Rebekkah	257	Rebekkah	268	Red	549
Reddy	562	Redi	549	Ree	191
Reeba	224	Reena	257	Reena	268
Reeta	224	Reeva	246	Rega	674
Regan	639	Reggi	551	Reggie	156
Regina	639	Regine	134	Rei	595
Reiko	224	Reina	652	Reine	156
Reini	551	Reja	617	Rejeen	663
Rejene	663	Relba	652	Remata	764
Remi	549	Remick	595	Remie	145
Remina	696	Remja	652	Remona	393
Remy	527	Rena	652	Renaat	775
Renae	257	Renae	268	Renata	775
Renate	279	Renato	371	Rence	189
Rene	156	Renea	257	Renea	268
Renee	652	Renell	123	Renelle	628
Renie	156	Renita	674	Rennetta	257
Rennetta	268	Rennie	112	Renny	584
Reseda	257	Reseda	268	Resi	516
Resida	652	Reta	628	Retha	617
Reva	641	Rexana	729	Rexanna	775
Rey	573	Reylana	764	Reyna	639
Rezi	584	Rezine	145	Rhea	685
Rheba	617	Rheta	617	Rhetta	639
Rheva	639	Rhiana	246	Rhianna	292
Rhoda	731	Rhodantha	898	Rhode	235
Rhodes	246	Rhodi	639	Rhodia	731
Rhodie	235	Rhodina	786	Rhody	617
Rhona	742	Rhonda	786	Rhonwen	257
Rhonwen	268	Rhue	887	Ria	191
Riana	257	Riana	268	Riane	652
Rianna	213	Riba	123	Rica	134

Ricadonna	887	Ricarda	279	Ricca	167
Richarde	663	Richel	551	Richela	652
Richella	685	Richelle	189	Richia	123
Rickee	156	Rickey	538	Ricki	955
Rickie	551	Ricky	933	Rida	145
Riena	652	Riesa	617	Rihana	246
Rija	112	Rijann	123	Rijanna	224
Rijean	663	Rijeanne	224	Rika	123
Riki	922	Rikki	944	Rila	134
Rilla	167	Rille	562	Rillete	189
Rimona	797	Rina	156	Rindi	999
Risa	112	Riska	134	Rita	123
Ritsa	134	Riva	145	Rivalee	279
Rivi	944	Rivkah	156	Rivy	922
Riza	189	Ro	696	Roalda	876
Roana	854	Roann	718	Roanna	819
Roanne	314	Robbi	641	Robbia	742
Robbie	246	Robbin	696	Robby	628
Robbyn	674	Robena	371	Robenia	371
Roberta	347	Roberte	742	Robertha	336
Roberthe	731	Robertine	797	Robi	628
Robin	674	Robina	775	Robinet	292
Robinett	224	Robinette	729	Robinia	775
Robyn	652	Robyna	753	Roch	628
Rochalla	887	Rochalle	382	Rochell	281
Rochella	382	Rochelle	786	Rochette	764
Roda	742	Roddana	843	Roddie	281
Roddy	663	Roderica	371	Rodericka	393
Rodi	641	Rodie	246	Rodina	797
Rohana	843	Rohane	347	Rohanna	898
Rohanne	393	Rohesia	393	Rois	617
Rokie	224	Rola	731	Roland	731
Rolanda	832	Rolande	336	Rolisa	742
Rollanda	865	Roma	742	Romain	797
Romaine	393	Romancita	854	Romella	314
Romelle	718	Romeyn	279	Romhilda	718
Romhilde	213	Romilda	729	Romilde	224
Romina	797	Romney	279	Romola	472
Romona	494	Romonda	448	Romy	628
Rona	753	Ronae	358	Ronalda	832
Ronalde	336	Ronaye	336	Ronda	797
Rondalin	786	Ronee	753	Ronel	281
Ronelda	336	Roni	652	Ronia	753
Ronica	786	Ronice	281	Ronli	685

Ronna	718	Ronnae	314	Ronnee	718
Ronni	617	Ronnica	742	Ronnie	213
Ronny	685	Rora	797	Rori	696
Rorie	292	Rorry	674	Rory	674
Ros	617	Rosa	718	Rosabel	369
Rosabella	494	Rosabelle	898	Rosaeen	865
Rosalee	843	Rosaleen	898	Rosalen	393
Rosalene	898	Rosalia	843	Rosalie	347
Rosalina	898	Rosalind	742	Rosalinda	843
Rosalinde	347	Rosaline	393	Rosalyn	775
Rosalynd	729	Rosalynde	325	Rosalyne	371
Rosalynn	731	Rosalynne	336	Rosamond	459
Rosamonda	551	Rosamund	156	Rosamunda	257
Rosamunda	268	Rosana	865	Rosann	729
Rosanna	821	Rosanne	325	Rosaria	819
Rosario	415	Rose	213	Rose Ann	325
Rose Anne	821	Rose Lynn	235	Roseann	325
Roseanna	426	Roseanne	821	Rosel	246
Roselane	898	Roselani	393	Roselin	292
Roseline	797	Rosella	371	Roselle	775
Rosellen	731	Roselyn	279	Rosemaria	459
Rose-Maria	459	Rosemarie	854	Rose-Marie	854
Rosemary	336	Rose-Mary	336	Rosemond	854
Rosemonde	459	Rosemund	551	Rosena	369
Rosene	764	Roseta	336	Rosetta	358
Rosette	753	Roshelle	764	Rosia	718
Rosie	213	Rosina	764	Rosita	731
Rosja	729	Roslin	696	Roslind	641
Roslindis	652	Roslyn	674	Roslyne	279
Roslynn	639	Rosmunda	156	Rossanne	336
Rosy	685	Rothnee	764	Rouvina	191
Roux	966	Row	652	Rowe	257
Rowe	268	Rowena	314	Rowenna	369
Rox	663	Roxana	821	Roxane	325
Roxann	775	Roxanna	876	Roxanne	371
Roxelana	459	Roxet	281	Roxey	246
Roxi	663	Roxina	729	Roxine	224
Roxy	641	Royal	718	Royale	314
Royall	742	Royane	336	Royce	213
Royceen	764	Roz	685	Roza	786
Rozalee	821	Rozalen	371	Rozalie	325
Rozalin	775	Rozalind	729	Rozaline	371
Rozalle	358	Rozalynne	314	Rozamond	437
Rozanna	898	Rozanne	393	Roze	281

Rozeel	729	Rozeen	742	Rozele	729
Rozelin	279	Rozella	358	Rozello	854
Rozene	742	Rozenn	292	Rozie	281
Rozin	641	Rozina	742	Rozine	246
Rozyte	281	Ruana	551	Rubee	426
Ruberta	944	Rubetta	966	Rubette	461
Rubi	325	Rubia	426	Rubie	821
Rubina	472	Ruby	393	Ruchi	325
Rudella	911	Rudelle	415	Rudi	347
Rudia	448	Rue	898	Ruella	966
Rufina	426	Rula	437	Rumunda	742
Ruperta	999	Rurika	426	Rusti	336
Rusty	314	Ruth	314	Ruth Ann	426
Ruthann	426	Ruthanne	922	Ruthe	819
Ruthi	314	Ruthie	819	Ruzina	448
Ryann	189	Ryanne	685	Rycca	145
Ryda	123	Ryla	112	Ryma	123
Saadi	257	Saadi	268	Saba	235
Sabeena	382	Sabena	786	Sabin	189
Sabina	281	Sabine	685	Sabinna	246
Sabinus	494	Sabra	235	Sabriam	279
Sabrin	189	Sabrina	281	Sabrine	685
Sabrinna	246	Sacha	235	Sachi	134
Sachiko	753	Sada	257	Sada	268
Sadella	729	Sadey	639	Sadi	156
Sadie	652	Sadira	257	Sadira	268
Sadye	639	Sadzi	145	Safarin	235
Safarina	336	Sagara	382	Sage	685
Sagi	189	Sagita	213	Sagitta	235
Saidee	257	Saidee	268	Sain	167
Sairey	685	Saja	224	Sakari	235
Sakima	279	Sakina	281	Sakti	156
Sakuna	584	Sakura	538	Sal	145
Sala	246	Salaidh	279	Salama	382
Salena	797	Salene	292	Salil	178
Salim	189	Salima	281	Salina	292
Sallee	279	Salli	178	Sallie	674
Sally	156	Saloma	887	Salome	382
Salomi	786	Salvia	281	Salvina	246
Sam	156	Samala	382	Samale	786
Saman	213	Samantha	325	Samara	358
Samaria	358	Samaya	336	Sameh	641
Samein	617	Samella	729	Samelle	224
Sammie	696	Sammy	178	Samora	854

Samuela	189	Samuella	123	Samuelle	527
Samuru	753	Sancha	281	Sanchia	281
Sancia	292	Sande	617	Sandee	213
Sandi	112	Sandie	617	Sandra	213
Sandrine	663	Sandro	718	Sandy	189
Sandye	685	Sani	167	Sanna	224
Santina	246	Sanura	562	Sanya	246
Sapata	314	Sapphira	257	Sapphira	268
Sapphire	652	Sappho	753	Saqu	494
Sara	213	Sarad	257	Sarad	268
Sarah	292	Saraha	393	Saraid	257
Saraid	268	Saree	213	Sarena	764
Saretta	753	Sarette	257	Sarette	268
Sarey	685	Sari	112	Saria	213
Sarika	235	Saril	145	Sarine	663
Sarita	235	Sarolta	865	Sasa	224
Sascha	246	Sasha	213	Sashenka	786
Satinka	213	Saundra	516	Saura	516
Savanna	369	Savannah	358	Saveta	775
Savilla	224	Savina	213	Saxona	832
Sayde	639	Saydesa	742	Sayre	685
Scarlet	696	Scarlett	628	Scarletta	729
Schifra	191	Scylla	189	Sean	663
Seana	764	Season	371	Sebastiana	821
Sebastiane	325	Sebastianna	876	Sebastianne	371
Sebastienna	371	Sebastienne	775	Sebbie	156
Secunda	944	Seda	652	Sedee	652
Sedna	617	Sedye	134	Seema	257
Seema	268	Segolene	371	Seja	628
Seki	538	Sela	641	Selda	685
Seleen	696	Selena	292	Selene	696
Selestina	235	Selewine	652	Selia	641
Selie	145	Selima	685	Selimah	674
Selina	696	Selinda	641	Seline	191
Selma	685	Semele	685	Semelia	281
Semira	652	Sena	663	Senalda	742
Senta	685	Seonaid	314	Sephira	674
Sephora	371	Septima	652	Sera	617
Serafina	731	Serafine	235	Seraphina	731
Seraphine	235	Serene	663	Sergine	145
Serhilda	674	Serhilde	178	Serilda	685
Serilde	189	Servane	213	Sesha	617
Sessue	437	Setsu	843	Severine	617
Shada	246	Shae	696	Shahar	281

Shaina	257	Shaina	268	Shaine	652
Shakeh	617	Shalom	775	Shamie	641
Shammara	382	Shana	257	Shana	268
Shanan	213	Shanda	292	Shandee	292
Shandeigh	663	Shandell	663	Shandie	696
Shandra	292	Shandy	178	Shane	652
Shani	156	Shanie	652	Shanin	112
Shanleigh	652	Shanley	663	Shanly	167
Shanna	213	Shannah	292	Shanneh	696
Shannen	663	Shannon	764	Shanon	718
Shanta	279	Shantee	279	Shappa	257
Shappa	268	Shar	191	Shara	292
Sharai	292	Sharee	292	Sharen	652
Sharena	753	Sharette	246	Shari	191
Sharie	696	Sharie Lea	336	Sharin	156
Sharita	224	Sharity	191	Sharla	235
Sharlanna	347	Sharlannah	336	Sharleen	281
Sharlene	281	Sharline	685	Sharllyne	696
Sharlyne	663	Sharma	246	Sharmell	617
Sharmin	191	Sharmina	292	Sharol	731
Sharole	336	Sharon	753	Sharona	854
Sharra	292	Sharra-Lee	336	Sharri	191
Sharron	753	Sharry	178	Sharyeen	235
Sharyl	112	Sharynne	685	Shaun	459
Shauna	551	Shawn	112	Shawna	213
Shawnee	213	Shay	178	Shayla	213
Shaylah	292	Shaylyn	145	Shaylynn	191
Shaylynne	696	Shayna	235	Shayne	639
Shea	696	Sheba	628	Shee	191
Sheehan	246	Sheela	235	Sheelagh	292
Sheelah	224	Sheena	257	Sheena	268
Sheeree	292	Sheila	639	Sheilah	628
Shel	538	Shela	639	Shelagh	696
Shelbi	551	Shelby	538	Shelia	639
Sheliah	628	Shell	562	Shelley	145
Shelli	562	Shellie	167	Shelly	549
Shemara	742	Shena	652	Shenla	685
Shenoa	358	Sheona	358	Sher	595
Shera	696	Sheralea	336	Shera-Lea	336
Sheran	652	Sherbina	674	Shere	191
Sheree	696	Sheren	156	Sherena	257
Sherena	268	Sheri	595	Sherie	191
Sherill	562	Sherilyn	562	Sherilynn	527
Sherilynne	123	Sherlee	639	Sherley	112

Sherline	189	Sherole	731	Sheron	257
Sheron	268	Sherona	358	Sherri	595
Sherrie	191	Sherril	538	Sherrill	562
Sherrin	551	Sherron	257	Sherron	268
Sherry	573	Sherye	178	Sheryl	516
Sheryle	112	Sherylen	167	Sherylyn	549
Sherylyne	145	Sherylynn	595	Sherylynne	191
Sheylah	696	Sheyona	336	Shiari	191
Shifra	167	Shifrah	156	Shika	123
Shina	156	Shir	999	Shira	191
Shirah	189	Shiran	156	Shiri	999
Shirie	595	Shirin	955	Shirina	156
Shirl	933	Shirlee	134	Shirleen	189
Shirlene	189	Shirley	516	Shirlie	538
Shirlina	189	Shirline	584	Shizue	887
Shizuka	415	Shona	753	Shoshana	854
Shumana	595	Shura	494	Shuri	393
Shushanah	549	Sian	167	Sianna	224
Sib	933	Sibbie	551	Sibby	933
Sibeal	663	Sibel	562	Sibell	595
Sibella	696	Sibelle	191	Sibeta	652
Sibie	538	Sibilla	191	Sibille	595
Sibley	549	Sibyl	944	Sibyline	595
Sibylla	178	Sibylle	573	Sid	955
Sidney	584	Sidonia	718	Sidonie	213
Sidra	156	Sidria	156	Siegfride	191
Siera	617	Sierra	617	Sigfreda	696
Sigfrieda	696	Signa	145	Sigrath	191
Sigrid	933	Sigrud	336	Sigurd	336
Sihu	393	Siko	639	Sil	944
Sile	549	Sileas	652	Silence	134
Silivia	189	Silke	562	Silva	189
Silvain	145	Silvana	246	Silvano	742
Silvia	189	Silvie	584	Silvious	999
Sima	156	Simah	145	Simma	191
Simmie	595	Simona	718	Simone	213
Simonetta	358	Simonette	753	Sindee	112
Sindie	516	Sindy	988	Sine	562
Sinead	617	Siobahn	775	Sireen	167
Sirena	663	Sirene	167	Sisely	538
Sisika	145	Sisile	551	Sisle	551
Sisley	538	Sissie	538	Sissy	911
Sita	134	Siti	933	Situla	461
Siuban	483	Siusan	472	Siva	156

Skye	516	Skyla	145	Skylar	145
Skyler	549	Slena	696	Slenia	696
Sloane	393	Sodonne	865	Sofi	674
Sofia	775	Sofian	731	Sofie	279
Sofiya	753	Sofya	753	Sojee	729
Solana	898	Solange	371	Solann	753
Solanna	854	Soledad	336	Solenne	753
Soline	292	Solita	764	Solly	652
Solvig	663	Soma	753	Somhairle	371
Sommer	292	Sona	764	Sondra	718
Sonel	292	Songan	797	Sonia	764
Sonja	775	Sonni	628	Sonnie	224
Sonny	696	Sonya	742	Sonyura	145
Sonyusha	145	Soph	674	Sophey	257
Sophey	268	Sophi	674	Sophia	775
Sophie	279	Sophronia	437	Sophus	988
Sophy	652	Sora	718	Sorcha	731
Sosanna	832	Soso	325	Sozanna	819
Sozanne	314	Sozanno	415	Sozano	459
Spica	123	Spring	922	Stace	663
Stacey	641	Staci	167	Stacie	663
Stacy	145	Stafani	257	Stafani	268
Stalina	224	Star	134	Starlene	224
Starlin	123	Starr	134	Stasa	246
Stasie	641	Stefa	696	Stefanee	753
Stefani	652	Stefanie	257	Stefanie	268
Steffane	224	Steffany	696	Steffi	562
Steffie	167	Stell	595	Stella	696
Stellara	797	Stelle	191	Stepfanie	235
Stepha	696	Stephana	753	Stephane	257
Stephane	268	Stephanette	797	Stephani	652
Stephania	753	Stephanie	257	Stephanie	268
Stephannie	213	Stephena	257	Stephena	268
Stephenia	257	Stephenia	268	Stephenie	652
Stephi	595	Stephie	191	Stephine	156
Stepka	639	Stesha	639	Stevana	731
Stevania	731	Stevena	235	Stevenia	235
Stevie	178	Stevona	336	Stina	189
Storm	674	Stormi	674	Stormie	279
Stormy	652	Strella	696	Sudi	358
Sue	819	Sue Ann	922	Sue Anna	123
Sue Anne	527	Sueann	922	Sueanna	123
Sueanne	527	Suela	944	Suelita	966
Sugi	382	Suje	821	Sukey	819

Suki	336	Suky	314	Sula	448
Sumer	854	Sumi	358	Summer	898
Suni	369	Sunny	393	Surata	538
Surender	415	Suresh	819	Suri	314
Surina	461	Surinna	426	Surjid	369
Surya	483	Susan	472	Susana	573
Susanetta	123	Susann	437	Susanna	538
Susannah	527	Susanne	933	Suse	821
Susel	854	Susen	876	Susette	461
Susi	325	Susie	821	Susy	393
Suti	336	Sutki	358	Suzamni	494
Suzan	459	Suzanna	516	Suzanne	911
Suzeda	944	Suzel	832	Suzen	854
Suzetta	944	Suzette	448	Suzi	393
Suzie	898	Suzin	358	Suzu	696
Suzy	371	Suzzy	369	Svetlana	764
Svetta	696	Sybella	674	Sybil	944
Sybila	145	Sybilla	178	Sybille	573
Sybley	527	Sybyl	562	Syd	753
Sydel	562	Sydelle	191	Sydney	562
Syeira	685	Syl	742	Sylva	167
Sylvana	224	Sylvette	112	Sylvia	167
Sylviane	628	Sylvie	562	Syna	145
Syne	549	Tabatha	358	Tabbi	167
Tabbie	663	Tabbitha	279	Tabby	145
Tabia	246	Tabib	167	Tabina	292
Tabitha	257	Tabitha	268	Tabithe	652
Tace	652	Taci	156	Tacie	652
Tacita	279	Tacy	134	Tacye	639
Tadi	167	Tadita	281	Taffy	134
Taha	213	Tahir	112	Taipa	292
Taka	246	Takala	371	Takara	347
Takeko	369	Takenya	775	Taki	145
Tala	257	Tala	268	Talia	257
Talia	268	Talli	189	Tallia	281
Tallie	685	Tallou	189	Tallu	483
Tallula	527	Tallulah	516	Tally	167
Talmai	292	Talora	854	Talula	584
Talyah	224	Tamara	369	Tamarah	358
Tamarra	369	Tamas	279	Tamasine	731
Tamena	729	Tamera	764	Tami	167
Tamiko	786	Tamjin	134	Tamma	213
Tammany	246	Tammara	314	Tammi	112
Tammie	617	Tammy	189	Tamsin	134

Tamzan	213	Tamzen	617	Tana	279
Tanaka	393	Tandem	663	Tandi	123
Tandie	628	Tandy	191	Tangerine	213
Tanhya	246	Tani	178	Tania	279
Tanis	189	Tanja	281	Tanjey	663
Tannie	639	Tannis	145	Tannjet	663
Tanny	112	Tansley	696	Tansy	167
Tanya	257	Tanya	268	Tara	224
Tara Lee	358	Tara Lyn	281	Tara Lynn	246
Tara Lynne	742	Tarah	213	Taralee	358
Taralen	718	Taran	279	Tarana	371
Taras	235	Tareyn	652	Taronne	336
Tarra	224	Tarrah	213	Tarres	639
Tarris	134	Tarryn	156	Taryn	156
Taryne	652	Tasarla	369	Tasha	224
Tasia	235	Tasida	279	Tassie	641
Tasya	213	Tate	641	Tatiana	393
Tatiania	393	Tatianna	358	Tatienne	257
Tatienne	268	Tatum	483	Taura	527
Taurin	472	Taurina	573	Taurine	977
Taves	674	Tavi	167	Tavie	663
Tavis	178	Tavy	145	Tawia	279
Tawnie	639	Tawnya	213	Tawrina	235
Tawrine	639	Tawsha	279	Tayler	639
Taylor	731	Taylore	336	Tazee	213
Tazena	764	Tazenn	628	Teca	652
Tecla	685	Ted	562	Tedda	617
Teddi	516	Teddie	112	Teddy	584
Tedi	562	Tedra	663	Teena	279
Tekla	674	Temina	628	Temperance	731
Tempest	178	Tempesta	279	Tempeste	674
Tennora	336	Teodora	966	Teodore	461
Tera	628	Terchie	145	Teree	628
Terena	279	Terencia	213	Terentia	292
Teresa	235	Terese	639	Teresina	281
Teresita	257	Teresita	268	Teressa	246
Terez	112	Tereza	213	Teri	527
Teris	538	Terisa	639	Terra	628
Terri	527	Terrie	123	Terrill	584
Terrilyn	584	Terrilyne	189	Terrilynn	549
Terrina	674	Terry	595	Terrye	191
Terryn	551	Tertia	641	Teryn	551
Terza	617	Terzah	696	Tesia	639
Tess	549	Tessa	641	Tessi	549

Tessie	145	Tessy	527	Tetsu	854
Teva	663	Teya	696	Thada	257
Thada	268	Thadda	292	Thaddea	797
Thalassa	369	Thalia	246	Thanasis	281
Thea	617	Theadora	459	Theadosia	461
Theafania	832	Theana	764	Theano	369
Theaphania	832	Theckla	696	Thecla	674
Thecle	178	Theda	652	Thee	112
Thekla	663	Thelma	685	Thema	652
Theo	213	Theodora	955	Theodore	459
Theodosia	966	Theofanie	832	Theofila	314
Theofilia	314	Theola	347	Theona	369
Theone	764	Theophania	437	Theophanie	832
Theophila	314	Theophilia	314	Theora	314
Thera	617	Therasia	729	Theresa	224
Therese	628	Theresia	224	Thetis	549
Thetys	527	Thia	112	Thirza	191
Thomasa	865	Thomase	369	Thomasin	729
Thomasina	821	Thomasine	325	Thora	718
Thorberta	358	Thorberte	753	Thorbertha	347
Thordia	753	Thordie	257	Thordie	268
Thordis	663	Thyra	189	Thyrza	178
Tibelda	628	Tiberia	641	Tiena	674
Tierney	156	Tifaine	641	Tiff	955
Tiffani	112	Tiffanie	617	Tiffany	189
Tiffi	955	Tiffie	551	Tiffy	933
Tilda	191	Tildi	999	Tildie	595
Tildy	977	Tilley	562	Tilli	988
Tillie	584	Tilly	966	Tim	966
Tima	167	Timi	966	Timmi	911
Timmie	516	Timmy	988	Timora	764
Timothea	371	Tina	178	Tina Maria	325
Tina Marie	729	Tine	573	Ting	955
Tini	977	Tiphaine	641	Tiphani	145
Tiphanie	641	Tiphany	123	Tiponya	731
Tirtha	134	Tirza	112	Tisa	134
Tish	922	Tisha	123	Tita	145
Titania	292	Tivona	729	Tivonia	729
Tivonya	797	Tiwa	178	Tizane	663
Tobe	246	Tobey	224	Tobi	641
Tobie	246	Toby	628	Tobye	224
Toinette	729	Toinon	336	Toireasa	437
Toki	641	Tokriva	786	Tola	753
Tolikna	731	Tom	663	Toma	764

Tomasa	876	Tomase	371	Tomasina	832
Tomasine	336	Tomi	663	Tommi	617
Tommie	213	Tommy	685	Tonda	729
Tonet	292	Toni	674	Tonia	775
Tonie	279	Tonis	685	Tonnae	336
Tony	652	Tonya	753	Tonye	257
Tonye	268	Topaz	786	Tora	729
Toranne	336	Toresa	336	Torey	292
Tori	628	Torie	224	Torranne	336
Torrie	224	Tory	696	Tosea	336
Toseia	336	Toshi	628	Tosia	731
Tosya	718	Totsi	652	Totty	641
Tourmalina	257	Tourmalina	268	Tourmaline	652
Toussainte	628	Tova	764	Tovah	753
Tovi	663	Toyace	336	Tracee	257
Tracee	268	Tracey	639	Traci	156
Tracie	652	Tracy	134	Traviata	382
Treacy	639	Trella	685	Trena	674
Trenna	639	Tresa	639	Trescha	652
Tressa	641	Treszka	641	Tricia	156
Triine	573	Trilbi	977	Trilbie	573
Trilby	955	Trina	178	Trine	573
Trinette	123	Trinidad	167	Trinity	977
Triphena	641	Triphenia	641	Trisa	134
Trish	922	Trisha	123	Triso	639
Trissie	549	Trissy	922	Trista	156
Tritha	134	Triva	167	Trivana	224
Trivann	178	Trivanna	279	Trivanne	674
Trix	988	Trixe	584	Trixee	189
Trixi	988	Trixie	584	Trixy	966
Truda	461	Trude	865	Trudey	843
Trudi	369	Trudie	865	Trudka	483
Trudy	347	Trula	459	Truna	472
Truwa	472	Tryphaena	729	Tryphena	628
Tryphenia	628	Tuesday	955	Tuki	347
Tula	459	Tulann	461	Tulanne	966
Tullia	483	Tupi	393	Tupia	494
Tupisa	415	Tusa	437	Tusya	415
Twila	112	Twilla	145	Twyla	189
Twyleen	145	Twylene	145	Tybi	922
Tybie	527	Tyee	191	Tyna	156
Tyne	551	Typhena	628	Tyra	191
Tyree	191	Uda	448	Udele	472
Udella	911	Udelle	415	Uke	821

Ula	437	Ulane	988	Ulani	483
Ulena	988	Ulima	472	Ulina	483
Ulla	461	Ulli	369	Ulrica	461
Ulrika	459	Ultima	494	Uma	448
Umeko	562	Una	459	Undine	854
Unity	358	Upala	516	Urania	551
Urice	832	Urielle	461	Urmi	347
Ursa	415	Ursala	549	Ursel	843
Ursie	819	Ursola	145	Ursula	742
Ursule	246	Ursulette	786	Ursulina	797
Ursuline	292	Ursy	382	Ushe	898
Ushi	393	Uta	426	Utina	472
Uzomee	134	Vada	281	Val	178
Vala	279	Valada	325	Valana	336
Valaree	371	Valaria	371	Valborga	876
Valburga	573	Valda	224	Vale	674
Valeda	729	Valema	729	Valencia	764
Valene	235	Valenka	753	Valente	257
Valente	268	Valentia	753	Valentina	718
Valentine	213	Valera	775	Valeria	775
Valerie	279	Valery	652	Valerye	257
Valerye	268	Valeska	718	Valida	224
Valina	235	Vallerio	314	Valli	112
Vallie	617	Vally	189	Valma	224
Valmarie	729	Valona	832	Valonia	832
Valora	876	Valorey	358	Valorie	371
Valory	753	Valry	156	Vamana	347
Van	191	Vancy	112	Vanda	246
Vandele	279	Vanessa	729	Vangie	674
Vania	292	Vanina	257	Vanina	268
Vanna	257	Vanna	268	Vanni	156
Vannie	652	Vanny	134	Vanora	898
Vanya	279	Varaza	336	Vardis	191
Varenka	729	Varina	292	Varma	281
Varni	191	Varrna	292	Varuna	595
Varvara	382	Varya	224	Varyusha	527
Vasfa	224	Vashti	167	Vasya	235
Vasyuta	551	Vatusia	573	Veda	685
Vedetta	235	Vedette	639	Vedis	595
Vega	628	Vegenia	279	Velda	628
Veleda	224	Velica	617	Velika	696
Vella	617	Velma	628	Velva	628
Velvet	145	Venetia	224	Venita	628
Ventura	922	Venus	819	Vera	641

Veradis	696	Verane	292	Verbena	224
Verda	685	Verde	189	Verdi	584
Verdie	189	Vere	145	Verena	292
Verene	696	Vergeen	674	Vergene	674
Verina	696	Verine	191	Verla	674
Verlee	674	Verlie	178	Verna	696
Verneta	224	Vernice	134	Vernine	156
Vernis	516	Vernita	628	Vernona	358
Verochka	382	Verona	393	Veronica	336
Veronika	325	Veronike	729	Veronikia	325
Veronique	189	Vespera	235	Vesta	674
Veta	663	Vevay	663	Vevila	628
Vi	944	Vic	977	Vicenta	652
Vick	999	Vicke	595	Vickee	191
Vicki	999	Vickie	595	Vicky	977
Victoire	292	Victori	696	Victoria	797
Victorie	292	Victorine	257	Victorine	268
Vida	189	Vidonia	742	Vigilia	156
Vignette	123	Vika	167	Viki	966
Vikki	988	Vikky	966	Viktorija	797
Vilhelmina	696	Villette	156	Vilma	123
Vin	999	Vina	191	Vincencia	628
Vincentia	617	Vinciane	685	Vinia	191
Vinita	123	Vinni	955	Vinnie	551
Vinny	933	Viola	775	Violaine	336
Violante	358	Viole	279	Violet	292
Violetta	325	Violette	729	Vir	944
Virgi	922	Virgie	527	Virgilia	156
Virginia	178	Virginie	573	Virgy	999
Virida	189	Viridiana	246	Viridis	999
Virina	191	Virna	191	Visolela	325
Vita	167	Vitia	167	Vitoria	764
Vittoria	786	Viv	988	Viva	189
Vive	584	Vivette	134	Vivi	988
Vivia	189	Vivian	145	Viviana	246
Viviane	641	Vivianne	696	Vivie	584
Vivien	549	Viviene	145	Vivienna	696
Vivienne	191	Vivyaan	224	Vivyan	123
Vivyanne	674	Volanda	876	Volante	358
Voleta	393	Voletta	325	Von	696
Vondila	775	Voni	696	Vonni	652
Vonnie	257	Vonnie	268	Vonny	639
Vrinda	145	Vyvyan	191	Vyvyana	292
Wakana	336	Wakanda	371	Wakenda	775

Walborga	887	Walburga	584	Walda	235
Waleska	729	Walker	617	Wallace	753
Wallie	628	Wallis	134	Wally	191
Wanda	257	Wanda	268	Wandie	652
Wandis	167	Waneta	731	Wanetta	753
Wanette	257	Wanette	268	Wapi	134
Warda	292	Wauna	516	Waunita	538
Welda	639	Welma	639	Wenda	652
Wendeline	641	Wendi	551	Wendie	156
Wendy	538	Wendye	134	Wenona	369
Wenonah	358	Wenowa	369	Wesley	178
Whitley	573	Whitney	595	Wicca	123
Wichasta	213	Wicia	189	Wikitoria	797
Wikta	191	Wiktorja	718	Wilda	134
Wileen	145	Wilf	955	Wilfreda	696
Wilfreida	696	Wilfrieda	696	Wilhelmina	617
Wilhelmine	112	Willa	123	Willabella	718
Willabelle	213	Willamina	224	Willetta	663
Willette	167	Willi	922	Willie	527
Willow	674	Willy	999	Wilma	134
Wilmette	178	Wilona	742	Wilone	246
Wilu	382	Win	911	Wina	112
Winda	156	Windy	933	Winema	652
Winfred	527	Winfrid	922	Winifred	527
Winifreida	628	Winifrid	922	Winifrida	123
Winifrieda	628	Winn	966	Winna	167
Winnah	156	Winne	562	Winni	966
Winnie	562	Winnifred	573	Winny	944
Winola	742	Winona	764	Winonah	753
Winter	538	Wisia	167	Wonona	461
Wren	516	Wuji	369	Wylma	112
Wyne	584	Wynn	764	Wynne	549
Wynnie	549	Wynny	562	Wynone	246
Xantha	235	Xanthe	639	Xaviera	718
Xaviere	213	Xena	628	Xene	123
Xenia	628	Ximena	663	Xylia	178
Xylina	134	Xylona	731	Yasmeen	281
Yasmin	189	Yasmina	281	Yasmine	685
Yasu	483	Yedda	663	Yerusha	977
Yetta	628	Yettie	123	Yetty	595
Yevette	663	Ynes	549	Ynez	527
Yoko	393	Yolanda	819	Yolande	314
Yolane	369	Yolanthe	371	Yona	731
Yonah	729	Yonina	786	Yonit	652

Yonita	753	York	696	Yosepha	358
Yoshi	674	Yoshiko	393	Yovela	358
Ysabeau	112	Ysabel	641	Ysabella	775
Ysabelle	279	Yseult	843	Ysobella	371
Ysobelle	775	Ysolbel	279	Ysolda	764
Ysolt	641	Yukiko	922	Yusepha	955
Yvet	549	Yvetta	663	Yvette	167
Yvon	674	Yvona	775	Yvonne	235
Zabine	663	Zabra	213	Zabrah	292
Zabreena	369	Zabrenna	729	Zada	235
Zadora	832	Zadri	134	Zaena	742
Zahara	371	Zaleya	797	Zaltana	393
Zamora	832	Zandra	281	Zandria	281
Zaneta	764	Zanna	292	Zanne	696
Zara	281	Zarah	279	Zareta	718
Zaria	281	Zariea	786	Zarifa	257
Zarifa	268	Zarina	246	Zarrna	246
Zea	685	Zeba	617	Zebaba	731
Zebeda	257	Zebeda	268	Zee	189
Zeena	246	Zel	527	Zelda	663
Zelde	167	Zele	123	Zelenka	292
Zelia	628	Zelie	123	Zelina	674
Zella	652	Zelma	663	Zena	641
Zenaida	786	Zenda	685	Zenia	641
Zenina	696	Zenna	696	Zennie	191
Zenobia	369	Zenona	393	Zenorbie	764
Zephyrine	189	Zera	685	Zerana	742
Zerdali	663	Zerla	628	Zerleen	674
Zerlina	674	Zerlinda	628	Zerline	178
Zeta	617	Zetana	764	Zetta	639
Zeva	639	Zeya	663	Zhorzh	652
Zia	189	Zigana	224	Zihna	134
Zilla	156	Zillah	145	Zilva	167
Zilvia	167	Zina	145	Zinia	145
Zinnia	191	Zippora	742	Zipporah	731
Zita	112	Zitao	718	Zitella	674
Ziv	933	Ziva	134	Ziyah	156
Ziyanta	246	Ziza	178	Zizi	977
Zizia	178	Zizis	988	Zjandre	696
Zjeria	696	Zoe	281	Zofia	753
Zofinka	731	Zohra	775	Zola	729
Zona	742	Zora	786	Zorah	775
Zorana	843	Zorina	742	Zorine	246
Zorya	764	Zsa Zsa	292	Zsa-Zsa	292

| Zuleika | 944 | Zuni | 347 | Zyta | 189 |
| Zytka | 112 | | | | |

MALE NAMES WITH REFERENCE NUMBERS

Aaeldert	393	Aage	775	Aarne	753
Aaron	854	Ab	123	Aba	224
Abana	371	Abasi	235	Abba	246
Abbas	257	Abbe	641	Abbey	628
Abbie	641	Abbot	764	Abbott	786
Abby	123	Abdel	696	Abdul	494
Abe	628	Abebi	641	Abel	652
Abelard	797	Abey	696	Abie	628
Abital	279	Abner	674	Abott	764
Abraham	358	Abrahan	369	Abram	268
Abramo	865	Abran	279	Abrasan	382
Absalom	819	Absolom	415	Aby	191
Acar	235	Acayib	235	Ace	639
Acey	617	Achille	685	Acie	639
Acker	652	Ackerley	268	Ackley	663
Ad	145	Adad	281	Adah	235
Adair	246	Adalard	325	Adalbert	729
Adalfuns	516	Adalwine	786	Adam	281
Adamec	729	Adamek	718	Adamer	786
Adamik	213	Adamnon	898	Adamo	887
Adamok	819	Adams	292	Adamson	854
Adan	292	Adao	843	Adar	246
Addam	235	Addie	685	Addison	753
Addy	167	Ade	641	Adeben	224
Adelard	729	Adelbert	224	Adelin	639
Adem	685	Aden	696	Aderet	268
Adham	279	Adhamh	268	Adhelard	718
Adigun	472	Adin	191	Adir	145
Aditi	167	Adiv	189	Adlai	279
Adlair	279	Adler	674	Adli	178
Admon	742	Adna	292	Adney	674
Adni	191	Adok	764	Adolf	742
Adolfo	448	Adolfus	156	Adolph	742
Adolphe	347	Adolpho	448	Adolphus	156
Adolpus	167	Adom	786	Adon	797
Adrial	279	Adrian	292	Adrianno	854
Adriano	898	Adriel	674	Adrien	696
Adrik	167	Adus	459	Aelfred	246
Aenas	764	Aeneas	369	Aeron	358
Aethelard	382	Aethelhard	371	Agdu	426
Agosto	415	Agu	472	Aguistin	461
Agustin	461	Ahanu	549	Aharon	843

Ahava	336	Ahdik	156	Ahearn	742
Aherin	641	Ahern	641	Aherne	246
Ahil	123	Ahir	189	Ahmad	279
Ahmed	674	Ahmik	156	Ahren	641
Aickin	112	Aidan	292	Aiden	696
Aiken	674	Aikin	178	Ailbert	674
Ailean	786	Ailemar	775	Ailfrid	145
Ailin	189	Aime	641	Aimee	246
Aimen	696	Aimol	775	Aindreas	718
Aineislis	617	Ainsley	674	Airel	639
Airleas	742	Akako	843	Akando	821
Akanke	797	Akar	224	Akela	753
Akiba	246	Akil	156	Akilah	246
Akim	167	Akin	178	Akins	189
Akio	729	Akiva	268	Akon	775
Akorn	775	Akron	775	Aksel	663
Akule	955	Al	134	Alabhaois	955
Alain	281	Alair	235	Alan	281
Aland	235	Alano	887	Alanson	854
Alard	279	Alaric	268	Alarick	281
Alasdair	382	Alastair	369	Alasteir	764
Alaster	764	Alban	213	Alben	617
Alberic	685	Alberik	674	Albern	617
Albert	674	Alberto	371	Albie	652
Albin	112	Albrecht	696	Alby	134
Alcot	786	Alcott	718	Aldabert	729
Alden	639	Alder	674	Aldin	134
Aldis	189	Aldo	775	Aldon	731
Aldous	189	Aldred	628	Aldric	112
Aldrich	191	Aldridge	696	Aldus	483
Aldwin	189	Aldwyn	167	Alec	663
Aleck	685	Aleister	268	Alejandro	448
Alejo	347	Alek	652	Alekos	369
Aleksandr	764	Aleksey	246	Aleron	382
Aleser	246	Alessandor	459	Alessandro	459
Alessio	358	Alex	696	Alexander	393
Alexandr	797	Alexandre	393	Alexandro	494
Alexandros	415	Alexi	696	Alexio	393
Alexis	617	Alexius	911	Alexsar	718
Alf	191	Alfaro	898	Alfeo	393
Alfie	696	Alfons	764	Alfonse	369
Alfonso	461	Alfonzo	448	Alford	742
Alfred	641	Alfredo	347	Alfy	178
Algar	213	Alger	617	Algernon	325

Algie	617	Algoma	854	Algy	189
Alhim	167	Ali	134	Alic	167
Alick	189	Alik	156	Alin	189
Alisander	742	Alison	797	Alistair	268
Alister	663	Alix	191	Alkas	268
Allan	224	Allard	213	Allayn	292
Allayne	797	Allen	628	Alley	641
Alleyn	696	Alleyne	292	Allie	663
Allin	123	Allison	731	Allister	696
Allistir	191	Alloys	753	Allvar	213
Allyn	191	Allyne	696	Almo	775
Almon	731	Alnaba	314	Alnath	292
Aloin	786	Alois	742	Alolphus	145
Alon	786	Alonso	494	Alonzo	472
Aloys	729	Aloysius	134	Alphie	696
Alphonsa	865	Alphonse	369	Alphonsin	729
Alphonso	461	Alphonsus	178	Alpin	167
Alric	167	Alrick	189	Alrik	156
Alroy	718	Alsandair	347	Alsten	628
Alston	729	Alta	257	Altair	257
Alten	617	Alter	652	Alther	641
Altman	257	Alton	718	Altsoba	887
Aluin	483	Aluino	189	Alumit	494
Alun	483	Alured	977	Alva	279
Alvah	268	Alvan	235	Alvar	279
Alvars	281	Alvie	674	Alvin	134
Alvis	189	Alvoid	729	Alvy	156
Alwin	145	Alwine	641	Alwyn	123
Alyne	663	Alysaundre	123	Alzubra	549
Am	145	Amable	797	Amadee	382
Amadeo	483	Amadis	292	Amado	887
Amand	246	Amando	843	Amasa	358
Amaury	527	Ambert	685	Ambie	663
Ambika	281	Ambrogino	494	Ambroise	371
Ambros	775	Ambrose	371	Ambrosi	775
Ambrosio	472	Ambrosius	189	Amby	145
Ame	641	Ameded	235	Ameer	246
Amelie	279	Amerigo	325	Amery	628
Amhlaoibt	819	Ami	145	Amie	641
Amiel	674	Amiliare	775	Amin	191
Amitan	224	Ammon	742	Amnon	753
Amoke	369	Amon	797	Amory	729
Amos	753	Amyas	235	Anael	786
Anastas	393	Anastase	898	Anastasio	999

Anastasius	617	Anastatius	628	Anastice	729
Anatholia	999	Anatol	819	Anatole	415
Anatolio	516	Ancell	652	Andeol	336
Ander	696	Anders	617	Andersen	268
Anderson	369	Andi	191	Andie	696
Andir	191	Andoche	325	Andonios	461
Andonis	764	Andor	797	Andras	213
Andre	696	Andrea	797	Andreas	718
Andrei	696	Andrej	617	Andres	617
Andrew	652	Andrey	674	Andrian	257
Andrien	652	Andris	112	Andrius	415
Andriyan	235	Andry	178	Andula	538
Andulka	551	Andy	178	Aneirin	617
Aneurin	911	Anevay	775	Anezka	764
Ange	639	Angel	663	Angell	696
Angelo	369	Angers	641	Angie	639
Angus	448	Angy	112	Aniceto	314
Aniol	786	Anka	279	Annan	268
Annesley	235	Annibal	268	Anntoin	786
Anscom	742	Anscomb	764	Anse	663
Ansel	696	Ansell	639	Anselm	641
Anselme	246	Anselmi	641	Anselmo	347
Anshelm	639	Ansley	674	Anson	729
Anstice	628	Anstiss	112	Anthelme	246
Anthony	797	Antin	134	Antoine	336
Anton	731	Antone	336	Antoni	731
Antonin	786	Antonino	483	Antonio	437
Antonius	145	Antons	742	Antony	718
Anum	494	Anwell	674	Anwyl	123
Anwyll	156	Anyon	786	Anzu	448
Aodh	731	Aoidh	731	Aoiffe	336
Apang	213	Apenimon	336	Apollo	448
Apollos	459	Aponi	731	Araldo	876
Aram	246	Arcadius	584	Arcady	257
Arch	123	Archaimbaud	639	Archambaud	639
Archambault	641	Archard	268	Archer	628
Archerd	663	Archibald	224	Archibaldo	821
Archibold	729	Archie	628	Archimbald	268
Archy	191	Arciet	652	Arcite	652
Ard	145	Arden	696	Ardie	641
Ardin	191	Ardlen	639	Ardley	652
Ardolf	742	Ardolph	742	Ardon	797
Ardy	123	Aree	292	Arel	639
Aren	652	Arend	696	Arens	663

Ares	617	Argemone	876	Argus	483
Argyle	685	Ari	191	Arian	257
Aric	134	Arick	156	Arid	145
Arie	696	Ariel	639	Aries	617
Aril	134	Arin	156	Ario	797
Aristide	674	Aristotetis	382	Aristotle	382
Arkin	178	Arko	729	Arlan	281
Arlay	213	Arledge	257	Arlen	685
Arlet	652	Arley	617	Arlie	639
Arlin	189	Arlo	731	Arly	112
Arman	292	Armand	246	Armando	843
Armel	674	Armen	696	Armin	191
Arminel	639	Armon	797	Armond	742
Armoni	797	Armstrong	718	Armund	448
Armyn	178	Arnald	235	Arnaldo	832
Arnall	224	Arnatt	292	Arnaud	595
Arne	652	Arnett	696	Arney	639
ARni	156	Arnie	652	Arnit	178
Arno	753	Arnold	731	Arnoldo	437
Arnon	718	Arnot	775	Arnott	797
Arnould	134	Arny	134	Aron	753
Arpad	224	Arpiar	279	Arri	191
Arrio	797	Arron	753	Arsene	268
Arshile	639	Arslan	292	Art	123
Artair	224	Arte	628	Artemas	775
Artemis	674	Artemisia	775	Artemus	977
Arther	617	Arthur	415	Artie	628
Artur	426	Arturo	123	Artus	437
Arty	191	Arundel	933	Arv	145
Arvad	281	Arval	279	Arve	641
Arvel	674	Arvey	628	Arvid	189
Arvie	641	Arvin	191	Arvy	123
Arza	281	Arziki	112	Arzit	112
Asa	213	Asabi	235	Asad	257
Asar	213	Ascot	764	Ascott	786
Ase	617	Asfour	178	Asger	685
Ash	191	Ashbey	696	Ashburn	472
Ashby	191	Asher	696	Ashford	718
Ashias	213	Ashley	617	Ashlin	189
Ashon	753	Ashton	775	Ashur	494
Asid	156	Asiel	641	Asiyah	279
Asker	639	Assid	167	Assunta	595
Astley	641	Astor	731	Aswad	213
Aswin	123	Aswine	628	Atanazy	347

Atar	224	Atek	641	Ateret	246
Athalaric	371	Athanase	876	Athanasios	988
Athanasius	685	Athelhard	775	Atherton	382
Atley	639	Atman	224	Attila	279
Attwood	448	Atuanya	652	Atwater	797
Atwell	641	Atwood	426	Atwoode	922
Atworth	786	Auban	573	Aube	922
Auberon	674	Aubert	944	Aubi	426
Aubin	472	Aubrey	999	Aubry	494
Aud	448	Audie	944	Audric	472
Audun	797	Audwin	459	Audy	426
Augie	977	August	718	Auguste	314
Augustin	764	Augustine	369	Augusto	415
Augustus	123	Augy	459	Aulii	437
Aurek	922	Aurele	538	Aurelio	639
Aurelius	347	Aurello	663	Aurthur	718
Austen	988	Austin	483	Autar	527
Ave	641	Avedig	663	Avel	674
Avenall	764	Avenel	235	Avenell	268
Averel	279	Averell	213	Averil	674
Averill	617	Avery	628	Averyl	652
Avi	145	Aviam	281	Avidan	246
Avidor	786	Aviel	674	Avir	145
Avit	167	Avital	292	Avivah	279
Avner	696	Avniel	639	Avram	281
Avrill	112	Avrille	617	Avrom	786
Awan	213	Awun	415	Ax	167
Axe	663	Axel	696	Axell	639
Axton	742	Aylmar	257	Aylmer	652
Aylward	213	Aylwin	123	Aylworth	775
Aymar	224	Aymer	628	Aymeric	652
Azad	235	Azami	235	Azariah	371
Azi	189	Azim	134	Azriel	628
Azrikam	257	Azur	483	Badem	617
Baden	628	Bafour	189	Baghel	628
Bail	156	Bailey	639	Bailie	652
Baillie	685	Baily	134	Bain	178
Bainbridge	628	Baird	167	Baka	246
Bakula	573	Bal	156	Balala	382
Balaniki	235	Balbo	775	Bald	191
Baldemar	742	Balder	696	Baldhere	281
Baldric	134	Baldrick	156	Balduin	459
Baldur	494	Baldwin	112	Bale	652
Balfour	123	Bali	156	Balin	112

Baline	617	Balint	134	Balki	178
Ballard	235	Baltek	696	Balthasar	371
Balthazar	358	Ban	178	Bancroft	797
Bandi	123	Bandric	156	Bane	674
Bank	191	Banky	178	Banning	167
Baptist	156	Baptiste	652	Baptistin	112
Bar	123	Barakah	336	Baram	268
Baran	279	Barclay	268	Bard	167
Barde	663	Bardo	764	Bardolf	764
Bardolph	764	Bardolphe	369	Bardrick	123
Bardulf	461	Bardulph	461	Bardy	145
Bari	123	Barika	246	Barima	268
Barlow	718	Barn	178	Barnaba	393
Barnabas	314	Barnabe	797	Barnabus	516
Barnaby	279	Barnard	224	Barnebas	718
Barnet	696	Barnett	628	Barney	652
Barnie	674	Barnum	426	Barny	156
Barol	753	Baron	775	Barr	123
Barret	641	Barrett	663	Barri	123
Barric	156	Barrie	628	Barris	134
Barron	775	Barry	191	Barse	639
Bart	145	Bartel	674	Barten	696
Barth	134	Barthel	663	Barthelemy	281
Barthelmey	281	Barthol	764	Bartholome	911
Bartholomeo	617	Bartholomeu	314	Bartholomeus	325
Bartholomew	966	Barthram	279	Bartie	641
Bartlet	696	Bartlett	628	Bartley	652
Barto	742	Bartoli	775	Bartolome	922
Bartolomeo	628	Barton	797	Bartram	281
Barty	123	Baruch	448	Barwch	191
Bary	191	Bas	134	Base	639
Basham	268	Basie	639	Basil	167
Basile	663	Basilio	764	Basilius	472
Basir	134	Bastian	213	Bastien	617
Basya	213	Basyll	178	Bat	145
Batini	191	Battista	292	Batya	224
Baudoin	123	Baudouin	426	Baudric	494
Baul	459	Bavol	797	Bax	189
Baxie	685	Baxter	617	Baxy	167
Bay	191	Bayard	246	Baye	696
Bayley	617	Bazir	112	Beach	641
Beacher	246	Beagan	753	Beagen	257
Beal	652	Beale	257	Beall	685
Bealle	281	Beaman	729	Beamer	268

Bear	628	Bearnard	729	Beathan	786
Beatie	246	Beattie	268	Beatty	641
Beaty	628	Beau	922	Beaufort	617
Beaumont	641	Beauregard	641	Beavais	775
Beavan	729	Beaven	224	Bec	551
Beck	573	Bediako	382	Bedir	562
Bedo	268	Bedrich	584	Beech	145
Beecher	641	Bekoe	742	Bela	652
Belamy	674	Belden	156	Beldon	257
Belen	112	Bell	584	Bellamy	617
Bello	281	Beltran	639	Bem	562
Bemossed	731	Ben	573	Benci	516
Bendek	145	Bendick	573	Bendict	573
Bendik	549	Bendix	584	Bene	178
Benedetto	369	Benedic	156	Benedick	178
Benedict	178	Benedicto	775	Benedik	145
Benedikt	167	Benedix	189	Benedykt	145
Benek	191	Bengt	573	Beniamino	371
Benito	292	Benjamen	281	Benjamin	685
Benji	584	Benjie	189	Benjy	562
Benn	538	Bennet	156	Bennett	178
Bennie	134	Benning	562	Benny	516
Bennye	112	Benoit	292	Benoni	235
Benot	292	Benson	246	Bent	595
Bentlee	639	Bentley	112	Bently	516
Benton	257	Benvenuto	191	Benyamin	652
Benzi	562	Berdy	549	Berenger	652
Beres	134	Beresford	742	Berg	595
Bergen	156	Berger	191	Bergess	123
Bergren	156	Berite	145	Berk	549
Berke	145	Berkeley	652	Berkie	145
Berklay	652	Berkley	156	Berkly	551
Berky	527	Bern	573	Bernard	628
Bernardin	674	Bernardo	325	Bernarr	674
Bernau	977	Berne	178	Bernhard	617
Berni	573	Bernie	178	Berny	551
Berri	527	Berrie	123	Berry	595
Bersh	527	Bert	549	Bertan	696
Berte	145	Berthold	213	Berthoud	573
Berti	549	Bertie	145	Bertik	562
Bertin	595	Berto	246	Bertold	224
Bertolde	729	Berton	292	Bertram	685
Bertramd	639	Bertrand	641	Bertrando	347
Berty	527	Berwin	538	Beryl	538

Besh	527	Bev	562	Beval	696
Bevan	628	Beven	123	Beverley	674
Beverly	178	Bevin	527	Bevis	573
Bevon	224	Biagio	797	Bialas	268
Bialy	134	Bian	178	Bic	955
Bick	977	Bickford	685	Bidu	369
Bil	955	Bildad	145	Bill	988
Billie	584	Billy	966	Bilten	538
Bily	933	Biminak	145	Bimisi	977
Bing	955	Bink	999	Binky	977
Birch	944	Birchard	189	Birk	944
Birke	549	Birket	562	Birkett	584
Birkey	527	Birley	538	Birney	551
Biron	674	Birtle	573	Bish	922
Bishop	696	Bitten	527	Bix	988
Bixby	988	Bjarne	685	Bjorn	685
Bjorne	281	Black	112	Blade	696
Blagden	639	Blain	112	Blaine	617
Blair	156	Blaire	652	Blaise	663
Blake	674	Blakeley	281	Blakey	652
Bland	156	Blandford	764	Blane	617
Blanford	729	Blas	167	Blase	663
Blasien	628	Blasius	472	Blayn	189
Blayne	685	Blayze	628	Blaz	145
Blaze	641	Bliss	977	Blodwen	213
Blom	696	Blum	393	Bly	753
Blyth	764	Blythe	549	Bo	628
Boas	731	Boase	336	Boaz	718
Bob	641	Bobbi	663	Bobbie	268
Bobby	641	Bobek	268	Bodaway	898
Boden	224	Bodi	663	Bodil	696
Bodua	167	Bogar	797	Bogart	729
Bogdan	797	Bogey	279	Bogie	292
Bohdan	718	Bohumil	988	Bohumir	955
Bonar	775	Bonaventure	292	Bonaz	764
Bond	628	Bonde	224	Bondie	224
Bondon	371	Bonds	639	Bondy	696
Bone	279	Boniface	371	Bonne	235
Booker	843	Boone	876	Boonie	876
Boony	358	Boot	347	Boote	843
Booth	336	Boothe	832	Bor	628
Bord	663	Borden	224	Bordie	268
Bordolphe	865	Bordy	641	Borg	696
Boris	639	Born	674	Bornie	279

Boske	257	Boski	652	Boswell	257
Bosworth	393	Both	639	Botolf	347
Botolph	347	Botolphe	843	Boton	393
Bour	922	Bourdolph	663	Bourke	549
Bourn	977	Bourne	573	Bow	674
Bowen	235	Bowie	279	Bowle	213
Bowman	775	Boy	696	Boyce	235
Boycey	213	Boycie	235	Boycy	617
Boyd	641	Boyde	246	Boyden	292
Boydon	393	Boyne	257	Boz	617
Bozsi	628	Brad	167	Bradan	224
Bradburn	448	Brade	663	Braden	628
Bradford	775	Bradlee	292	Bradley	674
Bradlie	696	Bradly	178	Bradney	696
Bradshaw	224	Brady	145	Brainard	224
Brainerd	628	Bram	167	Bramwell	685
Bran	178	Branch	191	Brand	123
Brandan	279	Brande	628	Branden	674
Brander	628	Brandie	628	Brandin	178
Brandon	775	Brandt	145	Brandy	191
Brandyn	156	Branko	797	Brannon	786
Brant	191	Brantley	617	Brass	145
Brawley	685	Braxton	764	Breck	573
Brede	167	Bren	573	Brendan	674
Brenden	178	Brendin	573	Brendis	538
Brendon	279	Brennan	685	Brennen	189
Brent	595	Brenton	257	Bret	549
Brett	562	Brevard	617	Brew	573
Brewer	178	Brewster	112	Briac	156
Brian	178	Briano	775	Briant	191
Briante	696	Brice	551	Bridger	549
Brien	573	Brieux	887	Brig	999
Brigg	977	Briggs	988	Brigham	134
Brinsley	595	Brion	674	Brishen	573
Brit	944	Britt	966	Broc	652
Brock	674	Brockden	279	Brockie	279
Brockley	281	Brocky	652	Brod	663
Broddie	213	Broddy	685	Broderic	292
Broderick	224	Brodie	268	Brodny	696
Brodrick	628	Brody	641	Brok	641
Bromley	279	Bron	674	Bronnie	235
Bronny	617	Bronson	347	Brook	347
Brooke	843	Brooker	843	Brooks	358
Brose	235	Brough	988	Brougher	584

Broughton	663	Bruce	854	Brucie	854
Bruis	336	Bruno	977	Bruns	382
Brush	325	Brutus	652	Bryan	156
Bryane	652	Bryant	178	Bryce	538
Brycen	584	Bryden	595	Bryn	775
Bryne	551	Brynn	731	Bryon	652
Bryony	639	Bryse	516	Bryson	663
Bua	426	Buck	371	Buckie	876
Buckley	887	Bucky	358	Bud	369
Budd	314	Buddie	819	Buddy	382
Budislao	112	Buiron	977	Bundy	393
Burbank	426	Burc	358	Burch	347
Burchard	483	Burckhard	415	Burdett	819
Burdon	922	Burell	887	Burford	933
Burg	393	Burgard	448	Burgess	821
Burian	472	Burk	347	Burke	843
Burkett	887	Burkhart	459	Burl	358
Burleigh	821	Burley	832	Burlie	854
Burn	371	Burnaby	472	Burnard	426
Burne	876	Burnell	843	Burnes	887
Burnett	821	Burney	854	Burnie	876
Burny	358	Burr	325	Burris	336
Burt	347	Burtie	843	Burton	999
Burty	325	Burura	729	Busby	336
Buster	854	Butch	369	Buz	314
Buzz	393	Byford	617	Bynshe	551
Byram	145	Byran	156	Byrann	112
Byrd	764	Byrdie	549	Byrle	538
Byrne	551	Byrom	641	Byron	652
Cab	156	Cad	178	Cadao	876
Cadby	178	Cadda	224	Caddaric	257
Caddock	775	Cade	674	Cadel	617
Cadell	641	Cadman	279	Cadmus	437
Cadogan	819	Cadwallader	843	Caesar	742
Cahil	156	Cailean	729	Cain	189
Caisey	628	Caiten	617	Cal	167
Calbert	617	Calder	617	Caldwell	639
Cale	663	Caleb	685	Calen	628
Caley	641	Calhoun	112	Calliope	371
Calliste	639	Callon	753	Calon	729
Calum	415	Calut	483	Calv	112
Calvert	639	Calvin	167	Calvino	764
Cam	178	Camden	674	Cameron	336
Camey	652	Camille	641	Camlo	718

Camm	123	Cammy	191	Camp	156
Campbell	641	Campy	134	Candide	674
Cannon	797	Canut	415	Canute	911
Canwall	213	Car	134	Caradoc	819
Caradock	832	Care	639	Carey	617
Carl	167	Carleton	347	Carlie	663
Carlile	696	Carlin	123	Carling	191
Carlisle	617	Carlo	764	Carlos	775
Carlten	641	Carlton	742	Carly	145
Carlyle	674	Carlysle	685	Carman	235
Carmen	639	Carmichael	731	Carmine	639
Carmon	731	Carnet	617	Carney	663
Carnit	112	Carny	167	Carol	764
Carollan	854	Carolos	472	Carolus	178
Carr	134	Carrick	189	Carrol	764
Carroll	797	Carsen	696	Carson	797
Carswell	663	Cart	156	Carter	652
Cartland	281	Carvel	617	Carvell	641
Carver	674	Carvey	652	Carvy	156
Cary	112	Caryl	145	Cas	145
Casar	246	Case	641	Casey	628
Cash	134	Casimir	189	Casimire	685
Caspar	224	Casper	628	Cass	156
Cassidy	178	Cassie	652	Cassius	461
Cassy	134	Castel	696	Castell	639
Castor	764	Catant	235	Catava	393
Caten	617	Cathmor	786	Cato	753
Caton	718	Caumlo	112	Cavan	235
Cavell	641	Cawley	696	Caz	123
Cazzie	617	Cece	167	Cecil	595
Cecile	191	Cecilio	292	Cecilius	819
Ced	573	Cedric	516	Celestin	156
Celio	268	Cemal	617	Cenred	134
Cerdic	516	Ceridwen	189	Cesaire	246
Cesar	641	Cesare	246	Cesaro	347
Chad	167	Chadd	112	Chadda	213
Chaddie	617	Chaddy	189	Chadwick	178
Chaim	167	Chal	156	Chale	652
Chalmer	696	Chalmers	617	Cham	167
Chan	178	Chance	617	Chanceller	279
Chancellor	371	Chancelor	347	Chancey	685
Chandler	652	Chane	674	Chaney	652
Channing	167	Chanoch	797	Chap	191
Chapin	156	Chapman	292	Chapmen	696

Chappie	674	Chappy	156	Charlemagne	336
Charles	663	Charleton	336	Charley	639
Charlie	652	Charlot	775	Charlton	731
Charltson	742	Charly	134	Chas	134
Chase	639	Chatham	279	Chaunce	911
Chaunceler	549	Chaunceller	573	Chauncey	988
Chavali	292	Chavi	167	Che	527
Chelovik	224	Chelton	235	Chen	573
Cheney	156	Chepe	191	Ches	538
Cheslav	617	Chesmu	876	Chester	156
Cheston	213	Chet	549	Chetwin	551
Chetwyn	538	Chev	562	Chevalier	292
Chevy	549	Cheyney	134	Chi	922
Chic	955	Chick	977	Chickie	573
Chicko	674	Chicky	955	Chico	652
Chiel	551	Chik	944	Chil	955
Chill	988	Chilo	652	Chilt	977
Chilton	639	Chim	966	Chimalis	112
Chip	999	Chips	911	Chito	641
Chizu	314	Chlodowig	336	Cho	628
Chretien	191	Chris	933	Chrisse	549
Chrissie	549	Chrissy	922	Christan	112
Christiaan	213	Christian	112	Christiano	718
Christie	551	Christoffer	281	Christoforo	922
Christoper	235	Christoph	628	Christophe	224
Christopher	224	Christophorus	639	Christos	663
Christy	933	Chucho	944	Chuck	371
Chuma	461	Chun	371	Churchill	314
Cian	189	Cicero	268	Ciceron	224
Cid	977	Cilombo	336	Ciprian	167
Cirillo	696	Cirilo	663	Cirio	639
Ciro	639	Claes	674	Claiborn	742
Claiborne	347	Claine	628	Clair	167
Clane	628	Clarance	753	Clare	663
Clarence	257	Clark	189	Clarke	685
Claud	415	Claude	911	Claudell	977
Claudian	562	Claudianus	876	Claudio	112
Claudius	729	Claus	472	Clavance	797
Clay	145	Claybirne	628	Clayborn	729
Clayborne	325	Claybourne	628	Clayne	696
Clayten	628	Clayton	729	Cleary	641
Cleave	213	Cleavland	742	Cleeve	617
Clem	516	Clemence	696	Clemency	178
Clemens	178	Clement	189	Clemente	685

Clementius	494	Clemmie	156	Clemmy	538
Clemson	279	Cleon	224	Clerc	595
Clerk	584	Clete	189	Cletis	595
Cletus	898	Cleve	112	Cleveland	246
Clevey	189	Clevie	112	Clif	933
Cliff	999	Clifford	641	Clift	955
Clifton	617	Clim	911	Clint	944
Clinton	696	Clive	516	Clodomir	358
Clovis	628	Cluny	393	Cly	764
Clyde	584	Clyve	584	Clywd	764
Cnut	314	Cob	652	Cobb	674
Cobbie	279	Cobby	652	Coblan	742
Codi	674	Codie	279	Cody	652
Coe	235	Coile	268	Col	663
Colan	729	Colas	775	Colbert	213
Colby	663	Cole	268	Coleman	369
Colet	281	Colier	268	Colin	628
Colis	674	Collayer	371	Colley	279
Collier	292	Collin	652	Collis	617
Collyer	279	Colman	764	Colomban	483
Colt	685	Colter	281	Colton	347
Colum	911	Columba	134	Columbo	639
Columbus	347	Colver	213	Colvert	235
Colyer	246	Coman	731	Comar	775
Comyn	617	Con	685	Conal	729
Conan	742	Conant	764	Conlan	775
Conlen	279	Conley	292	Conlin	674
Conlon	371	Conn	641	Connaire	347
Connall	718	Connel	279	Conney	224
Connie	246	Connor	347	Conny	628
Conrad	731	Conrade	336	Conrado	437
Conroy	369	Constant	797	Constantin	753
Constantine	358	Constantino	459	Conway	729
Coop	314	Cooper	819	Corbet	279
Corbett	292	Corbie	257	Corbin	617
Corby	639	Corcoran	426	Cord	674
Cordell	246	Cordie	279	Cordy	652
Corentin	268	Corey	213	Corguoran	764
Cori	639	Coridon	336	Cormac	718
Cormack	731	Cormick	639	Cornal	729
Cornall	753	Cornalle	358	Corneille	753
Cornel	224	Cornelius	538	Cornell	257
Corney	268	Cornie	281	Cornille	257
Corny	663	Corquoran	775	Correy	213

Corrie	235	Cort	652	Cortie	257
Cortlandt	718	Corty	639	Corwen	246
Corwin	641	Cory	617	Coryden	213
Corydon	314	Cos	641	Cosimo	382
Cosme	281	Cosmo	382	Costa	764
Costain	729	Costin	628	Court	955
Courtenay	685	Courteney	189	Courtland	189
Courtnay	189	Courtney	584	Covell	246
Covill	641	Cowan	742	Cowey	268
Cowie	281	Coyle	246	Cozmo	369
Craddock	775	Craggie	685	Craggy	167
Craig	112	Cran	189	Crandall	292
Crandell	696	Crane	685	Cranley	696
Cranston	775	Crary	112	Craw	189
Crawford	797	Crayton	786	Creigh	595
Creight	527	Creighton	279	Crepin	562
Crichton	639	Cris	944	Crisp	922
Crispen	573	Crispin	977	Crispinus	382
Crispus	336	Cristian	123	Cristobal	729
Cristoforo	933	Cromwell	292	Crosbey	246
Crosbie	268	Crosby	641	Crosley	257
Cross	652	Crow	685	Crowford	393
Culbert	819	Cull	393	Cullan	459
Cullen	854	Culley	876	Cullie	898
Cullin	358	Cully	371	Culver	819
Cur	336	Curcio	966	Curr	336
Curran	483	Curren	887	Currey	819
Currie	832	Curry	314	Curt	358
Curtice	887	Curtis	369	Cut	358
Cuthbert	887	Cutler	887	Cuttie	876
Cutty	358	Cvetan	652	Cy	731
Cyd	775	Cynric	999	Cyprian	145
Cyprien	549	Cyr	731	Cyrano	764
Cyrek	538	Cyrenaica	797	Cyriaque	999
Cyril	944	Cyrill	977	Cyrille	573
Cyrillus	382	Cyrus	325	Dabir	167
Dabney	696	Dace	674	Dacey	652
Dack	191	Dacy	156	Dael	674
Daelton	358	Dag	123	Dagaim	268
Dagan	279	Daganya	358	Daggi	191
Dagmar	268	Dagney	652	Dagny	156
Dagon	775	Dagwood	426	Dai	145
Daiden	641	Dainard	246	Dal	178
Dalbert	628	Dale	674	Dalis	189

Dalit	191	Dall	112	Dallas	224
Dallis	123	Dallon	764	Dalston	764
Dalt	191	Dalton	753	Daly	156
Dalziel	696	Dalziell	639	Damaris	292
Damase	797	Dame	685	Damek	617
Damhnait	257	Damian	246	Damiano	843
Damick	145	Damicke	641	Damien	641
Damon	742	Dan	191	Dana	292
Danby	191	Dandie	641	Dandin	191
Dandy	123	Dane	696	Dani	191
Danie	696	Daniel	639	Daniell	663
Danielle	268	Danior	797	Danit	123
Danladi	279	Dannel	685	Dannie	652
Dannisen	628	Danny	134	Dansan	268
Dansen	663	Danson	764	Dante	628
Dar	145	Darb	167	Darbee	268
Darbie	663	Darby	145	Darce	674
Darcey	652	Darci	178	Darcie	674
Darcy	156	Dare	641	Dareld	628
Daren	696	Darin	191	Dario	742
Darius	459	Darle	674	Darmel	628
Darn	191	Darnall	268	Darnell	663
Darol	775	Darold	729	Daron	797
Darrel	674	Darrell	617	Darren	696
Darrick	191	Darrill	112	Darrin	191
Darry	123	Darryl	156	Darsey	639
Darshan	292	Darsy	134	Darton	729
Daru	448	Darvin	145	Darwen	652
Darwin	156	Darwyn	134	Daryal	257
Daryl	156	Daryle	652	Daryll	189
Dasan	213	Dashiell	617	Daulo	178
Daun	494	Dav	189	Davaki	213
Dave	685	Daven	641	Davey	663
David	134	Davidde	674	Davide	639
Davidsen	696	Davidson	797	Davie	685
Davin	145	Davis	191	Davon	742
Davy	167	Dawid	145	Dawood	448
Dawred	641	Daye	628	De Witt	549
Dean	696	Deane	292	Dearborn	325
Deat	663	Decca	617	Decimus	832
Deck	595	Decker	191	Dedric	527
Dedrick	549	Dee	145	Deems	191
Degula	955	Deinard	641	Deiniol	235
Deiter	167	Dekel	191	Del	573

Delain	639	Delaine	235	Delainey	213
Delaney	213	Delano	336	Delbert	123
Dell	516	Delling	549	Delmar	628
Delmer	123	Delmor	224	Delmore	729
Delon	235	Delos	281	Delphin	595
Delphus	854	Delroy	257	Delsin	549
Delu	876	Delwin	584	Delwyn	562
Demas	696	Demeter	617	Demetre	617
Demetri	112	Demetris	123	Demetrius	426
Demmy	516	Demos	292	Demothi	292
Demp	562	Dempsey	156	Dempster	191
Demsey	178	Den	595	Denbay	696
Denby	595	Dene	191	Denebola	854
Denis	516	Denison	268	Deniz	584
Denley	112	Denman	696	Dennet	178
Denney	134	Dennie	156	Dennis	562
Dennisan	628	Dennison	224	Denny	538
Dent	527	Denten	178	Denton	279
Denver	145	Deny	573	Denys	584
Denzil	527	Deobald	347	Der	549
Derald	628	Derby	549	Derck	595
Dereck	191	Derek	167	Deric	573
Derick	595	Derk	562	Derle	178
Dermot	213	Dermott	235	Deror	246
Deroy	224	Derrack	696	Derrek	167
Derrick	595	Derrik	562	Derril	573
Derron	292	Derry	527	Derward	641
Derwin	551	Derwood	843	Deryk	549
Des	551	Desi	551	Desire	156
Desmand	696	Desmond	292	Desmund	898
Dessie	167	Dev	584	Devaki	617
Deverell	652	Devi	584	Devin	549
Devinder	189	Devland	628	Devlen	178
Devlin	573	Devon	246	Devy	562
Dew	595	Dewain	652	Dewayne	235
Dewey	178	Dewie	191	Dewitt	549
Dewy	573	Dex	516	Dexter	134
Dezi	538	Diamond	786	Diarmard	235
Diarmid	134	Diarmit	112	Diccon	663
Dichali	191	Dick	999	Dicke	595
Dickie	595	Dickon	652	Dickson	663
Dicky	977	Diderik	516	Didier	584
Dido	685	Diego	224	Diehl	562
Dierick	595	Dieter	167	Dietrich	584

Dietrick	527	Digby	922	Diggory	674
Dik	966	Dikla	191	Diklit	922
Dilan	134	Dill	911	Dillie	516
Dillon	663	Dilly	988	Dimitri	911
Dimitry	988	Dinka	123	Dinnie	551
Dinny	933	Dino	696	Dinos	617
Dinse	516	Dinsmor	652	Dinsmore	257
Diomede	731	Dion	696	Dionisio	314
Dionysus	999	Dirk	966	Ditka	189
Diverous	595	Dixil	944	Dixon	663
Dixy	988	Diza	134	Dmitri	911
Dmytro	685	Doane	393	Doba	764
Dobie	268	Doby	641	Dodek	213
Dohosan	494	Doirean	393	Dolan	731
Dolf	641	Dolfa	742	Dolfi	641
Dolfino	393	Dolph	641	Dom	685
Domenic	279	Domenico	876	Domhnall	797
Domingo	325	Dominic	674	Dominick	696
Dominik	663	Dominique	538	Dominy	628
Domnall	718	Domnin	696	Don	696
Donahue	685	Donal	731	Donald	775
Donall	764	Donalt	753	Donat	729
Donatello	988	Donatien	371	Donato	426
Donaugh	167	Donavon	494	Donevan	393
Doni	696	Donkor	325	Donn	652
Donnall	729	Donnell	224	Donnelly	292
Donni	652	Donnie	257	Donny	639
Donoghue	268	Donohue	281	Donovan	494
Doogan	472	Dor	641	Doral	775
Doran	797	Dorby	641	Dore	246
Dorek	268	Doren	292	Dorey	224
Dorian	797	Dorie	246	Dorin	696
Dorit	663	Dorjan	718	Dorn	696
Doron	393	Dorran	797	Dorren	292
Dorrit	663	Dory	628	Dosya	731
Dothan	718	Doug	922	Dougal	156
Dougan	178	Douggie	595	Douggy	977
Dougie	527	Douglas	167	Douglass	178
Dougy	999	Dov	685	Dovev	235
Dow	696	Doy	628	Doyle	257
Drake	663	Dreng	573	Drew	595
Driscol	628	Driscoll	652	Drogo	325
Dru	347	Druce	876	Drud	382
Drue	843	Drugi	325	Druon	999

Drury	325	Dry	742	Drydane	628
Dryden	527	Drystan	112	Duane	999
Duarte	966	Dud	382	Duddie	832
Duddy	314	Dude	887	Dudley	898
Dudly	393	Duff	371	Duffie	876
Duffy	358	Dugaid	461	Dugal	459
Dugald	494	Dugan	472	Duggie	898
Duggy	371	Duglass	472	Duke	865
Dukey	843	Dukie	865	Dukker	887
Duky	347	Dumaka	516	Duman	448
Dun	393	Dunc	336	Duncan	483
Dunham	437	Dunley	819	Dunmore	549
Dunn	358	Dunstan	483	Dunton	977
Dupett	865	Dur	347	Durand	448
Durant	426	Durante	922	Durell	819
Durriken	821	Durril	371	Durward	448
Durwin	358	Durwood	641	Durwyn	336
Dushin	393	Dust	371	Dustan	437
Dusten	832	Dustie	876	Dustin	336
Duston	933	Dusty	358	Duwayne	933
Dwaen	652	Dwain	156	Dwaine	652
Dwane	652	Dwayne	639	Dwight	988
Dyck	797	Dylan	112	Eachan	775
Eacheann	336	Eadgyth	617	Eadmund	988
Eadweard	347	Eadwin	652	Eadwine	257
Ealdfrith	652	Eamon	393	Eamonn	358
Ean	652	Eanruig	933	Earl	639
Earland	731	Earle	235	Earlie	235
Early	617	Earnest	281	Earvin	696
Eaton	371	Eatton	393	Eb	527
Ebbe	145	Ebbie	145	Ebby	527
Eben	178	Ebeneser	281	Ebenezer	268
Eberhard	257	Eberhart	235	Eberto	742
Ebner	178	Ed	549	Edan	696
Edbert	189	Edd	584	Eddie	189
Eddy	562	Edel	178	Edelie	674
Edelmar	224	Eden	191	Eder	145
Edgar	628	Edgard	663	Edgardo	369
Edik	562	Edin	595	Edison	213
Edlin	538	Edlyn	516	Edme	189
Edmidio	235	Edmon	246	Edmond	281
Edmondo	887	Edmund	887	Edolf	246
Edouard	685	Edric	573	Edsel	189
Edson	213	Eduard	988	Eduardo	685

Eduards	999	Eduino	595	Edvard	639
Edvin	549	Edwald	674	Edward	641
Edwin	551	Efrem	112	Efren	123
Egan	639	Egbert	123	Egide	123
Egidio	224	Egidius	832	Egmont	292
Egon	235	Egor	279	Ehren	145
Eidrich	562	Einar	652	Eirwen	112
Ejnar	663	Ejner	167	El	538
Elazaro	426	Elbert	178	Elden	134
Elder	178	Eldin	538	Eldon	235
Eldred	123	Eldredge	696	Eldric	516
Eldrich	595	Eldrid	527	Eldridge	191
Eldwin	584	Eldwyn	562	Eleazar	325
Elek	156	Elert	156	Elery	112
Elfirede	641	Elfrid	549	Elgar	617
Eli	538	Elia	639	Elias	641
Elick	584	Elie	134	Eliezer	628
Elihu	821	Elijah	639	Elinot	213
Eliot	257	Eliott	279	Elis	549
Elisee	641	Eliseo	742	Eliseus	459
Elish	538	Elisha	639	Elison	292
Elizer	123	Elizur	821	Ellard	617
Ellary	641	Ellef	134	Ellerey	641
Ellery	145	Elli	562	Ellice	191
Elliot	281	Elliott	213	Ellis	573
Ellison	235	Ellswerth	145	Ellsworth	246
Ellwood	865	Elme	178	Elmen	134
Elmer	178	Elmiro	279	Elmo	279
Elmore	775	Eloi	235	Elrad	674
Elridge	156	Elroy	213	Elsan	696
Elschem	112	Elsdon	246	Elson	292
Elstan	628	Elston	224	Elstone	729
Elsu	843	Elsworth	213	Elton	213
Elvera	279	Elviathan	742	Elvin	538
Elvira	674	Elvire	178	Elvis	584
Elvy	551	Elvyn	516	Elwell	156
Elwin	549	Elwood	832	Elwyn	527
Ely	516	Em	549	Eman	696
Emanuel	538	Emanuele	134	Emele	674
Emelen	639	Emeric	178	Emerson	718
Emery	123	Emie	145	Emil	573
Emile	178	Emilien	134	Emilio	279
Emlen	134	Emlin	538	Emlyn	516
Emmanuel	573	Emmanuil	977	Emmerich	112

Emmerie	685	Emmery	167	Emmet	112
Emmett	134	Emmit	516	Emmot	213
Emmott	235	Emmy	562	Emory	224
Emry	527	Emrys	538	Endre	191
Eneas	268	Engelbert	617	Englebert	617
Enguerran	584	Ennea	213	Ennes	123
Ennis	527	Enoch	279	Enos	268
Enrico	281	Enrique	448	Ensio	268
Ensor	268	Enyeto	753	Eogham	314
Eoin	257	Eph	562	Ephraim	617
Ephrem	112	Epiphane	292	Erai	696
Erasme	257	Erasmo	358	Erasmus	966
Eraste	235	Erastus	944	Erek	123
Erhard	639	Erhart	617	Eric	538
Erich	527	Erick	551	Erico	235
Erie	191	Erik	527	Erin	551
Erl	538	Erland	639	Erle	134
Erlin	584	Erling	562	Ermanno	358
Ermin	595	Ernald	639	Erne	156
Ernest	189	Ernesto	786	Ernestus	494
Ernie	156	Ernst	584	Erny	538
Errick	551	Errne	156	Errnest	189
Errol	235	Erroll	268	Erskin	584
Erskine	189	Ersok	235	Erssike	145
Erv	549	Ervin	595	Ervine	191
Erwin	516	Eryle	112	Erzsi	595
Esau	911	Esdras	663	Eshkol	257
Eskild	516	Esme	156	Esmond	257
Esra	617	Essien	178	Este	134
Esteban	213	Esten	189	Estes	145
Estevan	235	Estlin	527	Estonian	347
Etan	674	Ethan	663	Ethe	112
Ethelard	281	Ethelbert	685	Ethelmer	685
Ethelred	685	Ethne	167	Etienne	639
Eton	279	Ettore	742	Etu	821
Euell	461	Eugen	437	Eugene	933
Eugenio	134	Eugenius	742	Eurard	944
Eustace	562	Eustache	551	Eustashe	538
Eustasius	358	Eustatius	369	Eustazio	628
Eustis	843	Ev	549	Evagelos	865
Evan	696	Evel	178	Evelin	134
Evelyn	112	Even	191	Everard	281
Evered	685	Everet	663	Everett	685
Everilo	775	Everley	652	Everly	156

Evertson	731	Evin	595	Evyn	573
Ewald	639	Ewan	617	Eward	696
Ewart	674	Ewell	123	Ewen	112
Ewert	178	Ewing	584	Eyvta	641
Ez	584	Ezard	639	Ezechiel	641
Ezekiel	641	Ezequiel	911	Ezer	189
Ezhno	235	Ezia	685	Eziechiele	246
Ezkah	696	Ezra	685	Ezri	584
Ezzard	628	Fabao	887	Fabe	685
Faber	685	Fabian	246	Fabiano	843
Fabien	641	Fabio	786	Fabre	685
Fabrice	628	Fabron	742	Fadey	685
Fadil	145	Fagan	292	Fagin	191
Fagon	797	Fair	167	Fairdell	674
Fairfax	292	Fairlay	279	Fairleigh	663
Fairley	674	Fairlie	696	Fairly	178
Falconer	382	Falkner	674	Fane	628
Fanny	156	Far	167	Farand	268
Farant	246	Farl	191	Farlay	279
Farlee	292	Farleigh	663	Farlen	652
Farley	674	Farlie	696	Farlin	156
Farly	178	Farnall	281	Farnam	268
Farnel	652	Farnell	685	Farnley	639
Farold	742	Faron	729	Farquhar	549
Farr	167	Farrand	268	Farrant	246
Farrar	268	Farrel	696	Farrell	639
Farren	628	Farris	178	Farruco	191
Faulkener	573	Faulkner	977	Faust	494
Favian	268	Fax	134	Faxon	786
Fay	145	Fayette	281	Federico	742
Fedir	516	Fedor	213	Felic	538
Felice	134	Felicien	189	Felicio	235
Felike	123	Feliks	538	Felipe	178
Felips	584	Felix	562	Felizio	281
Fellips	527	Felmin	595	Felten	178
Felton	279	Fen	527	Fennie	178
Fenny	551	Fentan	696	Fenton	292
Feodor	819	Feodore	415	Ferand	663
Ferant	641	Ferd	516	Ferde	112
Ferdie	112	Ferdinand	663	Ferdy	584
Ferenc	156	Fereng	191	Fergie	145
Fergus	854	Ferguson	516	Ferike	189
Fernald	696	Fernall	685	Fernand	628
Fernando	325	Fernao	325	Fernley	134

Ferran	628	Ferrand	663	Ferrant	641
Ferrel	191	Ferrell	134	Ferreol	797
Ferris	573	Fess	584	Fidel	549
Fidele	145	Fidelio	246	Field	549
Fielding	573	Fields	551	Fife	538
Fil	999	Filbert	549	Filberte	145
Filberto	246	Filip	977	Filippo	652
Filley	516	Fillip	911	Fillmore	279
Filmer	549	Filmore	246	Fin	922
Findlay	178	Findley	573	Fineas	639
Finlay	134	Finley	538	Finn	977
Finnie	573	Finny	955	Fiora	764
Fiorello	832	Fiorenza	314	Firman	167
Firmin	966	Fisk	999	Fiske	595
Fitch	911	Fitz	977	Fitzalan	268
Fitzgerald	639	Fitzhugh	336	Fitzpatrick	134
Flann	112	Flavian	292	Flavien	696
Flavio	742	Flavius	459	Flem	549
Fleming	573	Flemming	527	Fletch	549
Fletcher	145	Flin	955	Flinn	911
Flint	977	Flip	977	Florent	279
Florentin	235	Florentine	731	Florenz	246
Florian	753	Flory	674	Floy	674
Floyd	628	Flynn	718	Fonda	764
Fons	639	Fonsie	235	Fonz	617
Fonzie	213	Forbes	292	Ford	617
Fordel	246	Forest	292	Forester	797
Forrest	292	Forrester	797	Forrie	268
Forster	292	Fortunat	167	Fortunato	764
Fortune	549	Fortunio	641	Foss	685
Foster	292	Fourier	562	Fowler	257
Foy	641	Fraine	628	Fran	123
Franc	156	Francelin	641	Francesco	393
Franchot	764	Francis	167	Francisco	797
Franciskus	494	Francisque	955	Franck	178
Francklin	167	Francklyn	145	Franco	753
Francois	764	Frank	145	Frankie	641
Franklin	134	Franklyn	112	Franky	123
Frankye	628	Frannie	674	Franny	156
Frans	134	Fransisco	775	Frants	156
Frantz	134	Franz	112	Franzen	663
Frasco	718	Frascuelo	641	Fraser	674
Frasier	674	Frasquito	189	Frayne	696
Fraze	652	Frazer	652	Frazier	652

Frean	628	Fred	516	Freddie	156
Freddy	538	Frede	112	Fredek	134
Frederic	145	Frederich	134	Frederick	167
Frederico	742	Frederigo	786	Frederik	134
Frederique	999	Fredi	516	Fredic	549
Fredric	549	Fredrick	562	Free	167
Freeborn	742	Freedman	213	Freeland	292
Freeman	268	Freemon	764	Freen	123
Fremont	281	Frewen	178	Frewin	573
Frey	549	Freyne	191	Frick	922
Fridolf	617	Friederike	639	Friedrich	538
Friedrick	562	Frisco	617	Frits	999
Fritz	977	Fritzie	573	Fritzino	639
Fulbert	843	Fulbright	314	Fuller	832
Fulton	977	Fyfe	516	Fyffe	573
Gabbie	628	Gabby	191	Gabe	696
Gabey	674	Gabi	191	Gabie	696
Gabin	156	Gable	639	Gabriel	639
Gabriele	235	Gabriello	369	Gaby	178
Gadiel	652	Gael	617	Gaelan	764
Gaetan	753	Gage	652	Gaho	764
Gail	112	Gaile	617	Gainer	639
Gainor	731	Gal	112	Gale	617
Galen	663	Galeno	369	Galit	134
Gallagher	718	Gallard	281	Galloway	876
Gallway	279	Galmier	652	Galor	718
Galt	134	Galton	786	Galvan	213
Galven	617	Galvin	112	Galway	246
Gamal	257	Gamali	257	Gamaliel	786
Gamiel	652	Gan	134	Ganin	189
Ganit	156	Gannie	685	Gannon	742
Ganny	167	Gar	178	Garald	257
Gard	123	Garde	628	Gardener	279
Gardie	628	Gardiner	674	Gardner	674
Gardy	191	Gare	674	Garek	696
Gareth	685	Garett	628	Garey	652
Garfield	628	Gari	178	Garik	191
Garland	213	Garlen	663	Garman	279
Garmon	775	Garmond	729	Garmund	426
Garner	639	Garnet	652	Garnett	674
Garnier	639	Garnock	786	Garold	753
Garolds	764	Garrard	224	Garraway	314
Garrek	696	Garret	696	Garreth	685
Garrett	628	Garrick	134	Garridan	279

Garrie	674	Garrik	191	Garrit	191
Garritt	123	Garrot	797	Garroth	786
Garrott	729	Garroway	819	Garry	156
Garson	742	Garth	189	Garton	753
Garv	123	Garvey	696	Garvie	628
Garvin	178	Garvy	191	Garwin	189
Garwood	472	Gary	156	Gaspar	268
Gaspard	213	Gasparo	865	Gasper	663
Gaston	764	Gatien	652	Gaud	426
Gauri	472	Gauthier	988	Gautier	999
Gav	123	Gavan	279	Gaven	674
Gavil	156	Gavin	178	Gawain	281
Gawaine	786	Gawen	685	Gawin	189
Gay	156	Gayelord	336	Gayland	281
Gayle	685	Gayler	685	Gaylon	742
Gaylor	786	Gaylord	731	Gayner	617
Gaynor	718	Gazit	189	Gearalt	731
Gearard	729	Gearey	257	Geary	652
Gene	134	Genest	167	Geno	235
Geof	246	Geoff	213	Geoffrey	786
Geoffroy	887	Geoffry	281	Geofroy	821
Georas	382	Geordi	224	Geordie	729
Georg	257	George	753	Georges	764
Georgie	753	Georgy	235	Ger	573
Geraint	652	Gerald	652	Geraldo	358
Gerallt	663	Geralt	639	Gerard	628
Gerardin	674	Gerardo	325	Geraud	922
Gerd	527	Gerek	191	Gereld	156
Gerhard	617	Gerhardt	639	Gerhart	685
Gerick	538	Gerik	595	Germain	674
Germaine	279	Germayne	257	Gernot	257
Gerome	729	Geronimo	876	Gerrald	652
Gerrard	628	Gerri	573	Gerrie	178
Gerrit	595	Gerritt	527	Gerry	551
Gersham	628	Gershom	224	Gervais	639
Gervase	235	Gery	551	Getty	595
Gherardo	314	Giacamo	854	Giacobo	437
Giacomo	459	Giacopo	483	Giamo	729
Gian	134	Gianni	189	Giavani	279
Gib	999	Gibb	922	Gibbie	527
Gibby	999	Gibor	696	Gibson	663
Gid	922	Gide	527	Gideon	279
Giff	911	Giffard	156	Gifferd	551
Giffie	516	Gifford	652	Giffy	988

Gil	911	Gilad	156	Gilbert	551
Gilberto	257	Gilbey	516	Gilburt	358
Gilby	911	Gilchrist	966	Gile	516
Gilead	652	Giles	527	Gilibeirt	551
Gilit	933	Gill	944	Gilleabart	786
Gilleasbuig	955	Gilles	551	Gillet	562
Gillett	584	Gillie	549	Gillies	551
Gillmore	281	Gillot	663	Gilly	922
Gilman	112	Gilmer	551	Gilmore	257
Gilmour	955	Gilot	639	Gilpin	944
Gilroy	685	Gino	639	Ginson	696
Ginton	617	Giordano	472	Giorgio	358
Giovanni	731	Giraldo	753	Giraud	426
Girvan	178	Girven	573	Girvin	977
Giselbert	167	Gisfrid	999	Giulio	911
Giuseppe	448	Giustino	966	Giusto	911
Givon	674	Gizus	371	Glad	156
Gladdie	696	Gladdy	178	Gladwin	167
Glanvil	145	Glanville	674	Glen	562
Glendale	246	Glenden	167	Glendon	268
Glenn	527	Glenndan	628	Glyn	764
Glynn	729	Godard	764	Godart	742
Goddard	718	Goddart	786	Godefroy	865
Godewyn	213	Godfree	786	Godfrey	268
Godfrith	696	Godfry	663	Godwin	639
Godwine	235	Godwyn	617	Golding	685
Goldwin	663	Gonsalve	325	Gontran	718
Gonzales	369	Gonzalo	459	Goodwin	336
Goran	731	Gord	628	Gordan	775
Gorden	279	Gordie	224	Gordon	371
Gordy	696	Gore	279	Gorman	775
Gosheven	775	Gostaff	742	Gothart	718
Gottfried	235	Gouverneur	472	Gower	235
Gowon	382	Gozal	797	Gradeigh	685
Gradey	696	Grady	191	Graede	224
Graehme	213	Graem	628	Graeme	224
Graham	213	Graig	156	Graige	652
Gram	123	Gran	134	Grandville	685
Grange	617	Granger	617	Granston	729
Grant	156	Grantham	281	Granthem	685
Grantland	281	Grantley	663	Granvil	112
Granville	641	Gray	156	Grayden	652
Graydon	753	Graye	652	Graysen	628
Grayson	729	Greagoir	358	Gredel	156

Greeley	685	Greely	189	Greerson	742
Greg	551	Gregary	639	Gregg	538
Greggory	213	Gregoire	753	Gregoor	854
Gregor	257	Gregorio	854	Gregorius	562
Gregory	235	Gregour	551	Greig	551
Greiogair	358	Grenville	145	Gresham	628
Grey	551	Greysan	628	Greyson	224
Griff	911	Grifferd	551	Griffie	516
Griffin	966	Griffith	922	Griffy	988
Griffyn	944	Grigori	652	Gris	988
Griswold	628	Griz	966	Grizemal	641
Grobber	224	Grove	224	Grover	224
Gruffyd	336	Gualterio	639	Gualtiero	639
Guarin	437	Guenole	167	Guerin	832
Guerric	819	Guglielmo	562	Guido	922
Guilbert	854	Guillaume	382	Guillermo	584
Guin	336	Gun	336	Gunar	437
Gunnar	483	Gunner	887	Guntar	459
Gunter	854	Gunthar	448	Gunther	843
Guriel	819	Gurion	933	Gurione	538
Gurisyne	821	Gurit	393	Gus	382
Guss	393	Gussy	371	Gustaf	472
Gustav	459	Gustave	955	Gustavo	156
Gustavos	167	Gustavus	764	Gustof	977
Guthnie	843	Guthrey	865	Guthrie	887
Guthry	369	Guy	358	Guyapi	437
Guyon	911	Gwenola	325	Gwyn	786
Gwynn	742	Haakon	865	Habib	134
Habibah	224	Hacket	663	Hackett	685
Had	134	Hadad	279	Hadar	235
Haddad	224	Haddan	235	Hadden	639
Haddon	731	Haddrian	235	Haden	685
Hadiya	213	Hadlee	268	Hadleigh	639
Hadley	641	Hadrian	281	Hadrien	685
Hadwin	145	Hagan	224	Hagen	628
Haggan	292	Haggen	696	Hagit	189
Hagley	674	Hagood	415	Haiden	685
Haig	167	Haile	628	Hailey	696
Haily	191	Hairdar	235	Hak	112
Hakan	268	Hakeem	257	Hakem	652
Hakim	156	Hako	718	Hakon	764
Hakum	459	Hal	123	Halbert	663
Haldan	224	Haldane	729	Halden	628
Hale	628	Haleigh	685	Haley	696

Halfdan	281	Halford	731	Halil	156
Hall	156	Hallam	292	Halley	639
Halliwell	674	Hallsy	145	Hallward	257
Halsey	617	Halstead	797	Halsted	696
Halsy	112	Halton	797	Halward	224
Ham	134	Hamad	279	Hamako	854
Hamal	268	Hamar	235	Hamdam	224
Hamdrem	628	Hamdun	437	Hamel	663
Hamelin	628	Hamelot	382	Hamelyn	696
Hamid	178	Hamil	167	Hamilton	742
Hamish	134	Hamlen	628	Hamlet	685
Hamlin	123	Hammad	224	Hammar	279
Hamnet	617	Hamo	731	Hamonet	314
Hanan	292	Handley	696	Hanford	753
Hanif	112	Hanit	167	Hank	167
Hanleigh	641	Hanley	652	Hannal	235
Hannibal	257	Hanno	797	Hanraoi	843
Hans	156	Hansel	685	Hanson	718
Hanssen	628	Hanuman	549	Harailt	246
Harald	268	Haratio	819	Harb	112
Harbert	639	Harbin	167	Harcourt	145
Harden	685	Hardey	617	Hardi	134
Hardie	639	Harding	167	Hardwin	145
Hardwyn	123	Hardy	112	Hareford	393
Harel	628	Hareth	696	Harfon	718
Harford	797	Hargrave	718	Hargreave	314
Hargreaves	325	Hargrove	314	Hari	189
Haridas	246	Harith	191	Harithah	281
Harivig	112	Harl	123	Harlan	279
Harland	224	Harleigh	685	Harlen	674
Harley	696	Harlin	178	Harlon	775
Harlow	775	Harly	191	Harman	281
Harmon	786	Harold	764	Haroun	145
Harp	167	Harper	663	Harris	191
Harrison	753	Harry	167	Hart	112
Harte	617	Hartford	729	Hartleigh	617
Hartley	628	Hartman	213	Hartmann	268
Hartmuth	461	Hartwell	639	Hartwill	134
Hartwood	415	Haru	483	Harun	448
Harv	134	Harve	639	Harvey	617
Harvie	639	Harwell	617	Harwill	112
Harwin	191	Harwood	483	Harwyn	178
Hasad	246	Hasen	652	Hasheem	235
Hashim	134	Hasin	156	Haskel	652

Haskell	685	Haslett	674	Haslitt	178
Hassan	268	Hassel	641	Hassin	167
Hastin	178	Hastings	167	Havelock	325
Haven	685	Havlock	729	Hawley	652
Hayden	663	Haydon	764	Hayes	674
Hayward	268	Haywood	461	Hayyim	189
Haze	674	Hazen	639	Hazlett	652
Hazlitt	156	Hazzel	696	Heall	652
Hearn	641	Hearne	246	Hearst	628
Heath	696	Heathcliff	696	Heathcliffe	292
Hebe	112	Hebert	134	Heck	549
Hector	246	Hedeon	786	Hedley	145
Hedvick	538	Heindrick	549	Heino	246
Heinrich	562	Heinrick	595	Heinrik	562
Heinz	538	Helaku	944	Helvan	628
Heman	685	Henderson	753	Hendrick	549
Hendrik	516	Heney	123	Henleigh	145
Henley	156	Henney	178	Henning	538
Henno	292	Henny	573	Henri	549
Henrik	562	Henrils	584	Henrim	584
Henrique	437	Henry	527	Henryk	549
Hephzibah	652	Herald	663	Herb	516
Herbert	134	Herbie	112	Herby	584
Herc	527	Hercule	459	Hercules	461
Herculie	459	Hereford	797	Hereld	167
Hereward	281	Herford	292	Heriberto	731
Herm	538	Herman	685	Hermann	641
Hermes	145	Hermie	134	Hermin	584
Hermon	281	Hermy	516	Hernando	347
Herold	268	Herrat	617	Herrick	549
Hersch	527	Herschel	156	Hersh	584
Hershel	123	Hertford	224	Herv	538
Herve	134	Hervey	112	Herwin	595
Hesketh	134	Hessin	562	Hever	134
Hew	549	Hewe	145	Hewet	167
Hewett	189	Hewie	145	Hewitt	584
Heyward	663	Heywood	865	Hezekiah	281
Hi	988	Hiatt	134	Hilaire	628
Hilario	729	Hilarion	775	Hilarius	437
Hilary	191	Hildebrand	685	Hildemar	617
Hildin	922	Hildon	628	Hilet	549
Hilger	595	Hill	955	Hillard	191
Hillary	134	Hillel	584	Hillerd	595
Hillery	538	Hilliard	191	Hillie	551

Hillier	551	Hilly	933	Hillyer	538
Hilmar	167	Hilton	696	Hinum	382
Hippolyte	279	Hiram	134	Hiroshi	685
Hirsch	922	Hirschel	551	Hisago	775
Hisako	729	Hiti	911	Hjalmar	279
Ho	685	Hoagy	742	Hobard	753
Hobart	731	Hobey	281	Hobie	213
Hod	639	Hodding	617	Hoebart	336
Hogan	729	Hoibeard	358	Hoireabard	459
Hoku	911	Holbrook	966	Holbrooke	562
Holcomb	325	Holcombe	821	Holden	224
Holecomb	821	Holecombe	426	Holim	663
Holleb	279	Holles	268	Hollis	663
Hollub	977	Holmes	279	Holt	641
Homart	753	Homer	235	Homere	731
Homerus	549	Homes	246	Honon	393
Honorat	461	Honore	843	Honorin	393
Honovi	382	Honus	955	Honza	731
Horace	325	Horacio	426	Horatio	415
Horatius	123	Horst	628	Hort	617
Horten	268	Horton	369	Hose	292
Hosea	393	Hoseia	393	Hoshi	685
Hoshie	281	Hototo	933	Houghton	639
Houston	674	Howard	786	Howe	246
Howell	213	Howey	224	Howi	641
Howie	246	Howin	696	Howlan	731
Howland	775	Hoyt	685	Hrodulf	933
Huata	516	Hubbard	472	Hubble	865
Hube	819	Hubert	832	Huberto	538
Hubie	819	Hudson	999	Huey	865
Hugh	358	Hughe	854	Hughie	854
Hughy	336	Hugibert	819	Hugo	966
Hugues	279	Huitt	336	Hulbard	483
Hulbert	865	Hulburd	685	Hulburt	663
Hulin	371	Hull	358	Hum	336
Humayd	459	Humbert	876	Humberto	573
Humbie	854	Humfrey	876	Humfrid	347
Humfried	843	Humfry	371	Hump	314
Humph	393	Humphrey	876	Hunfredo	551
Hunt	369	Hunter	865	Huntingdon	999
Huntington	977	Huntlee	494	Huntley	876
Huntly	371	Hurlbert	865	Hurlee	426
Hurleigh	887	Hurley	898	Hurst	325
Husain	459	Husein	854	Huso	999

Hussein	865	Husseini	865	Hut	314
Hute	819	Hutt	336	Huttan	483
Hutton	988	Hux	358	Huxford	966
Huxley	865	Hy	786	Hyacinthe	663
Hyatt	112	Hyde	516	Hyland	191
Hylton	674	Hyman	167	Hymee	112
Hymie	516	Hyram	112	Hywel	551
Hywell	584	Iago	775	Iaian	257
Iain	156	Ian	156	Ibraham	257
Ibrahim	156	Ichabod	786	Ifor	663
Igan	134	Igasho	775	Iggie	551
Iggy	933	Ignace	663	Ignacio	764
Ignacius	472	Ignate	652	Ignatia	257
Ignatius	461	Ignaz	123	Ignazio	729
Igor	674	Ihor	685	Ike	527
Ikey	595	Ikie	527	Ilario	731
Ilias	145	Imanuel	933	Immanuel	977
Imre	549	Inek	573	Ingamar	279
Ingar	134	Ingelbert	112	Ingelran	628
Ingemar	674	Inger	538	Ingeram	674
Inglebert	112	Inglis	977	Ingmar	178
Ingra	134	Ingraham	268	Ingram	178
Ingrim	977	Ingvar	178	Iniga	134
Inigo	639	Iniss	977	Innes	527
Inness	538	Innis	922	Innocent	224
Inteus	887	Ioakim	764	Iosep	281
Iowerth	268	Ira	191	Irv	944
Irvin	999	Irvine	595	Irving	977
Irwin	911	Irwinn	966	Isa	112
Isaac	246	Isaak	235	Isac	145
Isacco	775	Isador	753	Isadore	358
Isaiah	292	Isaie	617	Isak	134
Isambard	224	Isham	145	Ishmael	674
Isiah	191	Isidor	652	Isidore	257
Isidoro	358	Isidro	652	Israel	641
Issiah	112	Issie	527	Issur	325
Issy	999	Istas	145	Istu	336
Istvan	134	Isvald	134	Ituha	415
Itzhak	123	Ivan	191	Ivar	145
Ive	549	Iven	595	Iver	549
Ives	551	Ivo	641	Ivon	696
Ivor	641	Iwalani	246	Iwan	112
Iz	988	Izaak	213	Izak	112
Izzie	573	Izzy	955	Jabe	639

Jabez	628	Jacek	663	Jacinto	729
Jack	167	Jackie	663	Jackson	731
Jacky	145	Jacme	685	Jacob	764
Jacobo	461	Jacobus	178	Jacopo	426
Jacque	933	Jacques	944	Jae	617
Jael	641	Jaem	652	Jafar	279
Jaffa	246	Jaffe	641	Jafit	191
Jagger	663	Jahi	191	Jaime	652
Jaimie	652	Jaimy	134	Jake	639
Jakie	639	Jakob	753	Jakub	459
Jal	145	Jamaal	382	Jamal	281
Jambu	472	James	663	Jameson	325
Jamesy	641	Jamey	639	Jamie	652
Jamil	189	Jamill	123	Jamin	112
Jamison	729	Jammal	235	Jan	167
Janek	685	Janiuszck	426	Janka	281
Jankins	156	Jano	764	Janos	775
Januarius	876	Januisz	461	Janvier	617
Jaoven	314	Jaques	911	Jarad	257
Jarden	617	Jareb	639	Jared	652
Jarek	639	Jaret	639	Jarett	652
Jarib	134	Jarid	156	Jarit	134
Jarl	145	Jarlath	257	Jarlen	696
Jarman	213	Jaro	718	Jarod	753
Jaromey	336	Jaromir	753	Jaron	764
Jaroslav	898	Jarrad	257	Jarred	652
Jarret	639	Jarrett	652	Jarrid	156
Jarrod	753	Jarv	156	Jarvey	639
Jarvis	167	Jary	189	Jas	123
Jascha	246	Jase	628	Jasen	674
Jason	775	Jaspar	292	Jasper	696
Jaspir	191	Jasun	472	Javas	268
Javid	191	Javier	652	Javin	112
Jay	189	Jaye	685	Jayme	639
Jaymie	639	Jayson	753	Jaysone	358
Jean	663	Jecho	235	Jed	551
Jedd	595	Jeddy	573	Jedediah	281
Jededish	191	Jedidiah	685	Jedrik	573
Jedrus	865	Jeff	549	Jefferey	628
Jeffers	156	Jefferson	718	Jeffery	123
Jeffie	145	Jeffrey	123	Jeffry	527
Jeffy	527	Jehan	652	Jeks	549
Jem	551	Jemmie	191	Jemmy	573
Jeno	268	Jens	573	Jensen	134

Jensin	538	Jer	516	Jerad	652
Jerald	685	Jeramey	235	Jeramie	257
Jerdan	617	Jerdon	213	Jere	112
Jereld	189	Jereme	652	Jeremiah	246
Jeremias	268	Jeremie	652	Jeremy	134
Jerimiah	641	Jermain	617	Jermaine	213
Jerman	617	Jermayne	281	Jermyn	584
Jerol	246	Jerold	281	Jerome	753
Jeromy	235	Jerrald	685	Jerri	516
Jerrie	112	Jerrold	281	Jerrome	753
Jerry	584	Jervis	562	Jesper	191
Jess	538	Jesse	134	Jessee	639
Jessey	112	Jessie	134	Jessy	516
Jesus	832	Jeth	527	Jethro	224
Jevon	213	Jhae	696	Jhon	652
Jhone	257	Jim	955	Jimmi	999
Jimmie	595	Jimmy	977	Jimoh	641
Jin	966	Jiovanni	764	Jiro	617
Jivih	944	Jivvel	538	Jo	617
Joab	731	Joachim	775	Joaquin	156
Job	639	Joby	617	Jock	663
Jocko	369	Jodi	652	Jodie	257
Jodocus	696	Jody	639	Joe	213
Joel	246	Joerg	281	Joey	281
Joh	696	Johan	753	Johann	718
Johannes	325	John	652	Johnathan	821
Johnathon	426	Johnnie	213	Johnny	685
Johny	639	Jolan	797	Joliet	268
Jolon	393	Jolyon	371	Jon	663
Jonah	753	Jonam	718	Jonas	775
Jonathan	832	Jonathon	437	Jonati	786
Jone	268	Jonn	628	Jonno	325
Jonny	696	Jony	641	Jorah	797
Jordan	718	Jordane	314	Jordon	314
Jorgan	742	Jorge	281	Jorin	663
Joris	628	Jory	685	Jose	224
Josecito	876	Josef	281	Joseito	843
Joseph	281	Josephe	786	Josephin	246
Josephus	595	Josh	617	Josha	718
Joshia	718	Joshua	112	Joshuah	191
Josiah	718	Josias	731	Josse	235
Josselin	224	Josue	527	Jotham	764
Jourdain	112	Jozef	268	Juan	461
Jubal	461	Jud	358	Judah	448

Judas	461	Judd	393	Jude	854
Judicael	922	Judson	922	Juergen	448
Jule	843	Jules	854	Julian	494
Julie	843	Julien	898	Julio	944
Julius	652	Julyan	472	Jumah	448
Jun	369	Junichi	382	Junius	674
Jupe	887	Jurgen	843	Juri	314
Juris	325	Jurka	437	Juss	336
Just	347	Juste	843	Justen	898
Justin	393	Justinian	459	Justinien	854
Justino	999	Justis	358	Justus	652
Juvenal	944	Jynx	731	Jyotis	628
Kabil	178	Kabir	145	Kabran	292
Kadar	268	Kadin	123	Kadir	167
Kaese	235	Kaga	292	Kahaleel	371
Kahil	145	Kahlil	178	Kain	178
Kaine	674	Kaiser	639	Kaisy	112
Kal	156	Kalanit	235	Kalb	178
Kale	652	Kaleb	674	Kalig	134
Kalil	189	Kalkin	134	Kalle	685
Kalman	257	Kalmanu	551	Kaloosh	459
Kaluwa	516	Kalven	652	Kalvin	156
Kam	167	Kameke	281	Kameko	382
Kamel	696	Kanani	235	Kane	674
Kaneko	393	Kanoa	876	Kantu	494
Kapuki	426	Kapule	933	Kareef	281
Kareem	268	Karel	652	Karey	696
Karif	189	Karim	167	Karka	246
Karl	156	Karlan	213	Karle	652
Karlens	628	Karlik	178	Karlis	167
Karney	652	Karol	753	Karolek	371
Karoly	731	Karr	123	Karre	628
Karsin	189	Karsten	617	Kasch	156
Kase	639	Kaseko	358	Kasib	156
Kasimer	674	Kasimir	178	Kasin	189
Kaska	257	Kasoleo	966	Kasota	854
Kaspar	213	Kasper	617	Kass	145
Kasy	112	Kateb	663	Katike	663
Kato	742	Katus	459	Kavan	224
Kaveri	663	Kay	191	Kayne	652
Kazimir	156	Kazu	415	Kazuko	134
Kean	674	Keane	279	Kearn	674
Kearney	257	Keary	696	Keath	639
Keb	549	Kedar	663	Keddy	584

Kedem	112	Keefe	685	Keegan	257
Keegen	652	Keelan	213	Keelby	156
Keeler	652	Keeley	639	Keen	178
Keenan	235	Keene	674	Keir	527
Keith	538	Kelbee	674	Kelby	551
Keldon	257	Kele	156	Kelemen	652
Keler	156	Kell	584	Kellby	584
Kellen	145	Keller	189	Kelley	167
Kelly	562	Kelman	652	Kelsan	628
Kelsey	145	Kelson	224	Kelsy	549
Kelton	235	Kelvan	652	Kelven	156
Kelvin	551	Kelwin	562	Kem	562
Kemal	696	Kemble	123	Kemp	549
Ken	573	Kenan	639	Kendal	652
Kendall	685	Kendell	189	Kendrick	573
Kendricks	584	Kenelm	156	Keneth	189
Kenleigh	178	Kenley	189	Kenn	538
Kennan	685	Kennard	674	Kenne	134
Kennedy	156	Kennet	156	Kenneth	145
Kennett	178	Kennie	134	Kennith	549
Kenny	516	Kenon	235	Kenric	516
Kenrick	538	Kent	595	Kenton	257
Kenward	674	Kenway	617	Kenyon	213
Kenzie	167	Ker	527	Kerbay	628
Kerby	527	Keren	178	Kerey	191
Kerk	549	Kermie	167	Kermit	584
Kermy	549	Kern	573	Kerne	178
Kerr	527	Kerrin	573	Kerry	595
Kert	549	Kerwin	538	Kerwine	134
Kerwinn	584	Kery	595	Kesar	639
Kesse	145	Kester	156	Kev	562
Kevan	628	Keven	123	Kevin	527
Kevitt	516	Kevon	224	Key	595
Khalil	178	Kharouf	178	Khisto	641
Khoury	988	Kiden	527	Kiefer	189
Kiel	551	Kienan	639	Kieran	674
Kieren	178	Kiernan	639	Kieron	279
Kiffer	551	Kijika	156	Kiku	347
Kile	551	Kiley	538	Kilian	112
Killian	145	Killie	584	Killy	966
Kim	966	Kimball	156	Kimbell	551
Kimber	584	Kimble	527	Kimiko	685
Kimiyo	641	Kimmie	516	Kimmy	988
Kin	977	Kincaid	156	Kineks	516

King	955	Kingsley	573	Kingsly	977
Kingston	641	Kingswell	584	Kinnaird	178
Kinnard	178	Kinnell	595	Kinnie	538
Kinny	911	Kinsey	562	Kinsley	595
Kip	999	Kipp	977	Kippar	178
Kipper	573	Kippie	573	Kippy	955
Kirby	922	Kiritan	191	Kirk	944
Kirkby	944	Kirkley	551	Kirkwood	347
Kirwin	933	Kistur	358	Kit	944
Kito	641	Kittil	999	Kiyoshi	696
Kjeld	516	Klaas	268	Klair	156
Klare	652	Klaus	461	Kleber	178
Klemency	167	Klemenis	167	Klemens	167
Klement	178	Kleon	213	Klim	999
Kliment	573	Klyle	562	Klyment	551
Knight	966	Knolls	652	Knoton	358
Knowles	279	Knox	641	Knud	325
Knut	393	Knute	898	Kobi	641
Koby	628	Koenràad	426	Kolmin	652
Konane	336	Kono	371	Konrad	729
Konstantin	742	Konstantine	347	Kontar	797
Korb	641	Kordel	292	Kordula	191
Korey	292	Kormel	292	Kornek	292
Kornel	213	Kornelek	731	Korney	257
Korodon	922	Kort	641	Kory	696
Kosey	213	Kosse	246	Kostas	764
Kosti	652	Kostya	731	Kotha	731
Kovar	764	Krikor	641	Kris	933
Krisha	123	Krishan	178	Krishna	178
Krishnah	167	Krispin	966	Kriss	944
Krist	955	Kristafs	134	Kristian	112
Kristin	911	Kristjan	123	Kristmann	112
Kristo	652	Kristofer	224	Kristoffer	281
Kristofor	325	Kristoforo	922	Kristopher	224
Kristos	663	Kristsan	123	Krisus	347
Kriva	167	Kruin	371	Kryspin	944
Kuba	448	Kubes	854	Kulee	459
Kulen	819	Kumar	461	Kuper	898
Kurn	371	Kurt	347	Kurtis	358
Kuzih	393	Kwaku	494	Kwam	123
Kwamin	178	Kwasi	189	Kwesi	584
Ky	729	Kyle	538	Kylie	538
Kylin	988	Kynan	112	Kyne	551
Laban	213	Labhras	257	Labhruinn	459

Lach	156	Lache	652	Lachlan	246
Lacy	145	Lad	178	Ladd	123
Laddie	628	Laddy	191	Lado	775
Lafe	696	Laibrook	472	Laidley	685
Laird	178	Laith	145	Lajos	753
Lal	167	Lalo	764	Lamar	279
Lambert	628	Lamberto	325	Lammond	729
Lammont	797	Lamond	775	Lamont	753
Lance	628	Lancelin	617	Lancelot	371
Lancey	696	Lancilot	775	Land	134
Landan	281	Landbert	674	Landen	685
Lander	639	Landers	641	Landon	786
Landor	731	Landry	112	Lane	685
Laney	663	Lang	167	Langdon	764
Langford	775	Langley	674	Langsdon	775
Langston	753	Langstone	358	Langundo	167
Langworth	731	Lanie	685	Lannie	641
Lanny	123	Lanu	483	Larrance	729
Larry	112	Lars	145	Larson	797
Lasho	731	Laszlo	764	Lat	156
Latham	281	Lathe	641	Lathrop	729
Lathrope	325	Latimer	696	Lattie	674
Latty	156	Lauchlin	448	Laughton	178
Launce	922	Launcelot	674	Launder	933
Lauren	988	Laurence	527	Laurens	999
Laurent	911	Laurie	933	Laurier	933
Laurin	483	Laurince	922	Laurits	461
Lauritz	448	Laurn	483	Lavern	639
Law	189	Lawford	797	Lawler	628
Lawley	696	Lawney	628	Lawrance	775
Lawrence	279	Lawrie	685	Lawry	167
Lawson	753	Lawton	764	Lay	112
Layne	663	Layton	786	Lazar	224
Lazare	729	Lazaro	821	Lazarus	538
Leah	628	Leal	663	Lealand	764
Leander	235	Leandor	336	Leandre	235
Leandro	336	Leban	617	Lee	134
Leeland	268	Leger	112	Leggett	134
Leggitt	538	Leib	551	Leibel	189
Leicester	696	Leif	595	Leigh	595
Leighton	279	Leith	549	Leland	663
Lem	573	Lemar	674	Lemmie	123
Lemmy	595	Lemuel	415	Len	584
Lenaic	628	Lenard	639	Lenci	527

Lenn	549	Lennard	685	Lennart	663
Lennie	145	Lenno	246	Lennon	292
Lennor	246	Lennox	213	Lenny	527
Lensar	696	Lensiro	292	Leo	235
Leolin	224	Leon	281	Leonard	336
Leonardo	933	Leonce	729	Leone	786
Leoner	786	Leonerd	731	Leonhard	325
Leonid	235	Leonidas	347	Leonilde	764
Leopold	887	Leor	235	Lepp	584
Leroi	235	Leron	281	Leroy	213
Les	549	Lesley	156	Leslie	178
Lesly	551	Lester	167	Leupold	584
Lev	573	Leverett	628	Levern	134
Leverton	753	Levey	156	Levi	573
Levin	538	Levon	235	Levy	551
Lew	584	Lewas	696	Lewes	191
Lewi	584	Lewie	189	Lewis	595
Lex	595	Leyland	641	Leyman	617
Lezlie	156	Liall	191	Liam	178
Licien	527	Lief	595	Lien	584
Liggett	538	Lilian	123	Lin	988
Linc	922	Lince	527	Lincoln	617
Lind	933	Lindan	189	Lindberg	538
Lindell	595	Linden	584	Lindley	549
Lindon	685	Lindsay	123	Lindsey	527
Lindy	911	Linford	696	Linfred	595
Link	911	Linley	595	Linn	944
Lino	685	Linsay	178	Linsey	573
Linton	663	Linus	393	Lio	639
Lion	685	Lionel	224	Lionello	854
Lirit	955	Liron	685	Lisle	573
Litton	639	Livingston	696	Livo	674
Llew	527	Llewellyn	123	Lloyd	685
Llywellyn	595	Lock	685	Locke	281
Lockwood	988	Lodviska	753	Logan	764
Loic	663	Loman	731	Lomasi	786
Lombard	742	Lon	685	Lonato	415
London	382	Lonel	224	Lonnard	786
Lonnie	246	Lonny	628	Lono	382
Lorance	325	Lorant	718	Loredo	876
Loren	281	Lorens	292	Lorenz	279
Lorenzo	876	Lori	639	Lorimer	279
Lorin	685	Lorinc	628	Loring	663
Lorino	382	Lormer	279	Lorn	685

Lorne	281	Lorrie	235	Lorrimer	279
Lorry	617	Lory	617	Lothair	742
Lothaire	347	Lothar	742	Lothario	448
Lou	933	Loudon	639	Louie	538
Louis	944	Louison	696	Loulou	966
Lovel	213	Lovell	246	Lowe	281
Lowell	257	Lowis	696	Lowrance	371
Loy	617	Loyal	742	Loyd	652
Loyde	257	Loydie	257	Loydon	314
Luc	369	Luca	461	Lucais	472
Lucas	472	Luce	865	Lucerne	426
Lucho	955	Lucian	426	Luciano	123
Lucias	472	Lucien	821	Lucio	966
Lucius	674	Luck	382	Ludka	494
Ludlow	966	Ludo	977	Ludovic	955
Ludovick	977	Ludvig	393	Ludwig	314
Lugaidh	448	Luige	819	Luigi	314
Luigino	966	Luis	347	Luister	865
Lukas	461	Luke	854	Lukey	832
Lundy	314	Lunn	347	Lunt	314
Lusio	944	Lute	854	Lutero	551
Luthais	459	Luther	843	Ly	731
Lyall	178	Lyel	549	Lyell	573
Lyle	549	Lyman	112	Lyn	786
Lynall	134	Lynden	562	Lyndon	663
Lyndsay	191	Lynn	742	Lyon	663
Lyonel	292	Lyron	663	Lysander	628
Mac	178	Macaire	775	Macbeth	617
Mace	674	Macey	652	Mack	191
Mackenzie	246	Macknair	257	Maclean	764
Macnair	235	Macomb	742	Macy	156
Maddie	639	Maddis	145	Maddisen	696
Maddison	797	Maddock	786	Maddox	797
Maddy	112	Madid	134	Madisen	652
Madison	753	Madoc	729	Madock	742
Madog	764	Maecy	652	Mael	674
Maelmor	325	Maerwine	257	Magara	325
Magee	224	Magnus	483	Magre	628
Mahir	134	Mahmoud	123	Mahmud	426
Mahoud	178	Maimum	437	Maison	718
Maitland	292	Maixent	685	Maje	652
Major	753	Makan	224	Makara	369
Makis	178	Maks	178	Maksin	134
Mal	178	Malachi	292	Malachie	797

Malachy	279	Malan	235	Malcolm	786
Maldwyn	112	Malid	123	Malik	191
Malin	134	Malka	292	Mallory	786
Malo	775	Maloney	314	Malu	472
Malvern	674	Malvin	178	Manasseh	718
Manchu	426	Manco	731	Mandek	663
Mandel	674	Mander	641	Mando	742
Mandrill	112	Manfred	617	Manfried	617
Manga	279	Mango	775	Manleich	652
Manley	617	Mannie	652	Manning	189
Manny	134	Mano	797	Manoel	336
Manolo	437	Mansfield	652	Mansur	415
Manton	775	Manu	494	Manuel	933
Manuele	538	Manuil	437	Manus	415
Manuyil	415	Manvil	178	Manville	617
Mappin	156	Mar	145	Marald	224
Marc	178	Marceau	178	Marcel	617
Marcelin	663	Marcellin	696	Marcello	347
Marcellus	955	Marcelo	314	March	167
Marcin	134	Marcinek	652	Marcius	483
Marco	775	Marcos	786	Marcus	483
Marden	641	Mardy	167	Marek	663
Maret	663	Marice	674	Marick	191
Marid	189	Mariel	674	Marien	696
Marin	191	Marinos	718	Marinus	415
Mario	742	Marion	797	Marius	459
Mark	167	Markas	279	Markos	775
Markus	472	Marl	178	Marland	279
Marlen	639	Marley	652	Marlin	134
Marlo	775	Marlon	731	Marlow	731
Marlowe	336	Marly	156	Marmaduke	156
Marmion	742	Marnand	292	Marnin	156
Maro	742	Marquis	448	Marrand	246
Marreck	696	Marren	696	Marron	797
Mars	156	Marsden	652	Marsdon	753
Marsh	145	Marshal	279	Marshall	213
Marsin	112	Marson	718	Marston	731
Mart	167	Martainn	279	Martel	696
Marten	628	Martial	292	Martian	224
Martie	663	Martijn	134	Martin	123
Martino	729	Marton	729	Marts	178
Marty	145	Martyn	191	Marut	461
Marv	189	Marvan	246	Marve	685
Marven	641	Marvin	145	Marvyn	123

Marwin	156	Marwood	448	Maska	279
Maslen	641	Maslin	145	Maslon	742
Mason	718	Masow	718	Massey	641
Massimiliano	898	Massimo	718	Masud	494
Mat	167	Mata	268	Matek	685
Mateo	369	Mater	663	Mathe	652
Matheas	764	Mather	652	Mathew	617
Mathian	213	Mathias	268	Mathieu	955
Mathurin	415	Matias	279	Matope	347
Matro	764	Matsu	472	Matt	189
Matteo	382	Matthaeus	189	Matthaus	584
Mattheus	988	Matthew	639	Matthias	281
Matthieu	977	Matthiew	639	Mattias	292
Mattie	685	Matty	167	Mattys	178
Matus	472	Matvey	685	Maurey	922
Maurice	977	Mauricio	178	Maurie	944
Maurise	955	Maurits	472	Maurizio	134
Maury	426	Max	112	Maxence	292
Maxey	685	Maxi	112	Maxie	617
Maxim	156	Maxime	652	Maximilian	246
Maximilianus	551	Maximilien	641	Maximilienne	292
Maximillian	279	Maximin	112	Maximo	753
Maxwel	696	Maxwell	639	Maxy	189
May	123	Mayer	628	Mayfield	663
Mayhew	663	Maynard	224	Maynarm	224
Mayne	674	Mayo	729	Mayon	775
Mayor	729	Mazal	268	Mcgill	922
Mead	685	Meade	281	Medard	639
Medlar	628	Medwan	696	Medwin	595
Mehemet	696	Mehmet	191	Mehtar	652
Meier	145	Meir	549	Mel	573
Melaine	235	Melan	639	Melborn	257
Melbourne	156	Melburn	854	Melburne	459
Meldon	279	Melfort	268	Mell	516
Melvil	551	Melville	189	Melvin	573
Melvyn	551	Menard	641	Mendel	178
Mendie	145	Mendy	527	Mensah	696
Menteth	134	Mercer	178	Merdy	562
Mered	189	Meredith	191	Meredydd	156
Meredyth	178	Meriadec	224	Merideth	191
Meridith	595	Meridyth	573	Merill	516
Merithew	112	Merl	573	Merle	178
Merlin	538	Mernus	819	Merrack	696
Merrel	178	Merrell	112	Merrick	595

Merrie	145	Merril	573	Merrill	516
Merripen	178	Merritt	584	Merry	527
Mertin	527	Merton	224	Merv	584
Mervin	549	Mervyn	527	Merwin	551
Merwyn	538	Meryl	551	Meyer	123
Meyier	123	Meynard	628	Mic	977
Micah	167	Mich	966	Michael	696
Michah	156	Michail	191	Michal	191
Michale	696	Micheal	696	Micheil	595
Michel	595	Michele	191	Michelle	134
Michi	966	Mick	999	Mickey	573
Micki	999	Mickie	595	Micky	977
Migil	955	Miguel	854	Mihael	663
Mihail	167	Mihas	145	Mihiel	562
Mikael	696	Mike	562	Mikel	595
Mikelis	516	Mikey	549	Mikhail	189
Mikhos	663	Miki	966	Mikk	988
Mikkel	527	Mikkins	955	Miklos	617
Mikol	696	Miks	977	Mikulas	415
Mikus	371	Milap	156	Milbourn	955
Milbourne	551	Milburn	358	Milburne	854
Mile	573	Miles	584	Milford	685
Mill	911	Millard	156	Millardo	753
Miller	516	Milles	527	Millford	628
Millos	628	Milo	674	Milos	685
Milt	999	Miltie	595	Milton	652
Milty	977	Milward	178	Minal	134
Mine	595	Mineko	224	Miner	595
Minor	696	Mio	641	Mir	944
Mirit	966	Mirko	663	Miroslav	731
Mischa	178	Misha	145	Mitch	988
Mitchel	527	Mitchell	551	Mitros	674
Mitsos	685	Miyoko	347	Miyuki	347
Mo	641	Modred	235	Moe	246
Mohamet	393	Mohammed	369	Mohan	786
Moise	257	Moises	268	Mojag	731
Monro	393	Monroe	898	Montagne	358
Montagu	191	Montague	696	Monte	224
Montgomery	821	Monti	628	Monty	696
Mooney	876	Moore	843	Morcant	753
Mord	685	Mordecai	325	Mordy	663
More	246	Morel	279	Moreland	371
Morey	224	Morfin	663	Morgan	775
Morgen	279	Morgun	977	Morice	279

Morie	246	Morin	696	Moris	652
Morison	314	Moritz	652	Morlee	775
Morley	257	Morly	652	Morrell	213
Morrice	279	Morrie	246	Morris	652
Morrison	314	Morry	628	Morse	257
Mort	663	Mortemer	718	Morten	224
Mortie	268	Mortimer	213	Mortin	628
Morton	325	Morty	641	Morvan	742
Morven	246	Mory	628	Mos	652
Mose	257	Moses	268	Moshe	246
Mosi	652	Mosie	257	Moss	663
Motega	347	Motimo	314	Motka	786
Moyse	235	Moyses	246	Mozes	246
Muguet	246	Muhammad	562	Muir	347
Mulan	437	Mundan	494	Mungo	977
Munro	999	Munroe	595	Munsey	887
Mur	347	Murdoch	911	Murdock	944
Murlagh	448	Murphy	382	Murrah	437
Murray	426	Murrey	821	Murry	325
Murtagh	437	Murton	922	Murven	843
Murvyn	325	Muzio	933	My	742
Myca	156	Mycah	145	Mychal	178
Myer	527	Myles	562	Mylo	652
Mylon	617	Mylwen	562	Myrddin	966
Myrle	551	Myron	674	Myrvyn	549
Myrwyn	551	Nabal	213	Nabil	112
Nagid	178	Nahum	483	Nairn	112
Naldo	731	Nalren	641	Namid	145
Nandin	112	Nandor	753	Nanon	764
Nap	134	Napier	639	Napoleon	922
Narciso	797	Narcisse	617	Nard	191
Nasnan	279	Nasser	674	Nassor	775
Nat	178	Natal	213	Natale	718
Natane	731	Nataniel	764	Nate	674
Nathan	224	Nathanael	854	Nathanial	358
Nathaniel	753	Nathen	628	Natho	764
Nathu	461	Natka	292	Nattie	696
Natty	178	Naum	494	Nav	191
Nawat	235	Neacail	729	Neal	685
Neale	281	Neall	628	Nealon	347
Nealson	358	Nealy	663	Neathe	268
Ned	595	Neddie	145	Neddy	527
Nee	156	Neel	189	Nefen	178
Nehemiah	279	Nehru	843	Neil	584

Neill	527	Neils	595	Neilson	257
Neith	562	Nelek	112	Nell	527
Nellie	123	Nello	224	Nelly	595
Nels	595	Nelson	257	Nemo	292
Nenet	134	Neper	134	Nepter	156
Neree	652	Nero	257	Neron	213
Nessim	527	Nestor	281	Netis	584
Neto	279	Nev	595	Nevil	538
Nevile	134	Neville	167	Nevin	551
Nevins	562	Newall	674	Newbold	213
Newel	145	Newell	178	Newland	641
Newlands	652	Newlin	595	Newlyn	573
Newman	617	Newton	281	Nial	189
Niall	123	Nibaw	134	Nic	988
Nicaba	213	Niccolo	358	Niceto	213
Nichol	617	Nicholas	729	Nichole	213
Nicholl	641	Nichols	628	Nick	911
Nickey	584	Nicki	911	Nickie	516
Nickolas	753	Nickolaus	156	Nickson	674
Nicky	988	Nicodemus	584	Nicol	628
Nicolae	325	Nicolai	729	Nicolas	731
Nicoli	628	Nicolis	639	Niel	584
Niels	595	Nigan	189	Nigel	562
Nigell	595	Nihal	178	Nik	977
Niki	977	Nikita	191	Nikki	999
Nikky	977	Niklas	123	Niklos	628
Niko	674	Nikola	718	Nikolai	718
Nikolao	415	Nikolas	729	Nikolaus	123
Nikolay	786	Nikolia	718	Nikolos	325
Nikos	685	Nikula	415	Nikulas	426
Nil	988	Niles	595	Nils	999
Nilson	652	Ninon	663	Nirel	584
Nirveli	538	Nissan	134	Niven	551
Nivens	562	Nixon	674	Nnamdi	191
Noach	775	Noah	742	Noak	775
Nobe	279	Nobel	213	Nobie	279
Noble	213	Noby	652	Nodin	652
Noe	257	Noel	281	Nolan	742
Noland	786	Noll	628	Nollie	224
Nolly	696	Norber	279	Norbert	292
Norbie	279	Norby	652	Norm	696
Norman	753	Normand	797	Normane	358
Normi	696	Normie	292	Normy	674
Norrie	257	Norris	663	Norry	639

North	663	Northcliff	663	Northcliffe	268
Northrop	347	Northrup	944	Norton	336
Nortrop	358	Nortrup	955	Norvel	235
Norvie	292	Norvil	639	Norville	268
Norvin	652	Norvyn	639	Norward	753
Norwell	279	Norwin	663	Norwood	955
Norwyn	641	Nowell	279	Nowles	257
Noy	639	Numaris	415	Nuno	911
Nur	358	Nuri	358	Nuriel	887
Nuris	369	Nurit	371	Nuru	652
Nye	538	Nygell	573	Nyushan	483
Oak	729	Oakely	336	Oakes	336
Oakie	325	Oakleigh	325	Oakley	336
Oakly	731	Oaks	731	Oates	336
Oba	729	Obadiah	854	Obadias	876
Obed	268	Obediah	358	Oberon	876
Obert	246	Obie	224	Obo	325
Obour	628	Obram	764	Oby	696
Octave	393	Octavian	854	Octavien	358
Octavius	112	Octavus	112	Ode	246
Odell	213	Odey	224	Odi	641
Odie	246	Odilon	336	Odin	696
Odinan	753	Odinum	944	Odion	393
Odo	347	Odolf	347	Odon	393
Ody	628	Offin	685	Ogdan	775
Ogden	279	Ogdon	371	Ogie	279
Ogilvie	257	Ogin	639	Oglesby	224
Ogun	933	Ohanko	461	Ohin	641
Ojin	663	Okeley	731	Okely	235
Oki	628	Okon	371	Olaf	797
Olafur	191	Olar	731	Olav '	775
Ole	235	Olen	281	Olery	213
Oles	246	Olin	685	Olis	641
Oliver	279	Olivero	876	Olivier	279
Oliviero	876	Olli	663	Ollie	268
Olly	641	Olney	268	Olorun	685
Olvan	731	Olwen	246	Olwyn	628
Omai	742	Omar	742	Omarr	742
Omer	246	Omero	843	Onan	718
Onesime	718	Onfre	224	Onfroi	325
Onofredo	562	Onslow	358	Opie	279
Oral	731	Oram	742	Oran	753
Orazio	483	Orban	775	Ordando	448
Ordway	775	Orejtes	742	Orel	235

Oren	257	Oreste	731	Orestes	742
Orford	314	Orin	652	Orino	358
Orion	358	Orlan	786	Orland	731
Orlando	437	Orman	797	Ormand	742
Ormar	742	Ormen	292	Ormie	246
Ormin	696	Ormond	347	Ormund	944
Ornit	674	Oro	393	Orran	753
Orren	257	Orrick	652	Orrin	652
Orsini	663	Orson	369	Orton	371
Orunjan	123	Orv	641	Orval	775
Orvil	674	Orville	213	Orvin	696
Os	617	Osbert	257	Osborn	382
Osborne	887	Osbourn	685	Osbourne	281
Osburn	988	Osburne	584	Oscar	742
Osen	268	Osgood	933	Oshun	955
Oskar	731	Osman	718	Osmar	753
Osmond	358	Osmund	955	Osred	257
Osric	641	Ossie	224	Ossy	696
Oswald	742	Oswell	235	Otadan	821
Otes	235	Othello	876	Othis	628
Othman	718	Othniel	292	Otho	314
Otis	639	Otman	729	Oton	371
Ottah	731	Otti	641	Ottie	246
Otto	347	Ottorino	999	Ouray	178
Owain	718	Owen	213	Oxford	371
Oxton	347	Oz	685	Ozzie	279
Ozzy	652	Pablo	731	Pace	617
Packston	729	Paco	718	Pacome	358
Pacono	461	Pacorro	415	Paddie	663
Paddy	145	Padget	628	Padgett	641
Padma	268	Padraic	257	Padraig	292
Padriac	257	Page	652	Paget	674
Paige	652	Paine	639	Paki	191
Pal	112	Palani	268	Paley	685
Pali	112	Pall	145	Pallaton	821
Palm	156	Palmer	652	Panchito	775
Pancho	753	Panos	742	Paoll	742
Paolo	415	Paquito	189	Parge	652
Paris	189	Parish	178	Park	191
Parke	696	Parker	696	Parkin	156
Parlan	268	Parmatur	549	Parnell	696
Parr	178	Parrie	674	Parrisch	112
Parrish	178	Parrnell	696	Parry	156
Parsefal	786	Parsifal	281	Pascal	257

Pascale	753	Pascual	551	Pasha	279
Pasquale	112	Pat	191	Patamon	898
Pate	696	Paten	652	Patin	156
Paton	753	Patrek	628	Patric	134
Patrice	639	Patricio	731	Patrick	156
Patrin	156	Patrizio	786	Patrizius	494
Patsy	189	Patten	674	Patterson	382
Pattie	628	Pattin	178	Patton	775
Patty	191	Patwin	112	Pauel	911
Paul	415	Pauley	988	Paulie	911
Paulin	461	Paulinus	775	Paulo	112
Pauly	483	Pausha	573	Pavel	652
Pawel	663	Pawelek	281	Paxon	797
Paxson	718	Paxten	628	Paxton	729
Payat	279	Payne	617	Payton	731
Paz	167	Peadar	729	Pearce	213
Peder	123	Pedro	224	Peer	178
Peet	191	Peeter	696	Peirce	112
Peke	191	Pelham	641	Pell	549
Pelton	281	Pembroke	764	Pembrook	865
Pen	538	Penley	145	Penn	584
Pennie	189	Penny	562	Penrod	279
Pepe	156	Pepi	551	Pepillo	224
Pepin	516	Pepito	279	Peppi	538
Peppie	134	Peppin	584	Peppy	516
Per	573	Perc	516	Perce	112
Perceval	281	Percival	685	Percy	584
Peregrine	617	Peri	573	Peris	584
Perkin	551	Pernell	191	Pero	279
Perren	134	Perri	573	Perrin	538
Perry	551	Perth	584	Petar	696
Pete	191	Peter	191	Peterkin	178
Peterus	415	Petey	178	Peti	595
Petie	191	Petr	595	Petras	617
Petria	696	Petrie	191	Petrin	551
Peveral	257	Peverall	281	Peverel	652
Peverell	685	Peveril	156	Peverill	189
Peyton	235	Phelan	652	Phelips	584
Phellipps	595	Phellips	527	Phelps	584
Phil	999	Philbert	549	Philbin	977
Philemon	292	Philibert	549	Philip	977
Philipp	955	Philippe	551	Philips	988
Phillie	538	Phillip	911	Phillipe	516
Phillipp	988	Phillippe	584	Phillipps	999

Phillips	922	Philly	911	Philo	696
Philpot	696	Phineas	639	Pias	189
Pickford	641	Pickworth	696	Pierce	112
Piere	178	Pierie	178	Piero	279
Pierre	178	Pierrick	538	Pierro	279
Pierrot	292	Piers	584	Pierson	246
Pieter	191	Pietrek	123	Pietro	292
Pincas	178	Pinchas	167	Pincus	371
Pinkus	369	Pinon	685	Piotr	696
Pip	955	Pipal	189	Pippo	639
Pirro	674	Pitney	538	Pitt	922
Pius	382	Placide	685	Plato	731
Platon	786	Platt	156	Plenny	595
Pokuda	145	Pokuma	145	Pol	617
Pollard	786	Pollerd	281	Polloch	369
Pollock	393	Pollux	911	Pomeroy	898
Pompey	279	Port	696	Porter	292
Portie	292	Porty	674	Poul	911
Pov	628	Powell	292	Powl	663
Prane	639	Pranele	268	Pranute	955
Praxedes	292	Preben	156	Preetam	246
Pren	538	Prent	551	Prentice	189
Prentiss	573	Prescot	246	Prescott	268
Presley	191	Prester	112	Preston	268
Prewet	156	Prewett	178	Prewit	551
Prewitt	573	Price	516	Primael	652
Primo	628	Prince	562	Prinz	922
Prior	674	Privat	145	Proctor	336
Prosper	268	Pruitt	325	Prumer	821
Pry	775	Pryce	584	Pryor	652
Purcell	876	Purdy	393	Purvis	336
Putnam	494	Putnem	898	Quasimodo	786
Quemby	832	Quenby	843	Quenly	854
Quennel	437	Quent	865	Quentin	821
Quico	922	Quigley	876	Quill	358
Quillan	415	Quillon	911	Quimby	336
Quinby	347	Quincy	358	Quinlan	437
Quinn	393	Quint	369	Quintin	325
Quinton	922	Quintus	674	Quirin	347
Rab	123	Rabbi	145	Rabbie	641
Rabby	123	Rabi	123	Rabiah	213
Race	639	Rad	145	Radbert	685
Radborne	325	Radbourn	123	Radbourne	628
Radburn	426	Radcliff	145	Radcliffe	641

Raddie	685	Raddy	167	Radford	753
Radha	235	Radleigh	641	Radley	652
Radman	246	Radmen	641	Radmund	483
Radnor	797	Radolf	742	Radomil	729
Radovan	843	Radulf	448	Radvers	696
Rae	696	Raelle	268	Raf	167
Rafael	797	Rafaelle	336	Rafaello	437
Rafe	663	Raff	134	Raffaello	494
Raffaelo	461	Rafferty	639	Raffin	189
Rafi	167	Ragnar	235	Rahman	281
Rahmet	652	Raiden	696	Raif	167
Raimond	742	Raimondo	448	Raimund	448
Raimundo	145	Rainer	652	Rainger	639
Rainier	652	Ralegh	696	Raleigh	696
Ralf	191	Ralph	191	Ralphie	696
Ralston	729	Ram	145	Ramadan	347
Rambert	685	Ramda	281	Ramla	279
Ramman	246	Rammand	281	Ramon	797
Ramsay	235	Ramsden	652	Ramsey	639
Ramuntcho	145	Ranald	235	Rance	685
Rancell	652	Rand	191	Randal	235
Randall	268	Rande	696	Randell	663
Randi	191	Randie	696	Randle	639
Randolf	797	Randolph	797	Randy	178
Rane	652	Range	639	Ranger	639
Rani	156	Ranit	178	Rankin	134
Ranon	718	Ransell	639	Ransford	775
Ransley	674	Ransom	718	Ranulf	459
Rao	797	Raoul	134	Raphael	797
Rapier	674	Ras	112	Rasmus	461
Rastus	448	Ratri	123	Rauf	461
Raul	437	Ravi	145	Ravid	189
Raviv	189	Rawleigh	652	Rawley	663
Rawlins	156	Rawnie	617	Rawson	729
Ray	178	Rayburn	459	Raymie	628
Raymon	775	Raymond	729	Raymund	426
Raynard	279	Rayner	639	Raynold	718
Raynor	731	Razel	628	Razi	189
Razil	123	Razili	123	Read	641
Reade	246	Reading	674	Reagan	731
Reagen	235	Reamonn	358	Rearden	292
Reardon	393	Recardo	371	Red	549
Redbourn	527	Redbourne	123	Redcliff	549
Redcliffe	145	Redd	584	Reddin	549

Redding	527	Redford	257	Redley	156
Redman	641	Redmond	281	Redmund	887
Redpath	639	Redvers	191	Redwald	674
Redwall	663	Reece	639	Reed	145
Reede	641	Rees	112	Reese	617
Reeve	641	Refael	292	Reg	573
Regan	639	Regen	134	Regg	551
Reggie	156	Reggis	562	Reggy	538
Regi	573	Reginald	617	Reginauld	911
Regis	584	Rehard	639	Reid	549
Reiko	224	Reilly	549	Reinald	639
Reinaldo	336	Reinaldos	347	Reinders	112
Reinhard	685	Reinhold	224	Reinold	235
Reinwald	685	Rem	549	Remi	549
Remick	595	Remin	595	Remington	257
Remmie	189	Remus	854	Ren	551
Renado	393	Renald	639	Renaldo	336
Renan	617	Renard	696	Renato	371
Renaud	999	Renault	911	Rendor	292
Rene	156	Renford	268	Renfred	167
Renfrew	178	Rennard	652	Rennet	134
Rennie	112	Renny	584	Renshaw	617
Renton	235	Renzo	246	Resel	145
Reuben	472	Reudy	821	Reuel	437
Reuven	494	Rex	562	Rexford	279
Rey	573	Reyhan	628	Reylan	663
Reynard	674	Reynold	213	Reynolds	224
Rez	584	Rhett	538	Rhodes	246
Rhys	797	Riamund	448	Rian	156
Ric	933	Rica	134	Ricard	178
Ricardo	775	Riccardo	718	Rice	538
Ricehard	663	Rich	922	Richard	167
Richardo	764	Richart	145	Richerd	562
Richey	595	Richi	922	Richie	527
Richman	123	Richmond	663	Richy	999
Rick	955	Rickard	191	Rickert	573
Rickey	538	Ricki	955	Rickie	551
Rickward	156	Rickwood	358	Ricky	933
Rico	639	Ricy	911	Riddock	641
Rider	549	Ridge	527	Ridgeway	652
Ridgley	538	Ridley	551	Ridpath	134
Riekchen	191	Rienzo	246	Rigby	977
Rigg	955	Rik	922	Rikardo	764
Riki	922	Riley	516	Rimhel	562

Rimhen	584	Rimiel	573	Rimlal	112
Rimnir	999	Rimon	696	Rimshu	347
Rin	955	Rinaldo	731	Ring	933
Ringo	639	Riobard	764	Riocard	775
Riordan	797	Rip	977	Ripley	584
Risley	527	Risto	639	Riston	685
Ritch	944	Ritchard	189	Ritchie	549
Ritter	549	Roald	775	Roan	753
Roand	797	Roark	729	Roarke	325
Rob	628	Robard	764	Robb	641
Robbert	268	Robbi	641	Robbie	246
Robbin	696	Robby	628	Robers	235
Robert	246	Roberto	843	Robin	674
Robinet	292	Robinson	347	Roble	257
Roc	639	Rocco	369	Roch	628
Rochester	753	Rock	652	Rockey	235
Rockie	257	Rockley	268	Rockly	663
Rockwell	279	Rocky	639	Rod	641
Rodas	753	Rodd	685	Roddie	281
Roddy	663	Roden	292	Roderic	279
Roderich	268	Roderick	292	Roderigo	821
Rodge	224	Rodger	224	Rodhlann	775
Rodi	641	Rodie	246	Rodman	742
Rodmond	382	Rodmund	988	Rodney	279
Rodolf	347	Rodolfo	944	Rodolph	347
Rodolphe	843	Rodolpho	944	Rodric	674
Rodrick	696	Rodrigo	325	Rodrigue	527
Rodrique	538	Rodwell	268	Roe	292
Roelie	731	Rog	674	Rogan	731
Rogatien	358	Rogelio	819	Roger	279
Rogerio	876	Rogers	281	Rohan	742
Rohin	641	Roi	696	Roland	731
Rolando	437	Roldan	731	Roley	213
Rolf	696	Rolfe	292	Rolland	764
Rollie	268	Rollin	628	Rollins	639
Rollo	369	Rolly	641	Rolon	382
Rolond	336	Rolph	696	Rolphe	292
Rolt	652	Roly	617	Roma	742
Romain	797	Roman	797	Romaric	775
Romeo	843	Romford	358	Romney	279
Romuald	123	Ron	652	Ronald	731
Ronaldo	437	Ronan	718	Rondle	235
Ronit	674	ronn	617	Ronnie	213
Ronny	685	Ronson	325	Rooney	832

Roparz	764	Roper	279	Rorie	292
Rorke	224	Rorry	674	Rory	674
Ros	617	Rosco	347	Roscoe	843
Rosell	279	Roslin	696	Roslyn	674
Rosmer	257	Ross	628	Rossano	472
Rosse	224	Rosselin	213	Rossie	224
Rosslyn	685	Rossy	696	Roswald	742
Roswall	731	Roswell	235	Roth	617
Rothwell	235	Roupen	538	Rourke	527
Routledge	178	Rouvin	999	Rover	246
Rowad	797	Rowan	718	Rowe	257
Rowell	224	Rowen	213	Rowland	786
Rowlando	483	Rowley	268	Rowney	281
Rowsan	729	Rowson	325	Roxbury	966
Roy	674	Royal	718	Royall	742
Royce	213	Royd	628	Royden	279
Roydon	371	Royes	281	Roz	685
Ruan	459	Ruark	426	Rube	821
Ruben	876	Rubert	843	Rubey	898
Rubin	371	Ruburt	641	Ruby	393
Ruck	358	Rudd	382	Ruddie	887
Ruddy	369	Rudi	347	Rudie	843
Rudiger	821	Rudo	944	Rudolf	944
Rudolfo	641	Rudolph	944	Rudy	325
Rudyard	461	Ruelle	461	Rufe	865
Ruff	336	Ruffen	887	Rufford	977
Rufin	325	Rufo	966	Ruford	911
Rufus	674	Rugby	371	Ruggiero	551
Ruir	393	Rule	832	Rumer	843
Rumford	955	Rupert	898	Ruperto	595
Rupprecht	898	Ruprecht	821	Rurick	358
Rurik	325	Rus	314	Rusell	876
Rush	393	Rushford	911	Ruskin	382
Russ	325	Russel	854	Russell	887
Russet	843	Rust	336	Rustie	832
Rustin	382	Rusty	314	Rutger	898
Rutherford	527	Rutland	459	Rutledge	472
Rutley	832	Ruttger	821	Ruy	371
Ryan	134	Ryane	639	Rycroft	696
Rydder	562	Ryder	527	Rye	573
Rylan	167	Ryland	112	Ryle	516
Ryley	584	Rylie	516	Ryman	178
Rymner	573	Ryon	639	Ryton	652
Ryun	336	Saber	639	Sabin	189

Sacha	235	Sachael	764	Sacher	639
Sacheverell	742	Sachi	134	Safford	786
Sahen	652	Sahile	639	Saki	134
Sal	145	Saleem	281	Salem	685
Salim	189	Sallie	674	Sally	156
Salmalin	279	Salmon	742	Salomo	483
Salomon	448	Salomone	944	Salton	729
Salus	459	Salvador	832	Salvadore	437
Salvator	819	Salvatore	415	Salvidor	731
Sam	156	Samborn	731	Sami	156
Samir	156	Samman	257	Sammi	191
Sammie	696	Sammon	753	Sammy	178
Sampson	797	Samson	729	Samuel	988
Samuele	584	Samy	134	Sanat	281
Sanborn	742	Sancho	786	Sander	617
Sanders	628	Sanderson	371	Sandford	729
Sandie	617	Sandor	718	Sandro	718
Sandus	426	Sandy	189	Sanford	775
Sansom	729	Sanson	731	Sansone	336
Santo	786	Santon	742	Sarge	685
Sargent	663	Sargie	685	Sarngin	191
Sarojin	775	Sarsour	123	Sartan	281
Sascha	246	Sasha	213	Saturnin	448
Saul	448	Sauncho	189	Saunder	911
Saunders	922	Saunderson	674	Saundor	112
Savile	685	Saville	628	Saw	167
Sawny	191	Sawyer	641	Sawyere	246
Sax	178	Saxe	674	Saxon	731
Sayer	685	Sayers	696	Sayre	685
Sayres	696	Scanlon	786	Schuyler	843
Scoey	224	Scot	663	Scott	685
Scotti	685	Scottie	281	Scotty	663
Scoville	257	Scully	382	Seabert	257
Seabright	628	Seabrock	382	Seabrook	955
Seager	281	Seain	663	Sealey	224
Seamus	966	Sean	663	Seann	628
Searl	641	Searle	246	Seaton	382
Seb	538	Seba	639	Sebald	617
Sebastian	729	Sebastiano	426	Sebastien	224
Sebert	156	Sebrock	281	Sebrook	854
Sedgeley	641	Sedgequick	472	Sedgley	145
Sedgwick	549	Seeley	628	Seely	123
Seetin	189	Seeton	786	Sef	573
Segar	685	Segel	123	Seger	189

Seif	573	Seigneur	448	Seker	134
Selby	549	Selden	145	Seldon	246
Selig	527	Selmar	685	Selmer	189
Selvin	549	Selwen	156	Selwin	551
Selwyn	538	Semyon	281	Sen	562
Senior	268	Sennett	167	Senon	224
Senwe	123	Seosaidh	358	Sepp	562
Septimus	865	Seraphin	639	Sereno	764
Serge	189	Sergeant	268	Sergei	189
Sergent	167	Sergie	189	Sergio	281
Serle	145	Servan	617	Seth	527
Seton	281	Seumas	966	Seumus	268
Severin	112	Severn	112	Sevilen	145
Sewald	641	Sewall	639	Seward	617
Sewell	134	Sexton	257	Sextus	819
Seymour	538	Shadwell	663	Shae	696
Shaine	652	Shalom	775	Shamus	459
Shan	156	Shanahan	393	Shanan	213
Shandy	178	Shane	652	Shanley	663
Shann	112	Shannan	268	Shannon	764
Sharif	167	Sharmin	191	Shattuck	494
Shaughn	426	Shaun	459	Shaver	641
Shaw	156	Shawn	112	Shay	178
Shayn	134	Shayne	639	Shea	696
Sheane	257	Sheehan	246	Sheff	538
Sheffie	134	Sheffield	112	Sheffy	516
Shel	538	Shelby	538	Sheldan	639
Shelden	134	Sheldon	235	Shell	562
Shelley	145	Shello	268	Shelly	549
Shelton	213	Shem	549	Shen	551
Shep	573	Shepard	628	Shepherd	112
Shepley	189	Shepp	551	Sheppard	696
Shepperd	191	Sheppy	538	Sheratan	775
Sherborn	279	Sherborne	775	Sherbourn	573
Sherbourne	178	Sherburn	876	Sherburne	472
Sheremen	696	Sheridan	696	Sherlock	281
Sherlocke	786	Sherm	549	Sherman	696
Shermen	191	Shermie	145	Shermy	527
Sherwin	516	Sherwood	898	Sherwynd	538
Shimeon	292	Shing	933	Shino	652
Shipley	584	Shipton	652	Shiro	696
Shizu	382	Shizuko	911	Sholom	371
Sholto	358	Shon	652	Shoushan	156
Shunnar	415	Shurik	325	Shurlock	988

Shurlocke	584	Shurwood	696	Si	911
Sid	955	Siddell	562	Sidnee	112
Sidney	584	Siegfrid	595	Siegfried	191
Siffre	549	Sig	988	Sigfrid	999
Sigfried	595	Sigismond	641	Sigismondo	347
Sigismund	347	Sigismundo	944	Sigmond	639
Sigmund	336	Sigsmond	641	Sigurd	336
Sigvard	178	Sigwald	123	Sil	944
Silas	156	Sile	549	Silva	189
Silvain	145	Silvan	145	Silvano	742
Silvanus	459	Silvere	189	Silvester	123
Silvestre	123	Silvio	685	Sim	955
Simba	178	Simen	516	Simeon	213
Simmonds	617	Simon	617	Simone	213
Simpson	696	Simson	628	Sinclair	134
Sinclaire	639	Sinclare	639	Sinnott	663
Siobham	764	Siomann	764	Sipatu	415
Sissil	966	Sivan	112	Siwald	145
Siward	112	Sixtus	314	Skeat	652
Skeet	156	Skeeter	652	Skeets	167
Skell	595	Skelly	573	Skelton	246
Skerry	516	Skip	911	Skipp	988
Skipper	584	Skippie	584	Skippy	966
Skipton	685	Sky	731	Skye	516
Skylar	145	Skyler	549	Slade	685
Slane	696	Slaven	641	Slavik	112
Slavin	145	Slawek	628	Sleven	145
Slevin	549	Slim	988	Sloan	797
Sloane	393	Sloffco	314	Sly	742
Smedley	112	Smedly	516	Smith	966
Smitty	977	Snowden	224	Socrates	371
Sol	641	Solamon	448	Sollie	279
Solly	652	Soloman	448	Solomon	944
Solon	393	Somerset	786	Somerton	832
Somerville	764	Sommerville	718	Son	663
Sonnie	224	Sonny	696	Soren	268
Sorrel	246	Sorrell	279	Southwell	549
Spalding	191	Spangler	652	Spark	112
Sparke	617	Sparkie	617	Sparky	189
Spaulding	494	Speed	134	Spence	178
Spencer	178	Spense	156	Spenser	156
Sprague	966	Sproule	527	Sprowle	279
Squire	898	Stace	663	Stacee	268
Stacey	641	Stacie	663	Stacy	145

Stafano	854	Staferd	641	Staffard	213
Stafford	718	Staford	742	Stamford	786
Stan	189	Stanberry	685	Stanbury	483
Stancio	729	Stancliff	189	Stancliffe	685
Standcliff	134	Standcliffe	639	Standford	742
Standish	134	Stane	685	Stanfield	639
Stanford	797	Stanhope	358	Stanislao	832
Stanislas	246	Stanislaus	549	Stanislav	279
Stanislaw	281	Stanleigh	685	Stanley	696
Stanly	191	Stanmore	336	Stanton	764
Stanway	224	Stanwick	191	Stanwood	483
Starling	191	Starr	134	Stas	145
Stasio	742	Steadman	775	Stearn	685
Stearne	281	Stedman	674	Steen	189
Stefan	652	Steffan	628	Steffen	123
Stein	584	Stene	189	Stephan	652
Stephanus	966	Stephen	156	Stephenson	729
Sterling	595	Stern	584	Sterne	189
Steve	178	Steven	134	Stevenson	797
Stevie	178	Stevin	538	Stevy	551
Stew	584	Steward	639	Stewart	617
Stian	189	Stiggur	382	Stiles	573
Stillman	191	Stillmann	156	Stilman	167
Stinson	652	Stirling	999	Stockley	292
Stockton	369	Stockwell	213	Stoddard	764
Stoke	257	Storm	674	Storr	639
Stowe	281	Strahan	279	Stratford	764
Strothers	257	Stroud	977	Struthers	854
Stryker	538	Stu	336	Stuart	459
Styles	551	Suffield	821	Sullie	876
Sullivan	472	Sully	358	Sultan	426
Summer	898	Sumner	819	Sunki	382
Sutcliff	336	Sutcliffe	832	Sutherlan	911
Sutherland	955	Sutton	911	Sven	516
Svend	551	Swain	123	Swayne	696
Sweeney	696	Swen	527	Sweyn	595
Swinton	696	Syd	753	Sydney	562
Sylas	134	Sylvain	123	Sylvan	123
Sylvere	167	Sylvester	191	Sylvestre	191
Syman	189	Symington	641	Symon	685
Symphorien	257	Tab	145	Tabb	167
Tabbie	663	Tabby	145	Taber	641
Tabib	167	Tabor	742	Tad	167
Tadd	112	Taddeo	314	Taddeusz	911

Taddy	189	Tadeas	775	Tadek	685
Tadeo	369	Tades	674	Tadeus	977
Tadewi	628	Tadio	764	Tadzi	156
Tadzio	753	Taffy	134	Taggart	292
Taillefer	257	Tailor	753	Tait	145
Taite	641	Takis	156	Takuhi	437
Tal	156	Talbert	696	Talbot	797
Tales	663	Tallie	685	Tally	167
Talman	257	Talmon	753	Talor	753
Tam	167	Tamaki	281	Taman	224
Tamas	279	Tamjin	134	Tammany	246
Tammie	617	Tammy	189	Tan	178
Tancred	652	Tanek	696	Tanguy	437
Tann	134	Tanner	639	Tanney	617
Tannie	639	Tanno	731	Tanny	112
Tano	775	Tanton	753	Tarek	641
Tarleton	336	Tarn	178	Taro	729
Tarrance	718	Tas	134	Tassos	753
Tate	641	Tauno	178	Taurin	472
Tav	167	Tave	663	Tavey	641
Tavis	178	Tavish	167	Tawno	731
Tawrin	134	Tayib	123	Tayler	639
Taylor	731	Taylore	336	Tazu	415
Teador	369	Teagan	753	Teagon	358
Teague	595	Teak	641	Tearlach	775
Tearle	257	Tebald	628	Ted	562
Tedd	516	Teddie	112	Teddy	584
Tedman	663	Tedmond	213	Tedmund	819
Tedrick	527	Telek	178	Telem	191
Telfer	123	Telfor	224	Telford	268
Telfour	527	Telis	562	Telly	562
Tem	562	Teman	628	Temp	549
Temple	178	Templeton	753	Tenison	246
Tennison	292	Tennyson	279	Teodoor	562
Teodor	865	Teodorico	595	Teodoro	562
Teos	235	Terance	213	Terell	189
Terence	617	Terencio	718	Terike	145
Terrance	213	Terrel	156	Terrell	189
Terrence	617	Terri	527	Terrill	584
Terris	538	Terry	595	Tervor	268
Tevis	573	Teyte	123	Thacher	639
Thackeray	742	Thad	156	Thaddaus	516
Thaddee	292	Thaddeus	911	Thady	134
Thain	167	Thaine	663	Thane	663

Thanos	775	Thatch	156	Thatcher	652
Thaw	167	Thaxter	696	Thay	189
Thayer	685	Thayne	641	Thebault	988
Thedas	663	Thedric	584	Thedrick	516
Theo	213	Theobald	314	Theodoire	459
Theodor	854	Theodore	459	Theodoric	887
Theodorick	819	Theon	268	Theophane	832
Theophile	718	Theophilus	527	Theron	268
Therstan	696	Theudobald	652	Thibaud	472
Thibaut	459	Thierry	584	Thom	652
Thoma	753	Thomae	358	Thomas	764
Thomasin	729	Thompson	393	Thomson	325
Thor	617	Thorald	786	Thorbert	257
Thorbjorn	393	Thorburn	988	Thordis	663
Thoren	268	Thorfinn	685	Thorin	663
Thorleif	213	Thorley	224	Thormond	358
Thormund	955	Thorn	663	Thornburn	944
Thorndike	235	Thorndyke	213	Thorne	268
Thorneley	775	Thornely	279	Thornie	268
Thornley	279	Thornly	674	Thornton	347
Thorny	641	Thorold	382	Thorp	685
Thorpe	281	Thorstein	292	Thorsten	292
Thorton	382	Thorvald	731	Thumas	461
Thurlow	999	Thurmond	955	Thurstan	494
Thurston	999	Tibal	178	Tibbald	145
Tibble	595	Tibbles	516	Tibold	628
Tibor	641	Tidzio	652	Tiebold	224
Tiebout	562	Tierman	628	Tiernan	639
Tierney	156	Tiffany	189	Tilden	551
Tiler	551	Tilford	663	Tilton	639
Tim	966	Timie	562	Timin	922
Timmi	911	Timmie	516	Timmy	988
Timofie	235	Timon	628	Timoteo	887
Timothea	371	Timothee	775	Timotheus	584
Timothie	279	Timothy	652	Timur	369
Tinbury	371	Tink	999	Tinkler	538
Tino	674	Tiobaid	786	Tiobald	729
Tiomoid	314	Tirell	584	Tirrel	551
Tirrell	584	Tito	641	Titos	652
Titus	358	Tivon	628	Toba	742
Tobal	775	Tobalito	494	Tobbar	764
Tobe	246	Tobiah	731	Tobias	753
Tobie	246	Tobin	696	Tobit	663
Toby	628	Tod	663	Todd	617

Toddie	213	Toddy	685	Todor	369
Todorko	988	Todos	371	Toft	617
Tohon	369	Toiboid	382	Toland	753
Tolek	279	Toli	652	Tom	663
Tomas	775	Tomasek	393	Tomasjo	483
Tomasko	494	Tomaso	472	Tomasso	483
Tomaz	753	Tomcio	393	Tome	268
Tomek	281	Tomi	663	Tomislaw	764
Tomkin	641	Tomlin	652	Tommaso	426
Tommie	213	Tommy	685	Tomo	369
Tompson	314	Toms	674	Tomson	336
Tonek	292	Toni	674	Tonik	696
Tonnie	235	Tony	652	Toomas	472
Topaz	786	Topwe	257	Tor	628
Torald	797	Torbert	268	Torburn	999
Tore	224	Torey	292	Torin	674
Torley	235	Tormey	246	Tormond	369
Tormund	966	Tormy	641	Torr	628
Torrance	314	Torre	224	Torrence	718
Torrey	292	Torri	628	Torrin	674
Torry	696	Toshio	325	Toski	652
Totty	641	Toussaint	123	Tovi	663
Town	639	Towney	213	Townie	235
Townley	246	Townly	641	Townsend	246
Towny	617	Trace	652	Tracey	639
Tracie	652	Tracy	134	Trahearn	764
Trahearne	369	Trahern	663	Trask	156
Traver	663	Travers	674	Travis	178
Travus	472	Traye	696	Tredway	696
Trefor	281	Trehearn	268	Trehern	167
Treherne	663	Tremain	628	Tremaine	224
Tremayne	292	Trent	595	Trentam	641
Trentham	639	Trenton	257	Trev	562
Trevar	663	Trevelyan	235	Trever	167
Trevor	268	Trey	595	Trigg	977
Trip	999	Tripp	977	Tris	933
Tristam	191	Tristan	112	Tristen	516
Tristin	911	Tristram	191	Trowbridge	224
Troy	696	Trueman	922	Truesdale	516
Trumaine	922	Truman	426	Trumane	922
Trumann	472	Trumble	821	Trusdale	911
Tuck	371	Tucker	876	Tuckie	876
Tucky	358	Tudal	494	Tudor	966
Tukuli	674	Tull	382	Tulley	865

Tullius	696	Tully	369	Tunu	674
Tupper	876	Turi	325	Turlough	325
Turner	876	Turpin	358	Tuxford	999
Twain	134	Twitchell	584	Twyford	663
Ty	729	Tybald	191	Tybalt	178
Tycho	628	Tye	595	Tyl	753
Tyler	538	Tymek	562	Tymon	696
Tymothy	639	Tynam	191	Tynan	112
Tynek	573	Tyonek	279	Tyrell	562
Tyrone	257	Tyrrel	538	Tyrrell	562
Tyrus	314	Tyson	663	Udale	977
Udall	415	Udeko	562	Udell	819
Udolf	944	Ugo	977	Uilleam	911
Uilliam	415	Uillioc	999	Ukrain	472
Ulberto	573	Ulfred	843	Ulger	819
Ulick	382	Ulises	854	Ullock	922
Ulmar	472	Ulmer	876	Ulric	369
Ulrich	358	Ulrick	382	Ulrike	854
Ulysses	843	Umberto	584	Umeko	562
Unwin	369	Upton	955	Upwood	674
Urbain	472	Urban	472	Urbano	178
Urbanus	786	Uri	393	Uriah	483
Urias	415	Uriel	832	Urit	325
Urses	821	Ursi	314	Ursis	325
Urson	966	Ushi	393	Uziel	821
Uzoma	134	Vachel	696	Vaclao	819
Vadim	134	Vadin	145	Vail	178
Vailintin	112	Vajos	764	Val	178
Valdemar	764	Valdimar	268	Vale	674
Valente	257	Valentijn	628	Valentin	617
Valentine	213	Valentino	314	Valere	279
Valerian	731	Valerius	988	Valiant	257
Valient	652	Valin	134	Valle	617
Valli	112	Vallis	123	Van	191
Vance	639	Vandute	966	Varden	641
Vardon	742	Vareck	696	Varian	292
Varick	191	Varin	191	Varne	696
Varner	696	Vartan	224	Vas	156
Vasileior	382	Vasileios	393	Vasilek	617
Vasilis	191	Vasily	167	Vasin	112
Vasos	764	Vasques	955	Vasquez	933
Vassili	191	Vassily	178	Vassy	145
Vasya	235	Vasyuta	551	Vaughan	562
Vaughn	461	Vaun	494	Vawn	156

Vedis	595	Velden	178	Velmos	235
Vencel	167	Venceslas	281	Vendel	178
Verall	617	Verden	145	Verdie	189
Verdon	246	Vere	145	Vered	189
Verge	123	Vergil	551	Verill	516
Verl	573	Verlin	538	Vermund	887
Vern	595	Vernan	652	Verne	191
Verner	191	Verney	178	Vernon	257
Verrall	617	Verrell	112	Verrill	516
Veryl	551	Veryle	156	Vianney	639
Vic	977	Vick	999	Vicky	977
Victoir	696	Victor	696	Victorien	257
Victorin	652	Vidor	685	Vik	966
Viktor	685	Vilem	527	Vilfredo	281
Vilhelm	549	Vilis	988	Viljem	538
Viljo	685	Vin	999	Vince	538
Vincent	516	Vincents	527	Vincenty	584
Vincenz	573	Vinie	595	Vinney	538
Vinnie	551	Vinny	933	Vinson	663
Virender	145	Virg	922	Virge	527
Virgel	551	Virgie	527	Virgil	955
Virgile	551	Virgilio	652	Virgy	999
Vishau	448	Vishnu	393	Vital	191
Vite	562	Vito	663	Vittorio	382
Vivian	145	Vivien	549	Vladamir	268
Vladimir	167	Vladislav	213	Vladlen	617
Von	696	Vonnie	257	Vyner	573
Vynie	573	Waban	235	Wace	685
Wade	696	Wadley	617	Wadsworth	775
Wagner	685	Wain	112	Waine	617
Wainwright	156	Waite	674	Wake	674
Wakefield	224	Wakeley	281	Wakely	685
Wakeman	775	Walby	189	Walcott	764
Wald	134	Waldemar	775	Waldemer	279
Walden	685	Waldo	731	Waldon	786
Waldron	786	Walenty	641	Walford	797
Walfred	696	Walker	617	Wallace	753
Wallache	742	Wallas	235	Waller	628
Wallie	628	Wallis	134	Wally	191
Walmond	731	Walmund	437	Walsh	189
Walt	112	Walter	617	Walters	628
Walther	696	Walton	764	Walwain	292
Walworth	753	Walwyn	178	Warburton	156
Ward	191	Warde	696	Wardell	663

Warden	652	Wardley	617	Ware	652
Warfield	696	Warford	764	Waring	189
Warley	663	Warmond	797	Warmund	494
Warner	617	Warren	617	Warri	156
Warrick	112	Warton	731	Warwick	167
Wash	156	Washburn	437	Washington	764
Wasi	167	Wasil	191	Wasyl	178
Wat	178	Watford	786	Watkins	167
Watson	742	Wattie	696	Watty	178
Waverley	213	Waverly	617	Way	134
Waylan	224	Wayland	268	Waylen	628
Waylin	123	Waylon	729	Wayne	685
Webb	595	Webber	191	Weber	178
Webley	189	Webster	112	Weddell	112
Welbie	112	Welborne	764	Welbourne	167
Welby	584	Welch	516	Weldon	281
Welford	292	Welland	628	Wellesley	641
Wellington	235	Wells	538	Welsh	584
Welton	268	Wemilat	652	Wemilo	235
Wen	516	Wenceslas	292	Wenceslaus	595
Wendall	628	Wendel	189	Wendell	123
Wentworth	292	Wenutu	235	Werner	112
Wernher	191	Wes	562	Wesh	551
Wesleigh	167	Wesley	178	Wessely	189
West	584	Westbrook	832	Westbrooke	437
Westby	584	Westcott	268	Westlay	696
Westleigh	189	Westley	191	Weston	246
Wetherall	235	Wetherby	167	Wetherell	639
Wetherill	134	Wetherly	178	Weylin	527
Whane	696	Wharton	729	Wheatley	279
Wheaton	325	Wheeler	674	Whistler	516
Whit	966	Whitaker	685	Whitby	966
Whitcomb	663	Whitcombe	268	Whitelaw	652
Whitfield	516	Whitford	674	Whitley	573
Whitlock	652	Whitman	167	Whitmore	213
Whitney	595	Whitny	999	Whittaker	617
Wiatt	191	Wicek	516	Wicent	562
Wicenty	549	Wichado	729	Wickham	145
Wickley	527	Wicus	393	Wido	696
Wilanu	448	Wilbert	538	Wilbur	314
Wilburt	336	Wilden	584	Wildon	685
Wilek	516	Wiley	562	Wilf	955
Wilford	696	Wilfred	595	Wilfrid	999
Wilfried	595	Wilhelm	551	Wilhem	527

Wilkes	527	Wilkie	516	Will	922
Willard	167	Willdon	628	Willem	562
Willet	549	Willey	595	Willi	922
William	167	Williamson	731	Willie	527
Willis	933	Willoughby	988	Willy	999
Wilmar	134	Wilmer	538	Wilmot	652
Wilmur	336	Wilny	922	Wilson	652
Wilt	911	Wilton	663	Wilus	393
Wimund	393	Win	911	Wincenty	595
Winchell	595	Windham	189	Windsor	663
Winfield	551	Winfred	527	Wingate	617
Winifield	551	Winifred	527	Winifrid	922
Winn	966	Winne	562	Winnie	562
Winny	944	Winslow	617	Winston	696
Winstonn	652	Winter	538	Winthrop	696
Winton	685	Winwald	145	Winward	112
Wirt	977	Wirth	966	Wit	977
Witha	167	Witney	516	Witny	911
Witt	999	Witter	595	Wittie	595
Witton	652	Witty	977	Wladimir	178
Wolcott	369	Wolf	652	Wolfe	257
Wolfgang	764	Wolfie	257	Wolfram	797
Wolfy	639	Wolseley	718	Wolsey	279
Wood	393	Woodie	898	Woodley	819
Woodly	314	Woodman	494	Woodrow	955
Woodruff	639	Woodward	494	Woody	371
Woolsey	876	Wooster	887	Worcester	729
Worden	257	Wordsworth	371	Worrall	729
Worrell	224	Worrill	628	Worth	663
Worthington	371	Worthy	641	Worton	336
Wray	134	Wren	516	Wright	944
Wulcott	966	Wunand	415	Wyanet	617
Wyatt	178	Wyborn	617	Wyborne	213
Wycliff	933	Wye	538	Wykeham	685
Wylie	562	Wyman	134	Wymer	573
Wyn	718	Wyndham	167	Wyndhann	134
Wyne	584	Wynn	764	Wyot	652
Wythe	549	Xanthus	448	Xavier	617
Xeno	224	Xenophon	843	Xenos	235
Xerxes	145	Xever	112	Ximenes	178
Ximenez	156	Xylon	639	Xymenes	156
Yachi	191	Yadid	167	Yadin	178
Yadon	775	Yakecen	281	Yakez	685
Yale	617	Yamka	246	Yamut	448

Yanaton	819	Yance	663	Yancey	641
Yancy	145	Yank	156	Yankee	257
Yann	189	Yannakis	224	Yannick	145
Yannis	191	Yarb	191	Yard	123
Yarde	628	Yardley	639	Yaremka	742
Yarin	134	Yasir	189	Yasu	483
Yates	617	Yazid	112	Yazim	112
Yehudi	819	Yehudit	832	Yemon	279
Yeoman	371	Yeremy	191	Yerik	595
Yever	123	Yew	538	Yoann	786
Yogi	652	Yogy	639	Yonit	652
Yori	674	Yorick	639	York	696
Yorke	292	Yorker	292	Yoshin	639
Youri	977	Yucel	843	Yuki	393
Yukio	999	Yul	314	Yule	819
Yules	821	Yuma	426	Yurgon	911
Yuri	371	Yuria	472	Yurik	393
Yusef	854	Yutu	696	Yvain	178
Yvan	178	Yves	538	Yvon	674
Yvor	628	Zacarias	336	Zaccaria	358
Zacchaeus	156	Zach	112	Zacharia	314
Zachariah	393	Zacharias	325	Zacharie	718
Zachary	281	Zacherie	213	Zachery	685
Zack	145	Zackariah	336	Zackary	224
Zackery	628	Zadok	753	Zahaval	358
Zahid	123	Zahur	472	Zaid	134
Zak	112	Zakarias	325	Zakeralio	448
Zaki	112	Zakkai	235	Zalman	224
Zaloc	753	Zamit	156	Zane	641
Zareb	617	Zared	639	Zarek	617
Zarka	213	Zayit	189	Zdenek	112
Zeb	516	Zebadiah	742	Zebedee	257
Zebulen	494	Zebulon	595	Zechariah	797
Zed	538	Zedekia	257	Zedekiah	246
Zedof	292	Zeeman	281	Zeger	167
Zeke	112	Zeki	516	Zelig	595
Zelimic	595	Zelotes	753	Zemer	134
Zenas	652	Zennie	191	Zenon	292
Zenos	257	Zeph	551	Zephan	617
Zephaniah	797	Zephyrin	584	Zeppo	246
Zerk	516	Zesiro	292	Zetadiah	742
Zeus	898	Ziven	584	Zivon	685
Zofka	775	Zoheret	797	Zollie	257
Zolly	639	Zoltan	797	Zoraster	325

Zory	663	Zsoka	729	Zubin	369
Zupeika	988	Zuri	382	Zuriel	821
Zygmont	663				

ADDENDUM

NUMBERS

A COMMON THREAD THROUGHOUT ALL LIFE

COMPANION BOOK

The companion book to *Baby Names – Why They Count* is *Why Do Numbers Count*. If you wish to understand numerology, you will find *Why Do Numbers Count* to be of considerable interest. It is written with a goal of making numerology credible and easy to learn

FOR MORE INFORMATION

As noted in this book, even though it is of great value to utilize a balanced first name, it is advisable to adopt a balanced surname as well – a surname which is in harmony with your given name and creates a balanced destiny combination.

I have a data base of 100,000 surnames and can provide you with a list of list of surnames that will best match your choice of a first name.

If you would like a list of suitable surnames or help choosing the right name name for your child, email me at:

lance@numbers-count.com

BABY NAMES
WHY THEY COUNT

For A Lifetime !!!

www.ingramcontent.com/pod-product-compliance
Lightning Source LLC
Chambersburg PA
CBHW020848090426
42736CB00008B/279